*I'm Not Blessed With*

# An Oral History of Bembridge
## Isle of Wight

# *I'm Not Blessed Well Jokin'!*

## An Oral History of Bembridge
### Isle of Wight

## Alan Robert Phillips

First published 2023
© 2023 Alan Robert Phillips

The right of Alan Robert Phillips to be identified as the Author of this work has been asserted in accordance with the Copyright, Designs and Patents Act 1988.

All rights reserved. No part of this book may be reprinted or reproduced or utilised in any form or by any electronic, mechanical or other means, now known or hereafter invented, including photocopying and recording, or in any information storage or retrieval system, without the permission in writing from the Author.

Countryside Books
35a Kingfisher Court, Hambridge Road
Newbury, Berkshire, RG14 5SJ
**www.countrysidebooks.co.uk**

ISBN 978 1 84674 425 9

British Library Cataloguing in Publication Data.
A catalogue record for this book is available from the British Library.

**Front Cover illustrations:**
Bembridge Harbour Regatta, 1900s;
Tuffley's Stores, Sherbourne Street, 1880s.

**Title Page:** Bembridge Station, 1920s.

**Back Cover illustrations:**
Yeats' Butchers Shop, High Street, prior to 1850: the man front right, with the tall hat and tunic, is most likely the village policeman;
A Bembridge Farming Scene, 1920s.

*All photos by kind courtesy of Bembridge Heritage.*

Produced by The Letterworks Ltd., Reading
Typeset by KT Designs, St Helens
Printed by **Short Run Press Ltd**

# Contents

|  |  | Page |
|---|---|---|
|  | Acknowledgements | 7 |
|  | Introduction | 8 |
| Chapter 1: | The Village As It Was – Mrs Ivy Bryant (Part 1) | 11 |
| Chapter 2: | We's Country Chaps – Mr Walter Sillence (Part 1) | 29 |
| Chapter 3: | A Fisherman's Life – Mr Ashford Caws (Part 1) | 43 |
| Chapter 4: | Round The World To Under Tyne – Miss Edith Woodford | 58 |
|  | *Reports:* Longevity in Bembridge; Granny Woodford; Alfred Morris | 61 |
| Chapter 5: | A Smuggling Background – Mrs Ivy Evans | 64 |
|  | *Archives:* Bembridge Lifeboats and Lifeboatmen | 69 |
| Chapter 6: | A Contented Life – Miss Amy Nightingale | 72 |
|  | *Features:* The Wallis Family; Bembridge Brewery | 77 |
| Chapter 7: | The Butler Family – Mr Harold Butler | 79 |
|  | *Obituaries:* William Jacobs; Harry Weaver | 91 |
| Chapter 8: | Shh!! Don't Say Another Word! – Mrs Ivy Bryant (Part 2) | 92 |
| Chapter 9: | Poaching, Piloting and Driving Bullocks – Mr Ashford Caws (Part 2) | 109 |
|  | *Interludes:* The Christmas Boys; Musical Evenings | 124 |
| Chapter 10: | Granny Pryke the Smuggler and Other Stories – Mrs Celia Blackman | 128 |
|  | *Press cutting:* Tales of Bembridge Smuggling | 135 |
| Chapter 11: | The View from Hillway – Mr William Langworthy | 137 |
| Chapter 12: | Mollie Downer 'The Witch' and the Smugglers | 146 |
| Chapter 13: | Early Days around Peacock Hill – Mr Ernest Butler (Part 1) | 152 |
| Chapter 14: | On the Home Front – Mrs Elsie Hibbert | 165 |
|  | *Curiosities:* The Boer War; Blanket Torn by Shell of Destroyer; Carriage Charges; Bembridge School | 178 |
| Chapter 15: | A Seaman's Story – Mr Frank Brooks | 180 |
|  | *Reports:* A Sunken Barge; Terrific Gale; Heroic Brothers; Island Fishermen in Peril | 187 |

## Contents *(continued)*

| | Page |
|---|---|
| **Chapter 16:** A Pride in His Work: The Local Carpenter – Mr Walter Sillence (Part 2) | 190 |
| **Chapter 17:** The Bembridge Lady Cab Driver – Mrs Maggie McInnes & Mrs Isidora Whitehead | 208 |
| **Chapter 18:** You Never Seen Anythin' Like It! – Mr Arthur Orchard | 214 |
| *Features:* Fire Safety; Hay Ricks Destroyed by Fire; Otters in East Wight | 221 |
| **Chapter 19:** More Village Characters and Tales – Mr Ernest Butler (Part 2) | 223 |
| **Chapter 20:** I'm Not Blessed Well Jokin'! – Mr Ashford Caws (Part 3) | 238 |
| *Feature article:* When the Sun always Shone, by Angela Whitcombe | 254 |

# Acknowledgements

I would like to acknowledge the late Mrs Isabel Moore for providing the original inspiration for this collection of recordings and for introducing me to my first interviewee, the redoubtable Walter Sillence.

The late John Woodford provided much encouragement for the project in the early days, and of course went on to produce several publications of his own in connection with Bembridge Heritage Society.

Mrs Monica Brooks assisted early on with transcribing some entries from the old Bembridge WI scrapbooks.

Special thanks are due to Bembridge Heritage for allowing very generous use of their photographic database, and all photos in the book derive from this superb collection unless otherwise stated; many of these were taken in the early 20th century by renowned local photographer Alfred Wilson. These are supplemented by several photos kindly provided by Peter Chick from his extensive collection, while Mrs Jan Field was also kind enough to allow reproduction of her rare family photo of the Bembridge 'Christmas Boys'.

I am particularly indebted to Ken Orchard for reading through and commenting on all the transcriptions that make up this volume, and answering various queries I have thrown his way. His local knowledge of Bembridge past and present has proved invaluable.

Special thanks are also due to Alex Batho at Countryside Books for steering me through the whole production process whilst communicating throughout in a straightforward language free of jargon.

Needless to say, any errors of fact or interpretation are purely my own.

# Introduction

This volume has had an excessively long gestation period. Its inception began in late 1974 when, as a fairly newly qualified librarian at Bembridge – in the old fire station building beneath the old Council chamber – one of my regular customers, the late Mrs Isabel Moore, suggested to me that some of the stories and reminiscences of older born-and-bred Bembridge residents ought to be recorded before it was too late, and proposed that I might consider doing so. This happened to coincide with my recent reading of some inspirational volumes on Suffolk by the pioneering oral historian George Ewart Evans.

So it was that in February 1975 I paid my first visit to 90-year-old Mr Walter Sillence at his home in Heathfield Road accompanied by an old reel-to-reel tape recorder. I could not have asked for a better informant: forceful in his style of delivery with a crystal-clear memory, and characteristic of all that was best about Old Bembridge and indeed Old England, yet also very much rooted in the present. For the following eighteen months or more, helped by a series of recommendations and introductions, I was warmly welcomed into the homes of all the 'Old Bembridgers' included in this volume. The range and depth of their recollections were outstanding; there was no doubt about their love of the village and they obviously took great pleasure in recounting their experiences. A couple more were recorded in a fresh bout of enthusiasm several years later, in 1984.

Ironically, several of the interviewees said to me, "You're too late, you should have spoken to my father or mother, they could have told you everything you want to know" – bearing in mind that they were referring to a generation born around the 1860s! From their own perspective they were perfectly correct; but what it goes to show is just how much lived history is being lost everywhere, all the time – and that, conversely, it is *never* too late to capture people's memories, at *any* time.

The physical recordings themselves were not of the best quality and there was inevitably a lot of peripheral material to be jettisoned, while transcriptions were of course in those days all laboriously handwritten. Tapes were recorded over and reused, consequently very little of any quality recordings survive. If I were embarking on this project today I would approach it very differently, but my main aim then was to get this material down on paper, as with the oral history publications I had already seen. It should be remembered that in the 1970s oral history recording was in its infancy and still something of a pioneer activity. There was no back-up support nor oral history courses to sign up for as there are today, nor was there any local heritage society: it was very much a one-off activity.

## Introduction

Then the task of sorting these myriad handwritten transcriptions, especially in the days before computer software, was a challenging prospect. This was compounded from 1978 by a demanding job commuting weekly to Surrey and then London, along with my being an early environmental campaigner on the Island throughout the 1980s. There were intermittent bouts of activity on the transcripts over the years including transferring them to a digital format, but it was in fact only retirement a number of years ago which again opened up the prospect of bringing these interviews to publication.

All the interviewees gave permission to publish their stories but have inevitably passed away in the intervening years: several were indeed born over 130 years ago. The majority were very aware of the value of their reminiscences and would certainly have wished to see them in print within their lifetimes, though a couple simply saw our discussions as 'ordinary talk' and were sceptical that anyone would wish to read about them. I have also been conscious over the years that other villagers, especially those who knew about the original recordings, would have wished to see this volume come to fruition somewhat sooner than it is now finally doing.

In any case, the main intention has been for these older residents to speak for themselves, and speak they do. I sincerely trust that as old as these reminiscences now are, the stories told and some of the larger-than-life characters recalled – almost always with affection and genial good humour – will be seen as part of the spirit of 'Old Bembridge'. In a few sensitive cases I have shortened an individual's name to Christian name with the first letter of the surname.

As the villagers speak they will be fleshing out many historical details. However, I make no attempt to provide any kind of formal, archival history of Bembridge; for that I would refer readers to volumes such as *Bembridge Apart: A Local History,* produced by Bembridge Heritage Society in 2002; or Ernest Du Boulay's much older volume *Bembridge Past and Present* (1911).

Some of the most popular stories are repeated several times, and I have not sought to restrict these; indeed, the tales will be told each in their own inimitable way. There may be some small inconsistencies in the various accounts, which is inevitable where interviewees are recalling events or characters from sixty to eighty years previously. What is truly remarkable is just how sharply focused these villagers' memories were, recalling events and situations with a degree of detail I have not encountered before or since.

Some annotated notes have been provided where appropriate, and some modern businesses have been identified where it seemed helpful. However, given the rate at which businesses, shops and house-names have continued to change, it would have been a tedious, and often fruitless, task to try and link up every single reference to its present name and location – which could then change again in a short space of time.

The vast majority of name spellings are, I believe, correct, or as correct as I can make them; though it is possible an error may have occasionally crept in with some of the less familiar names which are difficult to check.

The recordings are mostly transcribed verbatim, though various passages have often been reshuffled and reordered to provide some kind of overall coherence. Sometimes sections have required editing for readability: I have found it necessary to steer a middle course between authenticity – capturing the flavour of the local vernacular where it was strong – and readability, i.e. rendering dialogue in a reasonably comprehensible form to avoid the text becoming arduous. One example would be the frequent pronunciation of the word 'round' in the local vernacular as 'rownd'; another would be the pronunciation of 'out' as 'owt'. An absolutely authentic approach would require these to be transcribed in the vernacular every single time they are used, but alongside similar examples this could become tiresome to read; so for most purposes I have considered it safer to adhere to the standard spelling, reserving the 'rownd' or 'owt' versions for added effect in cases where the speaker accentuates the word, or the context makes it particularly appropriate to use.

To provide further variety, the transcripts are interspersed with a set of IW County Press reports, some entries from the old Bembridge WI scrapbooks, a couple more from the IW Records Office, and a captivating article about Bembridge taken from an old magazine.

Living as I now do in the West Wight, all of this material has long become isolated from its proper home. But reconnecting with Bembridge Heritage in recent times has proved a very rewarding experience. In particular, I am extremely grateful to Ken Orchard for reading and commenting on all the transcripts. I have been pleased to find that he not only recalls mention of most of the characters in the transcripts but is also familiar with their modern family members where they still live locally. All this has given an added fillip to finally bringing the project to fruition.

I am only too glad after all this time to be returning these unique recollections to Bembridge, which is where they truly belong and where they may serve to complement the excellent ongoing work to document the heritage of this very special village.

Alan Phillips
Shorwell
Isle of Wight
*bembridgeoralhistory@gmail.com*

# Chapter 1

# The Village As It Was
## – Mrs Ivy Bryant

Ivy Tuffley (Mrs Bryant)

*Mrs Bryant was born Ivy Tuffley in 1890 in Bembridge, where she lived until 1913, then spent 36 years away, returning in 1949 and living continuously in the village from then on. She was 84 years old when recorded at her home in Meadow Drive over a series of five visits from February to April 1975. Mrs Bryant's memory was particularly detailed on the layout of the old village, its shops and houses, and the minutiae of daily life, and she became a prolific informant and guide to Old Bembridge life and times. Where the names of commercial businesses can change so frequently today, I have for the most part retained the original names that Mrs Bryant used for them and were current at the time of recording.*

## Robert Tuffley & Family

I've heard that my great-grandfather Tuffley first came to Bembridge with the Moreton family as their estate manager, but it must have been the East Cliff ones, I should imagine. He was originally a stonemason from Tuffley in Gloucestershire. My great-grandparents were all buried up at the

Sherbourne Street with gate at end, c.1910.

church graveyard, but even when I was a kid most burials were done at the cemetery.

Anyway, my grandfather Robert Tuffley was born here in 1825, and at one time he had the shop in Sherbourne Street which they call Sothcott's now [*currently the Co-op*]. That was Tuffley's, it was started by him, then Sothcott's took it over about 1912 or 13. It wasn't a very big business or anything, but it looks from this [*Hill's Commercial Directory 1879*] as though he sold absolutely everything! A lot of them could only have been odd items. Then he had the Windmill afterwards. So he did quite a few things, you see, and then he used to drive into Newport once a week, where he had a wool store in Lugley Street!

My father Wallace Tuffley and his two brothers Thomas and Luther went to Dame Attrill's school [*in the High Street, beyond the Village Inn*]: it used to be an old, low cottage, I can just remember it. I don't think she taught them much, she was a very old lady *then*. But I can remember my grandpa telling me something and I've never heard it from anybody else. I was out for a walk with him one day, and we were going through Darts Lane, and there's a building there in the grounds of Balure, I think the Balure people used it as a potting shed and it's all covered in ivy. Well he said to me, "That's where I first went to school". But I've never heard it from anybody else.

My earliest memory of Bembridge was when we had whooping cough, and I remember my brother and I being wheeled in a sort of double pushchair

## Chapter 1 – The Village As It Was

round the embankment to the gasworks at St Helens, 'cause the smell of the gas was supposed to be a cure for it.

Well as a small child, we used to go up to the mill for days, you know – my grandfather owned the mill then, you see. And the wall at the top of the High Street by Bembridge Lodge always leant over as though it was going to fall – well we children would walk the other side of the road because we thought the wall was going to fall on us! Anyway, my brothers and I would go up for the day to Knowles Farm as it was called, and we used to collect the eggs and help with the haymaking. And they did a milk round for the village, they weren't the only ones of course, other farms like Stanwell Farm used to do one. We had two deliveries a day, but we often went up to get skimmed milk for puddings an' things like that. And then sometimes we were allowed to play in the mill, my grandfather was working it then. Another time p'raps we weren't allowed to go in, but we loved to go in if it was working, but not on our own. Oh we had happy times up there. They used to have a big rabbit warren up there, and we would crawl along on our tums so as not to make a noise, to watch the rabbits come out from the holes. 'Course, there was no myxomatosis in those days so they didn't mind the rabbits breeding.

We'd go up on Saturdays and Sundays: we had to be very good on Sundays. They had a Noah's Ark and it was kept in the side of their drawing room, in what they used to call a powder room in the old days. We were allowed to have this Noah's Ark on Sundays, and Sundays only. And then *always* after lunch my grandparents used to rest, and that was sacred: we either had to go out and play, or if we stayed in, well we just had to sit still. They rested for about three-quarters of an hour, and it was really strict. Then they'd set us on different jobs, helping and so on, and then we'd come home at night. We were living at Kensington Cottage then, at the top of the Ducie [*in Sherbourne Street*], where I was born. Anyway, then Farmer Morris had the mill after my grandfather.

Well my grandfather used to go out shooting of course with his gun and his dogs. And they were great church people, and I always remember, they didn't used to wash up on Sundays, they'd leave it all until Monday! But I used to think it was dreadful, even as a child, not to wash up. And another thing, he always used to start his tea with cake, and then he'd have his bread and butter; and I would go home and I'd say, "Well why can't *I* have cake first, grandpa always does". And something else up there we used to get very disgusted about: if we had jam we weren't allowed to have butter, and on a farm! At home well of course we always had bread an' butter *and* jam – I expect they thought my mother was extravagant.

But the toilet up at the mill was dreadful! There was nothing in the house of course, so we had to go into the orchard and there was this midden business. And there was a high seat like that and a low one, and it used to be *awful* – everything was in a pail which had to be emptied. We'd rather go out in the fields! And we always used to think there were animals around, it was such a big place and we were frightened to death of going in there.

After they retired, my gramp and gran [*Robert and Theresa*] moved down to Oxford Cottage at the Point. And they used to trudge up that Folly Hill every Sunday for Church, except *Litany* Sundays: my gran wouldn't go on those days 'cause she wasn't goin' to say she was a miserable sinner! Ah-ha-ha-ha! And you always did have the full litany in those days, once a month; 'course, they don't bother nowadays.

When we lived in Foreland Road, we were next door to the schoolmaster then, Mr Alfie Smith, in fact it was his house also and we paid him rent for it. They were a pair of villas: his was called Thameslea and ours was Quarryville. We used to have to pump our water there, and as children we had to do so many turns, in the morning and dinner-time. The pump was in the scullery, and there was a tank-room at the top.

The milkman who came to our house was Bob Jordan, came round with his yoke on his shoulders and two pails of milk.

We had a pet bird, and it died. And we had a curate living in the village then, a Reverend Wilson. We could've only been about four or five [*1894/5*]. And one of the assistants from our shop was living with us at the time, and he said we ought to go and get the parson to come and bury it – so very serious! So Wallace and I went to the curate's lodgings at Woodbine Cottage and asked if he would come and bury our bird. He took it very well, I can't remember if he said yes or no, but he went round to our mother in the shop and had a good laugh about it. This curate was a very handsome young man, all the girls ran after him, but he left Bembridge and died of consumption a few years afterwards.

We had 'whatnots' in the sitting-room in those days, about five little movable shelves which usually went in the corner, and all with little ornaments on and they all had to be dusted on a Saturday morning. And Sarah our housekeeper would go round with her finger afterwards to see they'd been dusted properly. Sarah Wearn came to us from Bembridge Farm when she was about seventeen, and she married, and she was a great Salvation Army person. Then we had a piano in the sitting-room as well, and old-fashioned sofas with just a headpiece at one end but not at the other. We had big overmantels above the mantlepiece, a big mirror with little shelves down on it, and we used to put ornaments on them. The sitting-room would only be used on Sundays.

[*Mrs Bryant added the following written piece about the mill in the old WI scrapbook.*] Although not in regular use for over fifty years [*previous to when the article appeared, perhaps in the 1960s or 70s*], the mill was worked for a time forty-two years ago by Mr Ernest Orchard. The mill owner Farmer Morris was 'a little bit scared' of the mill, bur Mr Orchard used to superintend matters, although he could never persuade the owner to stay inside the building while the mill was working. Mr Orchard ground fifteen to twenty sacks of wheat and barley at a time. He said that once the mill was in motion it could be left, as whatever the strength of the wind the speed of running was automatically controlled. The mill was used mainly for the production of animal feedstuffs.

## Round the Harbour and Back

Bembridge is very different to what it was when *I* was a girl, which is a good long time ago now. I remember there used to be a handrail running round from the St Helens end of the harbour to Bembridge, and water used to be piped through it right round to the Point. And until a few years ago, opposite the Brading Haven Yacht Club, they used to camp over that side, and often in the winter it was covered with water and yet I've seen tents down there, Boy Scouts and so on. But I thought then, fancy camping on that waterlogged land!

Well coming along on the same side there used to be a ladies' golf links, where all the water is now. Then you had the waterworks down there, with two cottages. I had a boyfriend living down there once! They used to pump the water up to the water tower near the Mill, and Pip Osborn went down and worked in them – he belonged to the Osborns that had the bakehouse in Sherbourne Street. The two cottages were made into one, and is called Home Farm now.

Somewhere near those cottages there was a market garden, Mr Burden used to run it and he used to come round with a horse and cart. Freddie Weeks lived down there before the market garden was there, I think his father had something to do with the ladies' golf club.

We never had many bad winters and we had hardly *any* snow. But I can just remember the other side of the embankment being frozen over, where there's a lot of water. That was in 1895 I think, I was only about five then, it was a very hard winter. Part of the harbour was frozen over and I can remember seeing people skating all round there. Then I don't remember anything else until my daughter was about fifteen and we had a very hard winter then and she went sliding, not skating, down over Lynchens. That would've been in the '30s sometime.

Now those two old houses opposite the Sailing Club, they were boathouses underneath and flats on top. The tollkeeper used to live in one of them, and later on I believe there was an antique shop there run by Miss Du Boulay. The toll house was on the opposite side of the road, where the Tollgate Café is now. Then there was the Sailing Club itself, of course, which was very

Toll Hut, Embankment Road.

snooty – you had to be somebody to belong to that. They used to blackball people, they'd be put before the committee and if they weren't just so they didn't get in!

Now down by the station there was Hapgood's the Tailors, and afterwards they ran the telephone exchange when that came here, as well as the tailor's shop. And Seymour Place, d'you know what we used to call that? – Bug Alley, ah ha ha! Now that was about the poorest sort of place in Bembridge – any Bembridge person wouldn't say Seymour Place, they'd say Bug Alley!

Then there was a boatbuilder's workshop along Station Road, I think it was run by a man named Damp. And we used to go to these Good Templar meetings down there, over the top of this boatbuilding place. And another Noah's Ark used to kept in there and we were allowed to have it on Sundays, and Sundays only. Doctor and Mrs Payne used to run it. My number was Fifty, and Mrs Payne used to call me 'Little Grandmother Fifty' – don't know why!

The Weavers owned the Marine Hotel, and I remember people by the name of Collins at the Pilot Boat when I was quite young. And the Spithead Hotel didn't use to close up in the wintertime like it does now, there was always somebody living there. I remember going to a ball there, it was just about my first dance, I was about 16 or 17, and it was very nicely done. Then there was also the Bembridge Hotel, almost opposite the Pilot Boat, they call it Old Bembridge House now. And coming up Point Hill, there was the Prince of Wales pub, the only people I remember there were Locks – the girls Kate and Beattie used to come to school with us. I believe some people by the name of Mursell ran the Crab and Lobster. Bembridge had quite a few pubs for such a small village. But I don't think the Spithead or the Bembridge Hotel had licences, I think they were more like guest-houses in the old sense. I went to those for dances an' that, but not the *pubs*, they were mostly for men, not ladies!

Mrs Blackman once asked me to deliver a paper or something for the British Legion to New Road, and I said, "New Road? Where's that?" And she said, "You call yourself a Bembridger and you don't know where New Road is?" So I said, "Well I've never heard of it!" So she said, "It's where the Bembridge Hotel is". But I don't think we ever called it *anything*!

Now just on the left, between the Pilot Boat and the Prince of Wales, I believe Alf Watson had the blacksmith's shop, where he shoed horses. At *one* time it was a barber's shop! Well then on the right was Frank Attrill's boat shop – he and his wife sold everything in the way of hardware and sailing things. How ever he took stock I don't know, it was absolutely choc-a-bloc!

Then after the Prince of Wales closed, the Attrills took it over, and Mrs Attrill used to run it as an ironmonger's shop. After that it became an antique shop, but I knew *that* wouldn't last, 'cause the road had become too busy by then. Of course, when it was a pub the roads weren't anything like. I remember the old Wesleyan chapel halfway up, where my aunt used to play the organ – her name was Elizabeth Couldrey – and we went to services there sometimes.

## Schooldays

When I first went to the infants' school, it was a Miss Selina Matthews, she was a nice old dear. And my friend Elsie and I used to be favourites, I think, we would get away with all sorts of things. But when we went to Mr Smith's school, which is the one opposite the church, Elsie and I always used to be in trouble because we talked so. Although he was Elsie's father, he was very strict with all his family at school and he never favoured *any* of them, in fact he used to cane them. But he was a good schoolmaster, he really was. We were taught the three Rs for one thing, properly, and tables, and then we would have drill in the yard if it was a fine day.

We started off in Standard 1 and Standard 2: that was a classroom off the big room and a lady teacher used to look after those two. We were taught needlework, properly too, which I don't think they teach *now*, not

Bembridge Junior School, 1909. Not everyone is happy!

in that way. I mean, we were never allowed to work without a thimble, but now, all the young people these days, they never wear a thimble for sewing. Then you got into Standard 3, 4, 5 and 6, and Mr Smith used to be in that room.

At playtime we'd play 'Here we come gathering nuts in May' and 'He' and 'Hide-and-seek'. And 'Weary Bug' – a lot of us used to link up hands and then run and try an' catch somebody, and then they'd have to join in till we got a big lot, you know.

And in those days we wore pinafores to school, then when we went home lunchtime we always had to take those off and put on another one, keep it clean for school. Something *very* wrong if you went without a pinafore! We used to make them by hand in the needlework class.

There was a Miss Mursell used to run the sweet shop in the High Street, where we could go and get four things for a penny: a farthing stick of liquorice, everlasting strip, and something else. And o' course we only used to get a penny a week pocket money in those days! We could never go to St Helens because you had to pay a penny to walk round the bank – the tollgate was down at the Point of course, I think it was tuppence for a bicycle and sixpence for a car, and it belonged to the railway.

On Sundays we'd go to Sunday School at 10am, then into the Church for the first part of the service, and come out before the sermon. On the way to Sunday School we would call at the post office to see if there were any letters. Then afterwards we would walk down to the cemetery at Lane End

## Chapter 1 – The Village As It Was

– the old cemetery, opposite the new one – and go round and look at the graves, see if there were any new ones, look at the flowers, anything like that. But I often think, what a *funny* thing it was for us to do! And it was more or less regular, if it was fine. Then we'd go to a service for children at three in the afternoon.

Well at Sandown we used to pay tuppence ha'penny for sausage an' mash, and fourpence for a meat pie, which we had twice a week, and then we'd pay fourpence for school dinners that the cookery classes had made, you see.

In our spare time we would go for long walks, right round to Whitecliff and then up to the monument and home by the road. You can't get right round the cliffs these days as we could once. Another walk we did was through the mill fields and the marshes to Brading, and home by train. In the spring we would go to Centurions Woods for wild daffodils and bluebells, and also under the downs for cowslips. Then to Steyne Woods for primroses, and I always remember on Good Friday afternoons we used to go and tie the primroses up in small bunches, take them to Church the next morning, and they were strung up on ropes and put round and round the pillars, decorating the Church for Easter.

In the summer we were always on the beach building sandcastles, picking up shells, shrimping and bathing. And we used to dig for sand sprats and cockles. When the tide was out we could walk right out to the Fort: you'd have to follow the tide out; if you waited till it was low you couldn't get out there before it turned and came in again. It was a good mile out to the Fort. Then sometimes we'd play cricket with the boys, and croquet, we had a croquet set we took down to the beach. And we used to play skipping and hopscotch, and we had wheeling hoops – the boys had iron ones, and the girls had wooden ones – of course, we could wheel these wooden hoops in the road, which you couldn't do today in Bembridge!

Well, we were dared to go down Hermit's Hole by my mother. When we couldn't go to school, when my youngest brother had scarlet fever – they were very particular in those days – the assistant in our shop [*Tuffley's*], he wanted to go down Hermit's Hole. And I said, "Oh, take me! It'll be alright going with you" – see, he was much older than I was, I was only a kid about twelve. And they say that if you go down, it's only a very narrow path, and then *steep* down to the sea, right down, and the sheep were supposed to go down there and then they'd have to come back, and they say that if you met one coming back you had to lay down and let it walk over you, otherwise they'd knock you over, you see. Well of course I was scared stiff as you might guess, but we didn't see any sheep. Whether that was true or not, I never heard of anybody meeting sheep down there, but that's why we were dared to do down there.

I remember once mother was in bed ill and she wouldn't let Sarah the housekeeper make the Christmas puddings, they were to be made up in her bedroom in big red crocks, earthenware mixing-bowls – they were really bread crocks for keeping bread in. And then we all had to go up and stir. There were my two brothers and myself, and we were allowed to stone a dozen raisins and then eat *one* – the big raisins, you can't hardly get them now. And all the currants and raisins had to be washed an' dried and picked over for stones that were in them, and the stalks had t'all be picked off – used to take a *week* to make the Christmas puddings.

Now, where Sir Francis Pittis is in the High Street, that used to be a little private school called Alton House run by a Miss Bailey and Miss Jameson. It was never very big, they only had a few pupils, not more than twenty, if that. The Jordans used to go there and I went there for music lessons for a little while, I don't think we had to pay very much. I think they were quite good teachers but I didn't like them very much, I didn't like music lessons, that was *my* trouble. This was years after Dame Attrill's school.

## Trains and Traps

At one time Sothcott's had stables coming up just opposite the chapel – they had a little wagonette sort-of-thing where you would sit each side, to meet the trains, and he would charge sixpence to bring you up to the village or right up to Whitecliff or Hillway. And they used to have a grocer's shop opposite the station. In St Helens they're always Southcotts, but at Bembridge Sothcotts, that's always been so.

Well as you know the water used to go right up to Brading. My mother told me she was one of the first to go round the embankment, that was after she was married, but she used to come down to Bembridge *before* she was married, and they would have to meet her at Ryde with pony and trap and then come all round the downs to Bembridge, through Brading and round by Hillway.

Well there were no motor cars in those days, so most people had John Bull or Mrs Bull with their landaus, or Sothcott's when they had their livery stables. Mrs Bull was always down at the station to meet the trains, and she used to wear a bowler hat, you know. She lived in Sherbourne House, one of the two cottages next to the Grange, and had her stables up there.

Then there used to be a man at the back of our shop that rented the stables or part of them, and he worked on his own. He had two horses and we had our pony. I heard that the first person to have a motor car in Bembridge was a man from the Garland Club who used to live up at Woodlands.

The railway line went right up St Helens and then Brading, it just used to run up and down, and at Bembridge they had a turntable, the engine

## Chapter 1 – The Village As It Was

Sothcott's Stores, Bembridge Point, c.1910.

would go to the end and then it turned round on this turntable. The station was built the wrong way round, you know, the road should've been the other side or something. That came up again when the train stopped running in the early '50s. All the people went up on the last journey, made an awful fuss and kept stopping the train and made a real commotion about it.

Well I went to the village school till I was twelve, and then I was the first girl to win a scholarship to the secondary school at Sandown, they were the first scholarships given. And we had to go by the eight o'clock train to Brading and then change for Sandown, and if we missed that one there wasn't another one till half past ten. So of course we were scared stiff of missing it! And that was where the 'five minutes bell' came in handy, down at the station. They used to ring it five minutes before the train went, either the station master or the guard. I used to go from Swains Road and p'raps I'd be up in Ducie Avenue and hear the five minutes bell go and have to rush down for dear life to get the train.

Going up in the train, we were the only two girls with about six boys. 'Course, we used to get up to all sorts of tricks. I remember once Dr Davis threatened to report us: we were slinging our satchels at each other in that *long* carriage, shouting and talking. That was as far as Brading. On the Sandown line, we were not allowed to travel with the boys. I suppose that was why we'd lark about with them on the Bembridge to Brading part. There was also a short carriage which was the smoking compartment.

Then coming home the pupils from Bembridge and St Helens were supposed to come out five minutes earlier to get to the station, because our train went at half past four, and lessons didn't stop until half past four. But very often the teachers wouldn't think about it and let you go. Well if you didn't catch *that* train, there wasn't another one till quarter to six. So of course we used to be all on forms, waiting to be let out, and then we had to go right underneath the subway and up on the other side. And in those days we weren't allowed to talk to the teachers like the kids do today, we were almost *scared* of them, frightened to say anything, we should've got told off! We often tried to put our hands up, but it didn't come off, they wouldn't take much notice.

We sometimes went to Ryde by train as a special treat, though not very often, and instead of getting out at the esplanade we'd get out at St Johns Road, because it was ever so much more to go to the esplanade, about fivepence or sixpence more. And then we used t'have to walk up the hill to the town, but that was a treat!

Then down at Bembridge station there used to be a Smith's bookstall with the papers then, there was nobody selling papers in the village, they were all delivered from the bookstall. They also ran a subscription library from there, and the manager had a mother-in-law living in the village. Well one day she was going down to the library to change her book, and he saw her coming, so he stopped the train, thinking she was going by train. And as she got there he said, "I've got your ticket for you". "No," she says, "I only came t' change m' book." And the whole train was waiting for her!

## 'Our Mertie' and Other Local Gentry

There were very few big houses in the village in those early days. Well, an uncle of Colonel Moreton's first came to East Cliff, and then Colonel Moreton must have had Hill Grove built and lived *there*. He had seven girls and one son. And they all belonged to the Earl of Ducie's family, which was why Ducie Avenue was called by that name. Cara was the eldest, she became Mrs Mackenzie. Hilda first married Sir Simon Lockhart, then later became Lady de Robeck. Muriel became Mrs Ismay, she married James Ismay, who was chairman of the White Star Line, and they lived down Ducie. Evelyn never married. Then there was Islay, who became Mrs Woodroffe; Margaret became Mrs Philips; and Audrey became Mrs Oppenheim. Their one son was killed in the First World War.

I can remember there used to be quite a big do when any of the Moreton

## Chapter 1 – The Village As It Was

Queen Mary, visiting Couldrey's furniture shop.

girls got married, and we'd be invited down to Hill Grove to see the presents all laid out. And then for two or three of the weddings there were so many of the village girls chosen, about a dozen of us, and we'd go dressed in white and throw flowers as the bride came out. We were quite small then, about seven. And I believe one year we had like Little Red Riding Hood cloaks, that would have been 1898: we were given a brooch with 1898 by Lady Lockhart at her wedding – she was Hilda Moreton, and married Sir Simon Lockhart.

Nearly all the houses in Ducie, you know, in my young days were occupied by the Moreton family. They would close Ducie Avenue every so often, they had barricades at the top of it and down by the Bembridge Hotel, so that they could claim it as a private road. And another one I remember was the Earl of Fitzwilliam riding round in this small carriage drawn by a donkey.

D'you know that Queen Mary used to come to Bembridge quite often? she would visit several people here. On one occasion William Couldrey rushed across from his antique shop on the corner there [*Sherbourne Street / High Street*] to his other shop, the Emporium, across the road and my aunt Elizabeth was in the shop, his wife, and he said, "Gimme a chair! gimme a chair!" So she asked, "What d'you wanna *chair* for?" And he wouldn't stop to tell her it was for Queen Mary in his antique shop, and my aunt said that everybody saw the Queen except her! I suppose if she'd looked out she would have seen quite a crowd across the road, but she didn't.

King Alfonso of Spain at Bembridge.

Captain Davenport and his family used to live in Westcliff, Pump Lane. They kept their horses and carriage in the coach house down there, well now that's been made into a proper house. And a Mr Durnford was a bachelor and professor at Cambridge University, he lived at Pitt House. All the daffodils used to grow right across his estate, and he used to like going down to see them. His butler's name was Mr Sheridan.

I remember the Countess of Limerick coming to Bembridge and staying at Woodlands, in the High Street. And Alfonso the King of Spain used to come here, 'cause he married Princess Beatrice's daughter, Princess Ina. Well, one old boy told me that when he visited some friends down Swains Road – I believe it was the Elms – the King of Spain would come up to him and say, "Come on, Alf, are you comin' out for a drink tonight?" I don't know whether he made the story up or not!!

Then the Prince of Wales used to come here, the one that later became Edward VIII. 'Cause really on the Island Bembridge came next to Cowes for aristocracy. They would come with their maids and valets and butlers and take one of the big houses, and then they'd take another house, p'raps, for the children and the nannies. But they don't come *now*. The real aristocracy treated you more or less like friends, they'd just talk to you and call you by your Christian name – you know, people that you've *known*, all your life.

## Chapter 1 – The Village As It Was

One was Merton Thomas, at Tyne Hall – 'Our Mertie', as we all called him. There was just him and his mother living there, I think I can just remember the old lady dying. And he was getting on *then*. Well after that he lived there on his own. He was very musical, he used to sing and play the piano when we had village concerts and that sort of thing. And I know the schoolmaster Mr Smith and his wife often used to go there, they were singers, and they'd have little singing parties down there. Then we'd have our Sunday School treats there, and there'd be dancing on the lawn and things like that. He was very good to the village really.

Well, he was a real old bachelor, *well* into his eighties. And I was down on holiday from away, and Mr Couldrey – who I used to call Uncle Will – said, "Have you heard the news? Mertie Thomas is married." I said, "I don't believe you." He says, "It's quite true, his sister's just been in the shop an' told us." It turned out he'd married a Mrs Handley, to do with the Handleys of Southsea, the well-known drapers. And it was quite an event, you know, for *him*, that time.

Well then, they left Tyne Hall and they went up to Bembridge House, in the High Street. And Mary Riddick and my daughter were great friends, my daughter was seven or eight. And it was one Easter, and Mary said to Pat, "I've got t'go up an' thank Mrs Merton Thomas for my Easter egg. Will you come with me?" So they went together, and Mrs Thomas opened the door to them. "Oh," she said, "you *must* come in and see my little Tommie". So o' course, they both thought they were going in to see either a dog or a cat or summing like that, but when they got in, there was this old man sat in the chair, with a rug all round him and a cap on his head, and it was her husband, old Mertie Thomas! They came home tickled pink! He couldna' been married very long even *then*. That must have been about 1930. Oh, he was quite a character!

## A Little Bit o' Cheese & Some Dough Cakes

I can remember the White House being built in Church Street, where the Bellevilles lived, they were out of the top drawer too. But there used to be two shops there before that was built, one of them was Henry Pocock, who was a boot and shoemaker. Then Tom Broomfield had a cottage round by there, and a stables. He had a covered wagon and he ran a carrier service backwards and forwards to Ryde. Of course, it's all changed such a lot since then.

I just remember old Mrs Varnham who used to live round in Harbour Mount, I can remember her as an old lady coming to Church. She was pushed about in a huge chair always.

Then Frederick Osborne lived at Myrtle Cottage, well that's the last cottage on the corner of Point Hill, he was a pilot and so were his two

Early Motor Bus in Sherbourne Street, 1905.

sons also. His wife was a funny little thing, she used to come into the shop [*Tuffley's*] every week and she'd say, "I want a little bit o' cheese, m'dear, only a little bit, and we don't want any rind, because we don't like *rind* an' some people do". We had this story every week. Melinda we used to call her, she let lodgings in the summertime.

The road from Sherbourne Street used to go round the corner and then down the hill, and there was a gate leading into Hill Grove. And then in the middle of the road they planted an oak tree and called it King's Oak, and that's why that house was named King's Oak – the Saviles lived there. But that's very much altered to what it was, I can just remember going round the corner like that, and down the hill. They used to call it Church Street right down to the Point until they put that oak there, and then it became Kings Road. 'Course, we always called it Point Hill, anyway.

Then you come on to those two little Fuchsia Cottages in Sherbourne Street, well one or two of the girls used to roll about in the road. And the railway guard Mr Lee lived next door to us when we lived in Kensington Cottage. Then Josiah Caws the pilot lived in Regent Cottage: he and my gramp and somebody else used to go down nearly every night to the bottom of the Ducie where there was a seat, and they'd sit there and 'look orf', as they called it. It was always "goin' down t'have a look orf"!

Where the Westminster Bank is now, that was two small cottages, two up and two down; well, two of the biggest families in Bembridge lived in

## Chapter 1 – The Village As It Was

those two cottages! Anyway, they were pulled down and the Westminster Bank built there. I believe my grandfather built right along there, he built Kensington Cottage I know and Sherbourne Cottages. And he also built Lindsey Cottage, at the top of Love Lane, where they lived for quite a time.

Next, you've got the Casket Restaurant, well that's where we used to take the mangling. Polly Attrill had that, and her mother let lodgings there: it was called Palmerston Lodge in those days. Well if you didn't have a mangle, you could take your things there: Polly Attrill had a big, old-fashioned roller-mangle out the back, it was a big, heavy box filled with stones, I was scared stiff of it! My brother and I would go with our 'help,' take our washing up there already folded in a big wicker washing-basket with a couple of handles. Then you had to put it on rollers and turn the handle, a heavyweight! which went over and flattened out all the washing. I think we had to pay a penny or tuppence a dozen articles, she had any *amount* of people who'd go there. Polly was always giving away religious tracts and she'd go about looking just like a gypsy, oh she was quite a character in the village, she was!

The Bannister family outside their home in the High Street (later Lloyds Bank), 1906.

Then Lloyds Bank on the corner, well the Bannisters used to live in that cottage before it became Mr Couldrey's antique shop.

William Jacobs lived in Sherbourne Street too, he was the old boy that had been a carrier; it was his son Henry Jacobs that delivered for our shop, he'd collect from the boat mostly, and from the station. But John Jones used to do most of the carrying of the luggage up from the station: he had a horse and one of these flat trolley-things, and where people used to send on luggage in advance or they wanted somebody at the station to meet them, he used to do that.

Now across the road was the old bakehouse run by the Osborns – there was a big bakehouse at the back of the shop, and they sold grocery and cakes such as lard cakes and well-known buns and bread. And we used to let our house [*Burton House*] in the summer and go up and live over the stables at the back of our shop. There was a flat over there, but we didn't have much in the way of cooking arrangements, and we used to take our joint into the bakehouse on a Saturday to be cooked, for a penny, I think it was. Also, my mother would make dough cakes and Osborns would bake the dough cakes for us, and they were lovely, the real old-fashioned ones. Then Miss Osborn, the daughter of the founder, left the shop and went across to Kensington Cottage to live. And their actual baker was a Chick, and he took on the business, and they only closed down not so long ago [*i.e. before 1975*].

Well then came our shop, Tuffley's. And over the shop we had storerooms, and then Love's the builders had their workshop up there – there are steps up the side – before they moved to Northclose Road. Then it was turned into a sort of room used for different things, and as kids we used to go up there to a PSA on Sunday afternoons, they called it 'Pleasant Sunday Afternoons', we had a little religious service there. We used to call that room 'the Shanty'. Where the Midland Bank is now there used to be big gates which were the entrance to the stables belonging to the shop. Levi Dyer kept his horses and cabs in there.

Mr Couldrey had his Emporium next door to us, of course, but before that my grandfather had *that* shop too, as a draper's shop. You see, you had Tuffley's written up on the *two* shops. Then on the side, round the back, we had our one and only bank, the Capital and Counties Bank. Two assistants would come out twice a week from head office in Sandown, and that served for the whole village.

# Chapter 2

# We's Country Chaps
## – Mr Walter Sillence (Part 1)

● It has been a life cycle in more ways than one for 93-year-old Walter Sillence, of Hathfield Road, Bembridge, who is probably the Island's oldest active cyclist.

Walter, 94 at the end of September, has been riding a bike for more than 80 years, and only a few years ago he used to ride to Sandown and back. Now he uses his machine to go about the village.

Walter, a retired joiner and born and bred in Bembridge, has had his bike for more than 25 years. "This one was built to last," he said. "A bike keeps you fit; cars always end up making people put on weight."

Walter Sillence with Bicycle, c.1978. (*IW County Press*)

*Walter Sillence was the first 'old villager' whom I interviewed, and of all my interviewees he left the strongest lasting impression. Born in Bembridge in 1884, at 90 years old he was, at the time of recording, the oldest born-and-bred resident in the village. The recordings were made during three visits to his home in Heathfield Road in January 1975. Apart from fourteen years spent in Yorkshire from 1918 to 1932, he lived the whole of the rest of his life in the village.*

*He possessed a remarkably strong and healthy constitution for a man of his advanced years – much as he himself describes the old lifeboatman Joey Attrill in the recording. He was still regularly riding his bicycle, and on the day of my first visit he had been climbing up his apple-tree! Something of his powerful delivery, as well as his forceful views on just about any and every subject, are hopefully captured in the transcription – this despite the fact that all who knew him could verify that a swear-word never crossed his lips.*

*Despite the fact that Mr Sillence was able to convey so much of the spirit as well as the humour of 'Old Bembridge', including clear memories of when he was just three years old, at the end of an evening's recording session he would say, "Well, mister, I dunno as I can tell yer much", dismissing our previous conversation as of no great consequence. Indeed, his preference for the present time over history (as evidenced in the section on 'School'), together with his ongoing interest in current events, proved that whilst he could recall the past in great detail, he did not dwell in it. I sometimes wonder whether, were he still with us to see this publication finally brought to completion, he might think the whole enterprise a completely wasted effort!*

## Early Days at Bembridge Lodge

I'm the oldest Old Bembridger that's born here. You got plenty older than me that's come here, retired – Bembridge has got like that – it's a place of *retired people*, that's what it's come to!

My father Eli Sillence come here to be head gardener at the Lodge [*in the High Street*], well that's over just ninety years ago, 'twas all one big estate then, and went right down to the Harbour. I was born in the Lodge in that cottage just as you go up into Old Garth – there used to be big iron gates in the front there – well that was head gardener's cottage just on the road there. And then an under-gardener lived in the stable yard.

I had to go to the Church of England school at three. How they used to get me to go to school, they'd say, "Go down ter see the ducks, go down ter see the ducks". In fact I got knocked over three times be an engineer that was up here for Steyne Wood Battery – he come along on his bike and just as he got near the Lodge gates there, ring his bell and I'd run for home and o' course got beat over three times – anyhow, **never killed me, mate**!

There was another private school run by old Gov'ness Attrill in one o'

## Chapter 2 – We's Country Chaps

they old cottages where that there grocer's shop is now [*now a private house a couple of properties along from the Village Inn*]. She used to get out and sweep the roads sometimes out front of her... I was proper frightened of 'er. They'd say, "Oh she'll take yer in an' give you a ...!" – I was only three, yer know. I never wanted to be anywhere near her, I was *scared* of 'er! Joey Attrill's sons went there, I know, Teddy Attrill and Johnny Attrill. But they didn't get much education with ol' Gov'ness Attrill. I'll tell yer what, Teddy Attrill said to Mr Smith, "I wish I'd 'a went ter *your* school!"

Well weekends, we youngsters was brought up t'have to work. After the Lodge, my father was a head-gardener at East Cliff, and his own garden had to be kept perfect. Well we boys had to keep every blinkin' weed all out o' that, aw! – hand-weeded. Then up the garden path there's this blessed old thorn-hedge, that had to be weeded, and the blessed ol' thorn 'ud be in yer finger and I've had me fingers bleeding many a time! I thought myself, "If ever I gets a house o' me own, I'll never have a blinkin' ol' thorn-hedge!" And I haven't either!

But we warn't good enough to dig my father's garden, anyhow, 'cos he'd say, "You're gettin' that in a hole!" – it had to be as level as a billiard table, see. I think he was very pleased to be left to do't hisself. At the same time, he would have his garden *right*. Now the man next door was a carpenter and there's come a dry summer. So he says, "I can't make out your father's garden, he don't seem to do no more 'n what I do, but his stuff looks orright, an' mine's all wilting!" Well he didn't dig the *depths* like my father, yer see, and got dried out. You gotta put the work into anythink, for to get the best results!

Then you had these old steel knives and forks, you had to rub them on a knife-board to clean 'em, and you'd have a bit o' chammy leather to tip in the knife-powder and clean the whole steel forks – well I've had they beggars stick in me fingers 'fore that, aw haw haw!

But my father didn't want me to go in for gardening, no. He says, "Yer don't get paid for what you *know*". Well, one time Sturgess was working as gardener down East Cliff, he come years after my father was working there. And he says, "Yer know these fellers that come down from th' army an' the navy, they don't know how to do greenhouse work, grow the stuff, nobody expects *them*, but they expects *me* to do't, 'cos I can do't, but" – he says – "they all gets the same *money* as I do!" There y'are, that's the differentials in paying, yer see.

## School – and Military Discipline

Now when I was in the infants' school, I *copied*. Well, the Vicar's gardener's son – ol' Canon Le Mesurier was the Vicar at that time – well he was a good

Bembridge Primary School, with headmaster Alfie Smith. Date unknown.

chap, some of us was up top next t'him, *we* never done no sums, we copied. Then ol' Canon Le Mesurier went away and took his gardener, and o' course, the gardener's son went an' all. So anyhow, then we had to go up in the big school, and I'm bothered if the blessed teacher that was in the infants' school come up with us. Every time sums – out four cuts, and I would always have another couple for acting about or summat. I was on average for twelve cuts, two years to get over that! Cuts on the hand, yer see – but there you are, you mustn't touch anybody today! That's one o' the silliest things *owt*, and another thing is this – taking that religious instruction out, it's detri-*mental*, there you did have the *rules* of religion, you had ter learn the Commandments an' all that. I'm doubtful now whether a lot of 'em knows the Commandments at all.

And we had sums, morning and afternoon, and the only time we went out of the school was over the wall into the field, to peg out a bit o' ground, then we'd have to go and find the area – well that was jolly good teaching, wasn't it? that was something to *learn*, to find the area.

We learnt to read and write an' draw, maps and all that, history, geography... I liked geography because reading yer paper yer know where things are, but I didn't like history, I didn't wanna give two buttons if anybody's *dead* – any of yer blessed kings and that – they's dead, well they're *finished* wi' me!

## Chapter 2 – We's Country Chaps

Well Alfred Smith was the schoolteacher as well as organist and choirmaster, and he had yer like soldiers. Friday arternoons he'd have yer out in the playground, drilling yer. Now, yer'd have ter "Wheel round! Come round!" If you warn't coming round straight he'd come along and hit you in the stomach – "You there, you're too far ahead!" – you had to be looking to come round straight as a line. Then he'd form you up in rows. You'd be lined up – "Odd numbers stand fast, even numbers – move! Form – Two D!" He wanted to form yer in fours, yer see. Well then – "Right dress! Rear rank, two paces ter the rear! One – two!" Now then, he'd say, "Form Four!" so you'd go back, now you're in fours. And he had yer drilled, and you'd be alright, he'd have yer right, yer see. March yer round, well there's no mistake, he had *discipline*, and he could use the cane too – and the same time, if he *did* use the cane, what a schoolmaster 'ud give yer at school warn't hurt yer a bit. It do help to keep order, whereas now they don't trouble a bit.

Well, they used to play Reary Bug in school. Now then, where there was a school wall, you'd have two hands, and all these others gotta run any time that they liked to get across. Then if you got caught you had to be 'it' until they got a reg'lar big lot, yer see. And when they caught 'em all, we used to call that Reary Bug.

Then we had rounders, and Friday afternoons was a long playtime, and we'd have the girls out there as well. But anyhow Smith, the fisherman's son, he could throw a ball pretty straight. Anyway, when the girls was in, we had to be catching, yer see, so he caught the ball, and as the schoolmaster's daughter's running through, he caught her in the ear and beat her over! They says, "Steady, Smith, steady!" He'd hit her real hard, knocked this gal right over! Yeah!

Another time we had a long playtime, and we'd had a real good running about. Then we got in and had to stand up fer singing! Cor! There's the chaps goin' all faint an' that – well I tell yer, I was in the back row. By crikey, my head starts spinning round – I thought, "I'm beggared if I'm not goin' next, I'm gonna sit down". *I* warn't gonna go out in the cold, so I sat down! He never see me sit down at the back! Ha-ha-ha! I got alright after I had a bit of a rest.

You had anything on in the school them times. I tell yer, once there was a Harry Weaver – they was sort o' singing. Someone says, "You little sprat!" and he say, "You lump o' fat! Mind-you-don't-put-yer-hands-on-me!" He come in comical, yer see.

I know when I went t'ambulance class once, when the doctor started to talk about crepitus, cor! we had a blinkin' feller pass out! That's when you get a broken bone and you hear the grating, yer see – and some fellers 'ud do that!

# A Village Church with a Cathedral Choir

Bembridge Church Choir.

Now, take the choir. Mr Smith, he would have it *right*. We bin in the school, choirboys goin' out to play at playtime. "Choirboys, I want yer!" Well, we'd be round the harmonium, he'd just get yer to learn the anthems and that which we had, we done the Hallelujah Chorus and all o' that. D'you know, they used to say one time, "A village church with a cathedral choir" – we went to Winchester and beat Southampton, Bournemouth an' all the lot of 'em, the village did! Yes, you had some real good solid bass there, too – Alf Weaver and Newton Newman, Ern Osborne, ol' Perce Weaver – I tell you, you had some real good singers. And we boys, we was trained up to it pretty well, but old Smith, he'd have the whole school on singing up high, 'Aa' and 'Aa' [*sings*], up, yer see.

Anyhow, there's a boy come from up there near the duck pond name Charlie Butler, he couldn't sing at all, so he stand with his mouth wide open. So Smith come round, he says, "You singin', Butler?" "Yessir." "Well I can't *hear* yer!" If you didn't have yer mouth open, he'd very soon put a pointer in: "Open yer mouth, open yer mouth wide!" Yes, you had to be smart with him, there's no mistake. He did have discipline, but now they're just as much th' other way. I think it's absolutely a disgrace.

Now I'll tell yer, when we was in the choir, we used to get up there early to get surplices on an' all. Anyhow, there's one boy not quite so old as me

## Chapter 2 – We's Country Chaps

be a month or so but bigger – oh he was *on* some, saying what he could do! So he says he'll "go an' hit him" – that was *me*, yer see! He come across, as though he was gonna hit me, yer know. "Right," I thought, "that's not gonna be good enough for me, mate!" As he let out, I knocked his hand away an' I caught him by the nose, and down his surplice the blinkin' blood, you could never see such a mess in yer life! Nippers had his surplice off, over school, under tap, and then he had to stand in all amongst the nippers so the men wouldn't see the blessed surplice all wet through, ah ha! Play the part, he never wanted another touch, I caught him a proper clip! I give him a proper solder right in the nose! He'd think he was gonna run over me like that, mate! Why, didn't I fetch the blood out of him, by Jove alive!

I tell yer another time – a nephew of mine who was in the choir, he had this 'ere stuff you could tear to make a 'phiwt' noise as if you'd split yer trousers. Anyhow, Reverend Sims-Williams was up here then. So when the Vicar bent down for something, my nephew just went 'phiwt!' and Sims-Williams thought he'd split his trousers! he looked a bit *uncomf'table*, I can tell yer! I bet he's some glad when he got home to see what was the matter!

If you happened to be hanging around the street of a night, the old bobby was round. Yer see, when we was out choirboys, we was on acting about an' that, and the policeman's name was Toomer. So see him comin': "Here comes Two More, here comes Two More!" We was big as the law! But we was very soon orf! He used to get round, I s'pose, ter shift yer round.

Well there 'twas, in Mr Smith you had a man who was *gifted*, yet he never had a music lesson in his life, couldn't understand people wanting a music lesson. Yet he could bring all that out in th' organ an' all, mate. You could reg'lar *feel* it. That's who made the church there, right enough – the choir. *Now*, well there ain't no choir at all now. When I was up last, I's to the organist, "How many?" "Oh, only about two in there now." Well there's nothing for a man to *want* the job now. But when you had yer full choir, several men each side and full up wi' boys, well then you wanted to be part of it, mate.

## Helping Out at the Slaughter House

The slaughterhouse for Jordan was that little lane going down on the left of Foreland Road, just after the shops, they call it Slaughterhouse Row. When I was a nipper I bin up there as far as Yaverland, down over Boscombe Shute,★

---

★Boscombe Shute does not appear to be recorded anywhere, though the same name is also used for fetching bullocks by Ashford Caws in his transcription, and therefore must once have been in standard use. It is most likely an earlier or alternative name, now redundant, for Marshcombe Shute in the Yaverland area.

and help a man fetch p'raps two bullocks for slaughter. They was out on the mesh [*marshes*], as they call it, where you'd get yer selected few they had marked, and we'd have to drive two, p'raps, to come to Bembridge. And then every time I'd have to go ahead on 'em round Sandown Road, to sort o' turn 'em to keep on going 'fore they could turn off. Well you wouldn't be able to drive bullocks along the road like we did, they gotta come in a cattle-truck *now*, in a proper van. And the roads were so narrow then – Foreland Road has been made ver' near twice as wide as it was. 'Cos you had sheep on the roads too, and pony and traps o' course.

But I had a proper good fright though once. I wasn't left school, I was helping Jordan the butcher in the summer holidays. There was me and Wreaf Woodford, he was only a young chap then, and the other man's name was Beer. And when Mr Jordan himself was there, we were gonna kill a bullock. He'd help pull and he'd say, "Now, boys, drive him up!" I had to drive the bullock up and he goes through into a calf-pen and comes out onto the block, yer see. Well now, when we's on our own, us three, well Beer would drive us up – there, just this youth and me only a nipper, to pull a *bullock* in! Cor!

Anyhow, then once the blinkin' bullock come near quick, mate! He comes through the sheep's pen, then the beggar's comin' right at yer! I dodged 'n, he at me again, I dodged 'n again and up over the wall like a shot, and shook like a leaf! I's pretty soon out of the way of him too! Afore all the rope run out, mate, Wreaf Woodford got a turn on, but he'd bin loose in the yard! Cor! Oh, I've had some rum 'uns there, yer know! Well, I tell yer, they used to let some o' Lacey's cows come in there then sometimes, so as to get a bullock in, 'cos that 'ud quieten 'em down.

But there's no fridges then, yer see. D'you know, Mr Jordan once lost a *whole* bullock – through bad weather, that's why! That's what yer had to put up with! Another thing – when I was there, you had to go round with a bundle o' withies and hit the meat, to beat the flies off – you had any amount of 'em on the meat then. But now they keeps 'em out.

So anyhow, in the slaughterhouse you'd also kill the sheep, then you'd pick up the blood in the trough, congealed, and put it in a bucket. Then they'd put it in a tub and take it out in a field, where they had a lot o' ground so they could bury it in this 'ere earth. And the same with all the old paunches and all that, yer see.

Well, another job I had to do was take the meat out on a wooden tray, haul it out on yer shoulder. Anyhow, old Mr Jordan one day, "Oh," he says, "er, I wancha ter take that meat down to Number Two Swains." So I takes it to Number Two. "Oh *we* haven't ordered the meat." So I went back to the shop, I says, "They haven't ordered that meat." "Well p'raps it's Number Two Maylands." So I tries again, same thing – no. "Oh well, put it on the slab, somebody'll be comin' for it." Well turned out it was for San Remo, that was the big house there down Swains. So when I eventually got down there, the ol' cook shot out at me – "What's the good o' bringin' it *now*?" she says, "I wanted that fer dinner! What use is it now?" So I told him, I says, "She didn't half...!" But he didn't care, he didn't care a bit, ol' Mr Jordan, he laughed some about it! I had a proper old telling-off with this ol' cook – "I can't get that ready fer dinner *now*!" Aw-haw-haw! Dear oh dear! He had a laugh, he never cared though, ol' Mr Jordan, no!

## Proper Old Stagers

Well my father went on from the Lodge to be head gardener for the Earl and Countess Fitzwilliam at East Cliff for fourteen years. They had a yacht under Tyne, *Kathleen*, it used to be anchored well out, and they'd come in on the rowing galley. Well they had several men on there for crew, and the oars would come right up in the air, just like in the Navy. And when the old Earl got aboard as they were goin' out for the yacht, well I know as a nipper there's all the crew up aboard 'er, then... just a word – away! Just like clockwork it was, yeah!

The Fitzwilliams had coal mines up the north, and they had the biggest private house in the country, that was Wentworth Woodhouse in Yorkshire – 'bout quarter of a mile long, that house was reckoned to be – then they had a house in London, and another one over in Ireland. And me father had to send the big hampers up to London – 'cos they had their hens, butter, Jersey cows, as well as greenhouse stuff, peaches, nectarines, melons, they even had strawberries at Christmas time, but there warn't a bit o' sweetness in 'em – forced, yer see. Then he had eight gardeners under him. And a footman reckoned my father the best packer of the lot! Now other people used to pack strawberries so tight that they moved, and you'd get 'em squashed. But when my father packed 'em, you could just open up and 'twas just as if they'd bin put there, he says – that was ol' Jock Lucas, and he looked after the vinery, too.

Then me father would get up at four o'clock every morning, 'cos he wanted to be up when the old Earl come along and, "Ow's the grapes?" He wanted to be able to pick a lovely bunch, yer see. Father used to take a pride in his work, there's no doubt about it, it had to be exactly. 'Course, when he took over at East Cliff, there warn't no lodge there for the head gardener, so we moved to Foreland Road, to a house called Madeira – there wasn't *many* houses in Foreland Road at that time. There was just the Limes and the Hollies, then Jordan's had these three Salisbury Cottages up near Slaughterhouse Row. Well then this coastguard feller Weeks and Walt Caws's father – he was a pilot – they had a pair of houses put up next to where my father lived. Weeks's was called Lucknow, and Caws's was called Cawnpore, but they's all renamed now, yer see.

Then the Thomases had Tyne Hall – they was proper ol' stagers, you had to be proper smart wi' them. I'll tell yer one thing about it though – they had a yard to get in the back door and they had this great big dog there, and he was a rotten thing to deal with. But the brewer come there and he *frightened* that dog – well how'd he do't? He got a bowler hat he wore, put it in his mouth, and crawled on his hands at him and sort o' went at the dog, like, and the dog shook and went into the blinkin' kennel out the way! And always when that brewer come, that dog was coward. Well I've seen *my* father just ketch a dog's eye and watch him, they're turned tail 'n gorn, mate! Oh I tell yer, dogs, they know if you're frightened o' them or not, they get that off d'recly.

Well you had a very good class o' people come here one time, for the Lodge [*Bembridge Lodge*]. *My* wife had the Duke of Richmond's grandchildren for lodgers once, and their two nurses, yeah! When we was living in the Cedars, there in Foreland Road.

Now then, Colonel Moreton was a man like that. Fellers used to be stood up at the top o' Foreland Road, no work, yer see. Colonel Moreton 'ud come along – "Nothing ter do?" "No." "Well," he says, "go an' get some barrels, there's a heap o' stones out in my field, wheel them up into other corner!" So they went down and shifted all this lot. "We've done that, sir." "Well," he says, "now wheel 'em *back* again!" Then he paid 'em! They had to do summat for to get paid! Ah ha! Yeah, ol' Colonel Moreton was a reg'lar sort.

## Loves the Builders

I started my apprenticeship as carpenter on April 4th 1899 when I was just under fourteen, there you are, and worked till I was seventy. I left school and started straightaway 'cos Loves *wanted* somebody, and if I hadna' went then somebody else would've had the job. We used to work ten hours a day weekdays, and we had to work till three o'clock Saturday when I first started, well then it got to one o'clock, then twelve o'clock.

Well there was George Caws, he was the eldest, then there was Love's sons, himself, Alf Love, Fred Love and Will Love, then Charlie come after, he's younger than me. Well all the lot of them's gone now. Mr Love used to live at that time in Number 1 the Cedars in Foreland Road. His carpenter shop first was over Sothcott's [*in Sherbourne Street*], up them wooden steps, and that's where I started with him, then he had this other one built down Northclose Road.

Well when I was an apprentice, there was just The Limes in Foreland Road – Dr Payne used to live there, and then a couple further on. I had to start work at six o'clock all the year round, and I had to feel along the

## Chapter 2 – We's Country Chaps

blinkin' hedge to know where to turn down Northclose Road to the shop, 'twas that there dark sometimes in wintertime! And then we only had little paraffin lamps to see with when we got there, they was hung up – how ever we saw I'm beggared if I knows now! Then we used to go back for breakfast – eight o'clock, half an hour for breakfast – then back again. Making a ten-hour day. I used t'have a game if I was getting bigger too. Ol' George Caws, I could go at him, yer know. I said, "Look out, I'll give you a bit of Old English!" and get yer fist like this, go in and push him up the end of the shop an' that – when I was getting a bit bigger, yer know.

Mr Love had an orchard put up down there, and he had the carpenter's shop put up down there, then since they've had a plumber's shop, a brick office an' all that, garage – well, it's all gone today, bungalows there now! Oh we used to do all the lot, we never had no joiners from Morey's or nothin' like that, we'd do it all, yeah, stairs an' everything. That's where you *learnt* your trade, yer see.

Like a plumber said to me about, "Oh, plumbin's the best trade." "Ah," I said, "I'll tell you what is the best trade – carpenter," I says, "Christ was a carpenter, he picked out the best one." He says, "I never knew that one before, mate!" You gotta have one always ready, yer know!

Well when I was working for Love's, we had an old bricklayer feller on with us, Ted Clarke, well he said he *cried* to go to school, but he always had to stop and look after the cows, and he was the oldest. Anyhow, he's taken ill there once and he come back to work: "Ah," he says, "Chaps, you know, it's not so easy ter die as what you thinks. When I was bad I *tried* to die an' couldn't!" Oh, we had some comical ones, yer know!

Old Mr Love, he was a smart feller. He could do a job and do it quick and make a good job of it, too. And he could paperhang. I'll guarantee he's paperhang quicker than two o' the fellers that you have today. And I'll tell yer another thing, when I's a boy, we went down Foreland House, I had to go down there and paste for him. And I used to race trying to beat him, yer see. He'd have a line o' paper – c'mon, ready, and then, it just suited him for me to be roustin' along, but he could whack it up, and 'twas there, 'twas alright! Well a lot of them, they don't know how to do that, yer see! He knew just how to go on. But he was *making* the firm, and you had to *work*, I can tell yer. He was just the feller to wake a boy up, I can tell yer that! And that's what a lot of 'em wants. They comes away from the school, they seems real duds – never bin woke up! There's no discipline!

## Stand Back Three Paces!

See, my feet – I was dished out to go abroad but I didn't pass. I was in the Naval Air Service, but I had to go afore Travelling Medical Board, three doctors at table: "Anythin' a matter 'a you?" "No, not's I know of," I says, "only rather bad on me feet". "Stand back three paces!" One o' these doctors went, "Oh this is true, if this man can possibly carry on 'ere, be all means let 'im stop 'ere". I wasn't troubled any more. But I done my bit then, I tell yer. I couldna' gone to France – with them blessed great boots I had one toenail come orf and another one almost orf. And when I come home I see the doctor. "Good gracious!" he says, "haven't you got a sick bed there, if you don't look out you'll have t'have some toes orf".

I was late going in, for the simple reason Love's had government contracts, yer see. We had anythink right round from Northwood Park at Cowes there, right round to Sandown Barracks and out on St Helens Fort sometimes an' all. Fifty houses in Ryde you had ter go to and ride yer bike out there to get to 'em. Then there's places where the airmen had their huts – on Northwood Park there was a place there, see, on Ludham Camp, that's Osbirn [*Osborne*]. Anywhere all on that you had to be goin', yer see. They don't know what work is today, mate. And I've had to ride with a bag o' tools with that lot, too. But you had to do it them days. Why? three men for a job, mate. Now you gets your cards and you're in somewhere else.

I tell yer, Charlie Love, the youngest one of all, we's on match-lining a shed near Cowes for the people that had to be looking out for the aircraft comin' over. Well anyhow, to save us having to bike all out there the next day we laid on the timber that night, had a sleep, got up next morning early, finished the job and come back then.

Then as I say, I bin on St Helens Fort an' that, I had to make the place round the light, I had ter make like a shed round this 'ere blinkin' light thing, yer see. That's one o' the jobs I had out there. And what with landing-places and one thing an' the other. Yer know, you'd never believe how the tide… if you don't have yer battens far enough apart, the tide'll come up and cut the boats right orf. We had it once there. Yet we had it apart, the battens on, where they landed, and a rough sea an' that, and the boats left in on there just bin cut off – you'd never believe the power of the sea.

## Guns and Sewers

Well when they made that fort on the down, Culver, they had to get the guns up there an' all that, yer know. I've seen guns brought up over Point Hill, reg'lar heavy and sink in the road and one thing an' the other. They'd have horses and that there, o' course there come traction engines then at the finish. I've seen a traction engine reg'lar lift up like that to go down her wheels. You had ter get everything over there, y'see.

There was Nodes Point and Culver, they reckoned a ship comin' into Portsmouth, if she gets onto one bow on, she'd be broadside on t'other one!

## Chapter 2 – We's Country Chaps

Hauling the 9.7 inch guns to Culver Battery, c.1928.

They reckoned they could fire 'em off like that. But anyhow that's all out o' date now.

Now when I was a boy my father Eli Sillence was Chairman of the Parish Council for years. I wouldn't have a public office for anything. Anyhow, they wanted to put the sewer and the water through Foreland Road, and the people: "Ooh, the rates'll be up somewhere!" Well then they elected a lot that the Rural District Council ignored 'em, then when the progressives got in again, they got the sewer and the water in. Now, how many would want it taken out now? Bembridge then was a place growing and getting for visitors, and you gotta *cater* for visitors! They're not gonna come to empty earth-closets after the towns! You had t'have yer pump water in the back garden, then you had to empty yer midden right up the top o' the garden, all the water draining this way.

## A Real Good Time

Bembridge one time used to have ***a real good time***. Ducie Avenue used to be illuminated for the regattas. Ol' William Couldrey had any amount of Chinese lanterns in his shop there, they call it the Emporium in them times. All down the Ducie yer see all strings o' these lanterns, and looked quite nice, yer know. Any amount o' people used ter come, fellers there 'long with these long feathers, ladies' teasers, an' all sorts.

And we'd be dancing on the lawns and that. Well I'll tell yer, meself an' others, well, we's country chaps, I says, "We'll have to get ter know how to do this dancing, we're right out of it all. Well you had a very good class o' people come for the Lodge! So, we used t'have dancing classes down at Bembridge Hotel then – 'twas on the right, what we used to call New Road just as yer go down Point Hill. Well anyhow, there's me and Frank Orchard, six of us went there, we was going ter learn dancing. Well we let six dances go by, so I says t'old Frank: "I'm goin' in this next one, chance what 'tis". "So'm I," he says. Gets in there – set o' Lancers! Cor! Pushed here and there an' all about, I couldn't see anything, just like summat flyin' by! But anyhow, you get used to it in the finish, you can do it alright. Well the two that we went in, we only take the sides, and the top and bottom they just put us through. So we done very well! I'm beggared if I coulda seen anybody.

And I learned how to keep in the ring proper. Well some people don't know how to do it and you know why? 'Cos they *locks their feet*! If yer's waltzing you gotta keep yer feet far enough back so you can swing, then if you got a dancer with yer well you can go round as pretty as you like. Well, after my father left East Cliff there's two or three fellers come there to be head gardener, but anyhow a man come there, Taylor, and his wife – she was a nice dancer, so I partnered her once for a waltz. She said, "Can you reverse?" "No," I says, "I can't reverse." "Well let's try." She being a dancer, I could reverse a treat. "I thought you said you couldn't reverse, you're reversin' beautiful," she says. That's because you got a *dancer*. But I'm beggared if I had some o' the girls you had ter pull round, you had a reg'lar stiff arm the next mornin'!

Well them days the Hampshire Friendly used t'have a dance; there was Primrose League, to do with the Conservatives; Lane End Regatta, you could dance down there; and you could have a dance on Tyne Hall lawn as well as in the church room, yer see. Yes, we fellers enjoyed the fun. And up near the Grange they had a new hall there put up, and I put down a secret nailed floor there – 'cos after they had it for dancing, then they made it for roller skating, so you had to put down a hardwood floor, yer see. Oh, I went up there to do skating, 'twas a laugh about that. A feller that was gonna be in charge of it, he go along, make out he could turn, yer know, quite to come back. So he'd go over every time. "An' yer nearly done it that time!" – get him to go up there right on these roller skates, yer see.

Well, one time o' day Bembridge had a very good football team. I didn't play a lot, but I *did* play some games. I had one feller, mate, in a game, he was coming 'long at me and jumping and he'd 'a caught in me ribs with his feet, jumpin' at yer. Well anyhow, I see'n comin', so I stuck m' heel and stopped. He went round and skidded along in the dirt and mud like that. "Well done, Walter!" That 'ere shook him up! He didn't expect... I could see I was gonna get him broadside on, mate. Stuck m' heel out and held back like that, and he went an' skidded by! Cor! That shook *him* up, I'll bet a shillin'!

# Chapter 3

# A Fisherman's Life
## – Mr Ashford Caws (Part 1)

Ashford Caws and John Luff. The latter sat in on one of the early recordings with Ashford Caws.

*Ashford Caws was born in Bembridge in 1887, had spent his whole life in the village, and was 87 years old when I recorded him, which made him the second oldest born-and-bred villager at the time. The recordings were made over four visits to his home between October 1975 and February 1976, and he turned out to be the most prolific informant. Mr Caws was still living at Yew Cottage in the High Street, which had been his and his wife's home for over 60 years; but the Caws family had also owned the adjoining cottage called St Helens View from the early days, and both properties were still in possession of the family at the time of the recordings. The two cottages adjoin the Village Inn, and St Helens View had formerly been Dame Attrill's private school. (The properties are now modernised, with a change of names.)*

*Mr Caws' grandson, the late Robin Caws, was greatly interested in the project, and had not only traced his family history, but was also able to pull* together the various threads regarding the two family homes, in large measure with information supplied by his great-aunt Dorothy, Ashford's sister. Therefore, by way of an introduction, the first section is largely based on notes garnered from Robin, interspersed with spoken parts "in quotes" taken directly from Ashford Caws' own account; the full recordings then follow on from there.

The Caws family tree, like most family trees, is complex, so I shall try to provide a simple outline of the earlier ancestors, putting more flesh on the bones, so to speak, as we move down the tree.

## The Caws Family Background

Robert Caws, a labourer of St Helens, married Hannah Heail in 1755, and their son John Caws was baptised in St Helens in 1758. John married Martha Hollis in 1779 and they evidently settled in Bembridge soon afterwards. John and Martha had three girls and five boys, one of whom, William, was baptised in 1783 and married Sarah Cooper in 1802. There was no church in Bembridge at this early period of the village's development – it first acquired its own church only in 1827 – and therefore baptisms and marriages for Bembridge would have taken place at Brading Church. William and Sarah Caws had seven boys and one girl, also called Sarah.

It is this second Sarah, or 'Sally', Caws who is the important link in our chain: she was born in 1825 and lived to the grand old age of 92, dying in 1917. In 1846 she married Charles Smith. Charles was a mariner like his father John Smith, and they were related to the Smiths down Lane End – Quilly and Henley. Being quite wealthy and owning several houses, Charles bought Yew Cottage from the owners of the Village Inn in 1858, and then had St Helens View built, which he and Sarah made the family home.

The story switches at this point to Sarah's brother Silas Caws, who was born in Bembridge in 1830 but moved to Portsmouth in 1857, marrying Emily Attrill there in the same year. Emily was also from Bembridge, and was reputedly the sister of the great Edmund 'Joey' Attrill (the second-ever coxswain of Bembridge's first lifeboat the *City of Worcester*). Silas was crewman on the yacht *Marequita*, given as his address at the time of his marriage, and where their children William and Laura were born, in 1858 and 1860 respectively. They then moved back to Bembridge in 1861 or 2 and stayed with Silas's sister Sarah – who everyone knew as Sally – at St Helens View. Within a year Emily had died, and Sarah, who by now was in the habit of taking children in off the street, took charge of her brother's children, William and Laura.

Silas then travelled across to Cowes to work on a yacht there, lodged in the area, and remarried. The daughter Laura was taken off somewhere – there

## Chapter 3 – A Fisherman's Life

is a gap in the story at this point – but William remained with his 'Aunt Sally' at St Helens View, for which Silas paid Sarah an allowance. But Sarah claimed it was not enough, an argument ensued, and as a result there was no further communication between these two branches of the family until the boy William was grown up. Silas in fact only visited Bembridge once again before he died in 1902. There was a thunderstorm that night, and Dorothy (William's daughter), then only a child and scared of thunder, spent most of the time under the stairs, so she caught only the barest glimpse of Silas. It must have been rather uncomfortable under the stairs, because the meat and the coal used to be kept in there as well.

William retained his father's surname (rather than his aunt's surname Smith) and became known locally as Billy Caws – though Aunt Sally continued to call him 'Willy'. She lived in the back bedroom of St Helens View and had a habit of calling to him over and over again to come forward until he did so. Billy married Jane Butler and they had three surviving children: Ashford (our subject) born in 1887, Dorothy in 1893, and Herbert in 1896. Being that Great-Aunt Sally lived until 1917, Ashford of course remembers her very well: "She fell over and broke her hip when she was 90 and she recovered from that – 'course, there warn't no hospital they could take 'em to *then*. And she had another set o' teeth come through, she could crack a *brazil* nut with 'em when she was over 90!" (If Sally's husband Charles Smith seems to have disappeared from the story altogether, this is because he had already died in 1875, at the much younger age of 50.)

Ashford's father Billy Caws was a very popular character and was credited with the 'gift of the gab'. "He used to go round all the gentry and talked his way through the house. If you see 'n go in the back door, tradesman's entrance, warn't no good to wait out the back door fer '*im*, he might come out the front door!... Before my father was married, I think he was on the Earl o' Ducie's yacht as assistant cook." Billy also had a reputation for being very impetuous. On one occasion, he suddenly decided to cut down all the trees in the garden of St Helens View, where of course he had become the head of the house. They used to keep two pigs up the garden, and on another occasion Billy came charging up the passage with "Put the copper on!" as there had been an outbreak of swine fever, so the pig had to be killed quickly and cut up before it was taken away for destruction. "'Cos years ago we used t'have two pigs and we'd get 'em smoked up John Snow's [*at Hillway*]. We used to take 'em up about a month before Christmas and then bring 'em back just before. Then once my father come home and he says, 'Light up the copper, gonna kill the pig! Swine fever abowt! Kill 'm 'fore he gets it!'" Billy also once sold an enormous flatfish for a shilling, which was considered quite generous, considering that it was about eight times the normal size and the standard price was sixpence.

The kitchen at the back of Yew Cottage once had a lean-to where beer was brewed for the Village Inn, next door. The well in the corner of the kitchen is older than the house, twenty-four feet deep, and when previously last seen (in about 1955, when new floors were put down), it was said to have been 'beautifully made', in a spiral pattern of bricks. It was thought to have been used for storing smuggled goods. "Sarah Jordan, who had Waterloo Cottage, she used to reckon a lot o' smuggling went on up 'ere!" At the time of recording (1976) there was still a pump just outside the back door. And the cupboard in the kitchen was once full of barley salvaged from the wreck of the *Egbert* in 1867, the rescue which led to the presentation of the first Bembridge lifeboat, the *City of Worcester*. "That cupboard there was full o' barley once upon a time, a boat come in full of it, they smuggled the barley and they papered that all over so no-one should see't."

Of Billy Caws' wife, Jane Butler, we know that before she was married, she used to work for the Thomases at Tyne Hall, and that she was descended from the Butlers who once had Smugglers Cottage on the downs above Whitecliff Bay. Annie Butler, Jane's sister, looked very much like her, and the only way to tell them apart was that Annie had a wart on her tongue! Their father Billy Butler lived further up the High Street, in the former White Cottages. "He used ter say funny things" and grew radishes in his front garden. He had married their mother, Caroline Jones, in 1853, and she subsequently carried blocks of chalk down from the chalk pit at Longlands for the building of the Embankment; unsurprisingly, perhaps, she also lived to a great age!

Just before the First World War there were living at St Helens View: Billy and Jane Caws, the three children (already grown up) Ashford, Herbert and Dorothy, Aunt Sally, cousin Teddy Caws – "some relation, I don't quite know who", and Jim Harbour – "what they called Crabby Harbour, Aunt Sally used to sort o' look after 'n". In little Yew Cottage at the same time the Woodford family resided as tenants of the Caws. Charlie Woodford was an engineer on the *Island Queen*. They had twelve children – six boys and six girls – and a dog, and only two bedrooms between them. They would line up their shoes under a bed in the kitchen, and these would stretch the whole length of the kitchen wall. What's more, Billy and Jane used to let out the little room above the scullery of St Helens View to visitors in the summer. One such was Mr Pilditch, the family solicitor from London, who honeymooned on Billy's boat.

Cousin Teddy Caws was the singing sailor with a tenor voice who performed for the King of Spain. He was said to have been dismissed from the navy for drinking too much [*the navy, for drinking?*]. "Teddy was in the old navy, in the sailing-ships years ago, Teddy was. 'Cos when the choir had their sort o' dinner down the Bembridge Hotel, they used to get him to go and sing *Anchors Aweigh!* – proper ol' one, yer know." When he was quite old, he made an effort to go and see young Henry, Ashford's son, in his cot outside the back door of Yew Cottage, and was supposed to have said, "Yer a funny-lookin' bugger, ain't yer?" It is almost certain that a monumental inscription at Bembridge Holy Trinity Church for Edwin Charles Caws, giving his age at death in 1917 as seventy and his address as St Helens View, is this same Teddy Caws; it would also mean that he was born in 1846 or 7.

Billy Caws and both his sons, being fishermen, were also very good rowers, but whereas Ashford was more of a steady rower, Herbert went in for spectacular oarsmanship and was acknowledged to be the local champion. On one particular occasion Herbert had done half a day's fishing when someone passing him out at sea reminded him that the Regatta was on in Bembridge; whereupon he rowed round and arrived in time for the start of the race, won the race hands down, and then rowed home without stopping to collect his prize. He then went back out and finished his day's fishing!

It's an open question whether the reason why some Bembridge fishermen wouldn't learn to swim was due to the superstition that if the sea wanted them it could take them anyway. When asked about this, Ashford would simply say, "Well they just didn't bother, did they?"

The Caws tea garden was established in 1919 at the back of the two houses, which shared one garden, and it ran between the wars. Ashford and Herbert caught the lobsters and crabs, while their wives Ethel and Victoria made the cakes and jam. Tables were set round a square lawn, and there was a shelter at the back for when it rained, with a white rose trailing all over it; if that overflowed, visitors were ushered into the front room of Yew Cottage. A printed advertisement from the period reads:

**Caws Tea Gardens, High St., Bembridge**
**Lobster luncheons (1/6) and Prawn teas.**
**Fresh fish daily. Home made cakes and jam.**
**Eight minutes' walk from sea and station.**

Ethel Caws also used to be persuaded to do the catering for the coronation parties down Love Lane fields, where there were big marquees, and she appears to have done it just about singlehandedly. "Alf Watson, he done the hot water, and Jack Riddick supplied all the food. 'Bout tuppence for every person, to help pay for it, yer see. But she had money left over, she didn't use all of it."

"And the wife used to do the catering for the Women's Institute parties down the church room: they'd charge two shillings for a double ticket, plenty of everythin' down there. She used to have four shoulders o' bacon for half-a-crown each, two from Riddick's and two from down Sothcott's.

Caws Tea Garden at the rear of the house, next to the Village Inn.

They'd cook 'em, then they'd mince that up and make sandwiches o' that. And then they got Jack Mursell to make 'em a hundred or two sausage rolls. And they was never out o' pocket! She was a good caterer."

"Who the wife worked for down Pitt House, [*Walter*] Durnford, he was the Provost o' Cambridge, well he wasn't there only 'bout two months out o' the twelve. They was on board wages all that time, and they had to keep themselves, yer see [*board wages = wages paid in the form of board and lodging*]. Then instead o' give 'em a Christmas box, he used to pay 'em, and then Miss Durnford used to pay 'em too, so they had double pay that time. He gen'lly used to come down just bifore the boat race; he used to bring some chaps down with 'n, and the wife reckons they didn't half eat, them chaps!"

It appears that Victoria Caws' father from Yaverland had once lodged at St Helens View long before Victoria ever came to Bembridge, when Aunt Sally used to take in lodgers. Victoria first came to work at one of the big houses, either Hill Grove or the Lodge, before marrying Herbert. An inscription in Bembridge Church gives her age at death as 74 in 1974, which would give her year of birth as 1899 or 1900.

Ashford's sister, Dorothy, though small, had long Titian hair that flowed down behind her, and was considered a local beauty: lads would gather on street corners to whistle after her. As for their little brother Albert born in 1890, he was said to have been inadvertently frightened to death at the age of two by Aunt Annie (Butler), who approached him wearing a fox's stole. "Old Aunt Annie what lived up the road, she had one o' those fox's fur on, and she said, 'My pussy'll bite yer', and then he caught meningitis, an' he died." [*The likelihood is, however, that the child would have contracted meningitis irrespective of any fright.*]

## A Little Bit o' Fishin'

I lived in St Helens View [*in the High Street*], and I went ter school ol' Gov'ness Attrill, I just had to step over the hedge. She had dozen or fourteen boys, paid tuppence a week! She didn't want the *money*, yer know, I don't *think* she did! And her sister was a nurse, but she bin out abroad somewhere, I don't know where, and she's comin' up round by the church, well she was knocked down by a bike and broke her hip. So after that, 'course Gov'ness Attrill had ter look after her, so she had to give up the school, yer see. Alfred Attrill was her brother, an' then Charlie Attrill was architect for the seawall down Lane End.

She warn't strict! P'raps she'd send yer over the shop to get summing: "Well shall I give yer sixpence or a shillin's worth fer goin' over there?" You'd already paid tuppence 'fore you could go in the school: she was pretty dim, though! I went two years afterwards to the village school, twelve to fourteen. A lot of boys didn't always stop till they was fourteen, years ago, they wasn't so strict as they was afterwards.

I went fishing wi' my father [*William, or Billy, Caws*] straight from school, about fourteen. Well my father, he worked with Frank M–, I think he used ter drink a good bit. They both went fishin' in the winter, and in the summer they had a boat, the *Kohinoor*, and they used ter lend that to officers over Portsmouth, and dad used to go away down the West Country sometimes, as crew. Then she drove in and broke up down Under Tyne, I remember that, and then they had another one built up at Warsash, an Itchen ferryboat, they called that one the *Witch*. They used to go trawling and after oysters and scallops too, when they's about. Then he had a fifteen-foot pot boat called the *Jane*.

As a boy I done a little bit o' fishin' while he was away in the summer holidays, I used ter go 'long wi' Frank, and he used ter gimme a pound a week. Well I had to go and dig worms and bait hooks and shoot a trot, that's what I had to do, yer see. Pound a week was nearly as much as some o' the old people used to get, that time.

Well my father and me used to do pottin' and nettin', both of that. We'd be up and down the shore plenty o' time 'fore it got light, oh yeah. We'd reckon t'half finished getting our boxes in bifore the sun get up, we used to, but I don't think they do that now.

Dad used to go round the village selling his fish when I first started with him. But that's how it was we come to do teas – we didn't *have* to go round then, we could sell 'em 'ere, yer see. Then ol' Curtis used to come here, he'd

Dame Attrill's School, c.1900.

say, "Count me owt a thousand", so then he took nearly all the fish round – I seen 'n with twelve thousand shrimps. We'd let him have three or four thousand, 'course we used ter sell some ourselves.

Well *I* can't swim, never could! Well I'll tell yer one thing: people that don't swim don't seem to bother, do they? Now Pewey [*Charlie Mursell*], well they used to say he could swim like a duck, and yet he's as squeamish as yer like, nearly frightened ter get his feet wet! [*My brother*] Herb couldn't swim, nor my father. S'pose there warn't time for learnin' ter swim! though we used to go down shore as nippers.

One day my father and me was fishing off the fort [*St Helens Fort*] – 'cos when the tide goes up there's no tide up by the side o' the fort – we'd just started shooting and we heard a *hell* of a scream. Dad says, "Pull that net in! Let's go 'n see what that is!" And we pulled the net in – well, what happened was, Mrs Langton on the fort, she was lifting the boat up on the crane with her husband in the boat, and what I couldn't understand, they had a wire went over but they never had a *loop* in, and when they got up so far the boat slipped and shot out under, out into three foot o' water. If it pulled down on the ground, well he'd a bin killed. 'Course, I had to stop in and look after the boat: my father went and put a lifebelt round the ol' man, and then she lifted 'n up on that crane, no other way to get 'n up! Then they had to get the boat up afterwards. The ol' man got shook up a bit but he never had nothing broke!

And me and me father went out, we had a conga trot shot, and he's hauling this conga trot up and looked his hand there – it never *bled* – and he had like electric shock come over him. And I had ter bring him ashore, and Doctor Chambers, he lanced it and had a bath-towel and soaked the blood up. And about three weeks he's dead.

## A Fisherman's Daily Routine

'Course, different times o' the year, different things, yer see. As the days got out, you'd be out fishing earlier. Well, always reckoned to be down shore quite hour before the sun got up, if you know what time that would be. 'Course, they never used to alter the clocks them days, did they? In the spring o' the year from about middle o' March you'd put yer pots out for prawns and shrimps – me an' Herb 'ud have 'bout twelve dozen, I s'pose, I don't think we had quite so many when Dad was alive. You could use your prawn-pots for shrimps but you gen'lly used t'have 'em a little bit coarser for prawns, if you could. We used to put 'em out, then take the prawns and crabs and little ones out, then rebait them and chuck 'em over again, then leave the pots there till next morning. But when it got back to about the middle of July

Fishermen around the early 1900s.

you wouldn't do that kind o' thing, you'd bring all that lot in and have a new lot in. Then keep them in yer boat and then haul 'em in the morning, come home to breakfast. And then you might have to go down shore again, to go to yer lobster pots. 'Cos we used t'have three boats, one was always empty. We had a motor in one, Herb used to get in there – warn't no good ter me, I soon have a sailin'-boat, I can *handle* a sailin'-boat!

Well if you didn't go to yer pots, you'd have to go down and get king crabs. Time you walked down Under Tyne and back, take yer couple of hours; then after Dad died we went to Lane End in 'bout 1920, we found that was easier. Under Tyne is *awkward* place, you always gotta larnch yer dinghy to get in; down Lane End you haven't – sometimes you can walk in and walk out down Lane End. But when we was Under Tyne there was Ernie Baker, Dick Mursell, Reub Mursell, Walt Mursell an' his son Charlie, me an' Dad, there was always them Under Tyne at that time. There about *fifteen* fishermen in Bembridge years ago, and they all had four dozen an' a half pots each. And you had a devil of a job to get enough king crabs to bait yer pots up with, you had! Every one o' them fishermen wanted 'bout two hundred crabs every day, two in a pot. You worked *with* other fishermen and *against* 'em.

Then afterwards you would have p'raps the afternoon orf. I never used to sleep. In 1919 we started doin' teas out in the garden: the wife and her sister, an' Herb, and Mrs Seymour too to start orf. Used t'have to cut up lobsters, *I* did, and serve out prawns to people who wanted them. We only charged eighteen pence for a lobster tea, I bet they're 'bout couple o' pound now! And prawns 'ere was one and fourpence, but they used t'have about twenty. You'll get three and fourpence a hundred, yer see, so we was doing very well out o' that. 'Twas lobsters that we warn't doing much out of. We never *bought* lobsters: if we didn't *ketch* none, we didn't have any, they had to go without. An' Herb used to come and wipe up. My wife had a blessed great garden up there, used to go right out to where Staples' Yard is, come out by the club in Queens Road. Then if you growed any vegetables you didn't get much for 'em, well everything was cheap. I mean, they'd want a gallon o' peas fer a shillin', now they want about ten bob! Potaters 'bout five bob a hundredweight, that's *all*, years ago.

Well after tea you'd have to go down shore and put yer pots out again. Then we get back and what I liked to do, I liked to come home and the only really sensible meal we could *have* was in the evening when we come back, because you was sort o' messed about all the time, with the teas an' whatnot. And if I could get to bed by ten o'clock I was *orright*, yer see. I *never* wanted alarm clock, anywhen after two o'clock I was awake. But I used t'have to call Herb, I'd throw a stone up at his winder, he was over there [*at St Helens View*] for hisself for about five years, 'fore he got married.

## Chapter 3 – A Fisherman's Life

And then when the Second War come, they didn't allow no visitors on the Island, did they? So there was no visitors to come t'*have* yer tea. And another thing, you wanted a head like a lawyer to fill up the papers, blessed papers! How much tea yer want, how much sugar, an' all this, aw! Then health inspector an' all. So we had to pack in. And we sold all our stuff to Curtis.

In the summer, up between two and ha' past, bin down shore and half finished 'fore the sun got up, yeah. Sat'days and Sundays too – if yer didn't work Sundays you never had no fish for Monday, see. We only went potting up till September started, and then all the fishermen would bring their pots in. There was no sale for them, nobody 'ere to buy 'em, you understand.

So we done netting from September to about Christmas, we went netting for mackerel an' herrings an' whiting. And then we went what you calls 'splashing': you shoot a net round half-circle and then you go inside it and hit the water with yer oars and you drive the fish in there. You could get some bass and mullet at times. For herrings an' mackerel we drifted: shoot the nets over and then let 'em drive with the tide, chance whether you gets anything. Now my father went splashing but he never went drifting.

Then we used t'have to cook 'em and pack 'em up and send 'em to London, there was nobody here to buy them. In the spring of the year they'd fetch very good money, but afterwards they didn't seem to fetch so much then – they would now if you had 'em. I *have* got over a pound a hundred for 'em! You used to sell mackerel by the hundredweight but you gotta have hundred and twenty for a hundred, and same with herrings, a long hundred, yer see. It's like potaters: you get seven pound o' potaters, but you'd only get six pound of onions, fer a gallon. But anyhow we'd pick 'em out, all nice picked mackerel, and I think we got 'bout five bob a hundred for them – for four thousand, there you are.

And from Christmas up to middle o' March you'd make yer pots and tar them. And o' course, you'd have to paint your boat up if you get any weather to do it, and one bloomin' thing an' another, always summing ter do, y'know. Then up to middle o' March we went winkle-picking sometimes, I bin down along wi' my brother. But we didn't get much money for 'em, we only used to get about eighteen pence a gallon – but now they'd warnt 'bout two bob a pint, I s'pose. One day me an' Herb picked up twenty-four gallon, only had about three hours to do it, yer know, low tide. We used to sell them to a man up at Havant, and afterwards we sold it to Swadling up at Newport. And Swadling used t'have our crabs, live, that was when George Chiverton used to go up, he went up twice a week as carrier. He only paid five bob a score for crabs – they warnt that nearly for a pound now, yer know!

Now Mrs Goodall what lived down over St Jean d'Acre, down over Point Hill, she used to see me and my brother bring up some crabs in a basket, about couple o' score o' crabs, thought we had a bloody fortune!

Ha-ha-ha! Ten bob between us! Oh God A'mighty! 'Twill make yer feel tired, dunnit?

When the First War come on someone said, "They wants you fishin' chaps in the minesweeping," so I went over Portsmouth and went up to where I had to go to. So the officer there says, "Oh, they're full up now," he says, "have you got anything to do? D'you want to go straight in?" "No, 'course I don't!" "Orright," 'e says, "they won't want you for a twelvemonth." So he says to the chaps there: "Give him an armband" – navy armband – "there you are, take it to go home". So I come on back for a twelvemonth. And then I joined up. Peterhead in Scotland was my base during the War: they was trawlers adapted for minesweeping, and I eventually come home about May 1919 when the withies started getting dry.

## Herbert Caws c.1896-1953

Herb, my brother, was nine years younger than me, yer see, so I had a few years fishing wi' my father before he started. Then I went fishing mostly with Herb summertime, and we had nets, yer see, but Herb, 'e didn't like going netting wintertime, so sometimes I used to go along with Dick Mursell in the winter, then sometimes I was with George Bannister, all depend. And

Herbert Caws 'shoving' his fishing boat.

## Chapter 3 – A Fisherman's Life

that means to say, I had ter make up extry lot o' pots so Herb could have a gang o' pots himself. [*A gang equalled 4½ dozen shrimp pots; approximately one gang to a boat.*] We had a big shed up our garden for making the pots, me an' Herb used t'have a fire up there, 'cos when it's frosty weather – we don't get none o' that weather now – you can't make 'em up, the frost gets to the withies and they crack. And I used to do all the tops, and Herb used to do the bottoms. But he couldn't *sit* very long and make the pots – well fact is, he didn't make none till I finished. He'd do all the tarring, I couldn't tar very well, it used to make me feel bad. One year I made ten dozen pots: eight dozen shrimp pots, two dozen lobster pots. And at that time I had to soak 'em – that's why I don't like soaked withies, they're very poisonous. 'Cos I had poison hands at that time, all blue.

I went orf the Cole [*Rock*] fishing, and Herb used to go round the Ledge, yer see. He'd say, "You go orf there." "Ah!" I'd say, "but if it's rough in the mornin'?" "Ah!" 'e say, "well I'll come out with yer an' we'll get yours first an' then get mine afterwards." But he didn't have to come *that* many times, I could gen'lly manage. 'Course that would be when we was shrimping. When we was prawning in the spring we used to go *together*: prawning was nearly always double-handed. And o' course when you got to the summer you'd be on your own, yer see.

Me an' Herb was comin' in th'harbour one day, and Gerry Goodall says, "Got a nice bass?" – 'cos you could get one pretty cheap them days, yer know. So Herb says, "Yes." "Oh," he says, "one 'bout 'arf a crown – I ain't got no money," but we know'd that was alright. Well they's prickly things, they got nasty spikes attached to them, so we was gonna hand 't to him. "No," he says, "throw 'n." So we throwed 'n. He says, "You see me ketch 'n, didn' yer?" We seen him ketch 'n alright, but he didn't take 'n orf of a hook! He could'a say he caught 'n, couldn't he? Who's gonna know?

Well when the King o' Spain [*Alfonso*] come ashore fer sailing down Under Tyne once, Peter Laughrin said, "Gen'lemen, the King!" Herb went to tow one Frenchman orf down there, and he said, "I ain't got no money but I can give yer some spider-crabs". Well blimey, we used to throw them away!

So Herb's goin' in the harbour to row in the Bembridge Regatta, and there's Herbie Occomore, Ern Wade down there, oh several these chaps. So Gerry Goodall he says, "Ain't yer gonna take yer jerser orf, 'Erbert?" (he always called Herbert). Herb says, I don't think I shall want to take 'n off to beat these!" 'Course, he nearly rowed *round* them, come in first, yer see. So Ern Wade – before Ern was the harbour pilot then – he was gonna challenge Herb for five pounds. Herb says, "Yes! I'll row this, I'll row it at five pounds," he says, "but I warnts a longer distance than *that*! Rownd the Fort an' back!" Anyhow, Gerry Goodall says, "That's orright, 'Erbert, I'll put the pots down there, you leave her in like that" – but it *never* come orf. No, if he'd 'a went took her round the Fort, I know Herb 'ud beat him miles, I'm sure he would! He's one o' them kind – wiry! He used to do a day's work, go in the Regatta, win first prize, an' then go back to work again.

Herb only went to Ryde Regatta once or twice. *I* used to go ter Ryde Regatta 'fore any o' that – blessed hard work! And after I seen Dick Mursell, I didn't wanna go no more – where he done so much rowin', I've seen the blood down t' his socks, it's true, yes I have! And he said that was strain, an' I don't disbelieve it. Dick used to row in Sandown Regatta, he went 'long wi' Cap'n Parkes. I never rode single in Bembridge Regatta. I done a shoving one, only got a third prize, 'cos Dick Holbrook an' Dick Mursell they was great strong fellers, you couldn't hopin' to row against them. 'Course, Herb had a dinghy to row, I'll own, but he had to put half a hundredweight o' ballast in the stern to keep her trim, yer see.

Well Herb was just about the best rower round 'ere, mate. But he didna' weigh no more 'n six stone, it's a wonder where he got the strength from, that's what I said to the doctor. "Agh," he says, "that's just...", I dunno what he called it, some name he had for 't. I didn't go more than eight stone, so he wasn't near so big as me, but I had a *job* to row away from him! 'Course, fishermen used to cross oars an' push, yer see, but he couldn't do so much of *that*, but if he could sit down, yeah he was pretty good. And he didn't mind how long he sit down either: I've seen him sit down five or six hours and row, he didn't take any notice o' that. He'd soon do that than he'd do a pot.

I used to get Herb to get up an' haul sometimes, and I bet if he had to get up an' haul there'd be a blessed crab then, 'e couldn't get 'n out. He says, "Cor! can't get this crab owt!" 'Course, when it's fine weather, he already up to the pot and all ready for me t'haul 'm up, yer see, and then gotta chuck one over an' haul the next one in. But you didn't get a chance to get upright. See, if there's a bit of a breeze, sometimes I had t'help him – take one oar, and he'd look out and ketch 'n and ketch the same stroke. Well of course, that's what Dick Mursell said ter Ernie Baker and Reub [*Mursell*]: they went down t'haul some pots one day and was a fresh breeze, so Dick says, "Where yer bin to?" "Well, tryin' ter get some pots." "Is 'Erb back yet [*from the village*]?" "No." "What the hell d'yer think *you* gonna do, if they ain't owt?" [*Because the Caws brothers were known to manage in a rough sea better than most.*]

In the First War Herb was in the army, he was over at Le Havre working in the cookhouse. And he went down Cowes to work for a little while: he had ter sort o' look after a boat belonging to a chap from Brading, Dewi Buckett as he called 'n. There's some rope down there wanted in this boat. Dewi Buckett said, "Orright, strip orf!" 'Course, Herb was only a little thin chap, warn't bout as big as three penn'orth ha'penny. So he stripped orf an'

Dewi Buckett bound this rope right round 'n. "There y'are, put yer gear on agin" – and he come home like that wi' his clothes on!

Herb only went in the lifeboat once, he had enough o' the lifeboat, too many big blocks [*block and tackle*] for him there.

He died in '53 rescuing people down East Cliff. The boat was floundering, and they's shouting for help. Herb was down Swains and he heard 'em shouting, and he had to pull a dinghy down. An' o' course he wasn't very big, and he couldn't get 'em in the boat yer see, he had to tow 'em ashore hanging on the back. And *then* he had to go and pick up their dinghy and the stuff what was floatin', so he strained himself. He never done nothin' afterwards, never went down on the shore no more.

# Chapter 4

# Round the World to Under Tyne
## – Miss Edith Woodford

*Miss Woodford was recorded at her home in Church Row in the High Street during February 1983. She was born in Bembridge in 1896 and was 86 years old at the time of the recording. Her contribution is one of the shortest but nevertheless of a consistent quality one has come to expect of Old Bembridgers.*

I was born on August 29th 1896 in Oak Cottage, Steyne Road, which was all part of the Thornycroft estate then, just a few houses with fields all around. My father was working for the first Sir John Thornycroft as a gardener – before that he was on the railway when it first started. And my grandfather was Charlie Butler who fought in the Crimean War. Now when I was born they didn't know what to call me, you know, so somebody said, call me Kathleen. Well my grandfather was on the old Earl Fitzwilliam's yacht down here, you see, well *that* was called *Kathleen*, and my mother says, "No, you can't call her that, they'll think you're naming her after the Earl's yacht!"

I always remember mother telling me she had me out in a pram and the first Lady Thornycroft came along and said, "Hello, Edie!" So I said, "'Ello, Puddie!" There was a girl lived near us, Attrill, they used to call her Puddie and I suppose I just picked that word up, y'see! Then as a kiddie I used to play with Lady Margetson up Steyne Farm.

Bastiani the baker had one of those handcarts that he used to deliver the bread with, and I always remember when Queen Victoria died, he had this blessed great black bow tied on there! I was five years old then. And then the following year I was there when they planted the King's Oak [*at the top of Point Hill*] for King Edward – 1902.

Just after the First World War, I was working at what is now Warner's holiday camp, with the Waterlows – they used to call it Fuzzie Frieze – and when the war was over they sold that to Lord Herschell and bought a house in Tunbridge Wells, and I went with them and worked as lady's maid for thirteen years altogether.

Then I joined Cunard as a stewardess aboard their passenger liners. My first ship was the *Aquitania* which I joined on the 3rd September 1927, went

# Chapter 4 – Round the World to Under Tyne

to New York and then I transferred to the *Mauretania* and then several other Cunarders to the Mediterranean, India, West Indies, Palestine and Russia. It was my job to look after the lady passengers – 'course, it was just the elite in those days, European royal families and so on. That was till '38 when the war came, you see.

Then from 1946 I used to have five donkeys down the beach, Under Tyne, always one resting, and I used to give the children rides. And I had a little basket-cart, which I discovered afterwards once belonged to Queen Victoria, I didn't know at the time, it'd gone before I found out!

Mrs Parker in the almshouses used to come down the road on a Sunday morning with a coarse apron on full o' wood where she'd been up copse fetching wood, just as the people were coming out of church, ha!

Before the Embankment was built, when the water went up to Brading, the Lodge used to have bathing-huts down over; and from the Lodge there was a driveway down to the church.

I remember old Mrs Moreton, the Colonel's wife, she used to ride about in a governess-cart pulled by a donkey. And of course, there were no cars about in those days – Sir John Thornycroft had the first car that came to Bembridge, number H99.

Sir John Thornycroft's car (DL 22) at Steyne House, 1906.

Well it was election day, us kids were all down round Couldrey's Emporium 'cause we knew Colonel Seely was coming. So his car arrived, and as he went to Couldrey's, someone shouted "Turnjacket!" and Couldrey knocked him down – I think Seely was Conservative and turned Liberal, he'd crossed the floor of the House.

Now Mrs Barlow used to run the Garland Club and I used to do the deck and the bathing-huts. And I was out on the deck one day putting the chairs out, when someone came down and said, "Queen Mary will be coming down shortly, would you keep a place for her?" I think it was said for a joke. But anyway I put this table and so many chairs round – well she didn't come that day, but the very next day she *did*!

# Reports

## The Fifth Generation

*(From an entry in the IW Records Office)*

The Brading burial register carries the following entry for 17th June 1782:

'John Stone of Bimbridge, Mariner, aged 86 years who lived to see his Great Great Grand Daughter even the fifth generation, so that he might say: "Arise Daughter and go to thy Daughter for thy Daughter's Daughter has got a Daughter".'

## Longevity in Bembridge

*(Newspaper cutting about 1915, and written at a time when living to a ripe old age was nowhere near as common as it is today)*

There are not many places of the size of Bembridge, the population of which at the last census was 1,334, which have thirteen aged people living in their midst whose ages range from 80 to 96. The local list is headed by 'Granny' Woodford, whose correct age cannot be ascertained. Her baptismal certificate, however, shows that she was christened in 1819, ninety-six years ago, and she maintains that she can recollect the occasion, so that she must have been two or three years old at the time.

The following are included in the venerable list: Granny Woodford 96, Sally Smith 89, Joseph Bond 89, Robert Tuffley 89, Mrs Alfred Newman 88, George Weeks 88, Mrs John Holbrook 88, Isaac Toogood 87, Capt. Robert Dyer 85, Mrs Robert Tuffley 82, Josiah Caws 82, Capt. John Grainger 81, Robert Newman 80, their united ages making a total of 1124, or an average of 86.6 each, which says much for the salubriousness of the climate of the South of England.

## 'Granny' Woodford, Centenarian

*(Newspaper cutting November 1918; entry in the old WI Scrapbook)*

A venerable and well-known resident has passed away this week in the person of 'Granny' Woodford, as she has been familiarly known for many years. The deceased was born at Andover, Hants, her parents' name having been Sheppard. She has often related how when four years old she walked to church with her father to be christened. Her friends have a certificate of that ceremony which shows that it took place in 1819, just 98 years ago. They have not been able to get the register of her birth but by the above she appears to have been 102 at the time of her death. She has lived in Bembridge practically all her married life. Her husband, Mr William Woodford, predeceased her thirty years ago. She had a wonderful strength and energy for her age until a year or so ago, although being very deaf, this being her only ailment. She visited neighbouring towns or did shopping and made her bed as usual until the Monday previous to her death. During last summer she was to be seen looking over her her wicket gate in Church Row, High Street, her wrinkled, ever smiling face beaming out from under her mob cap. She was a picture of venerable old age and the admiration of everybody. She passed peacefully away at midday on Wednesday. The deceased had a family of five sons, of whom two are still living, also nineteen grandchildren and fifteen great-grandchildren.

## Mr Alfred Morris of Stanwell Farm, Hillway, Bembridge

*(IW County Press archive for 11th December 1937 – amended extract)*

For nearly 50 years the deceased had been one of the best known Island farmers, and at one time had more land under cultivation than any man in the county. Mr Morris was a native of Southampton and came of farming stock... In 1890 he married Miss Mary Jane Orchard of Wroxall and they settled at Stanwell, where there was then but a struggling farm. Mr Morris later acquired the Mill Farm, Bembridge, and Hill Farm, Rowborough, near Brading. He was a greatly esteemed and popular man. For nearly 40 years he attended Newport market regularly. It was his custom for the greater part of that period to ride from Stanwell to Newport on a grey mare, and he thus became a familiar figure in the country roads. A typical English farmer, he possessed a very genial nature, and made many friends in all walks of life. He was particularly interested in local history. He took a great pride

## Chapter 4 – Round the World to Under Tyne

Stanwell Farm, around 1870.

in Stanwell farmhouse and it was a great grief to him when in May 1915 it was destroyed by a serious fire. From the shell of the building, however, he erected the present house, the front door of which is reputed to have been a door of the ancient chapel at Woolverton in St Urian's Copse, near Bembridge... He was the last Island farmer to work a windmill. Some 35 years ago, with Mr Ernest Orchard, his brother-in-law, he set the sails of Bembridge mill, which stands on his land, and the machinery after several years was again in motion. Grinding corn in this way proved more expensive than modern methods, and the mill fell into disuse. The mill stones were latterly sold to the owner of St Helens Priory, but the wooden machinery remains intact.

# Chapter 5

# A Smuggling Background
## – Mrs Ivy Evans

*Mrs Evans was born as Ivy Clarke in Bembridge in 1906 and lived all of her life there. She was 78 years of age when I recorded her during one visit to her home in Lane End in August 1984. Her narrative runs so smoothly that it is possible that some of her written notes may have been incorporated into the original transcription.*

## Brandy for the Parson

Starting with my grandfather Tom Smith [1816–1887] as he was known to all, he was a fisherman and a smuggler and kept his own cows and sheep and pigs as well. He lived in the Thatched Cottage at the bottom of Lane End, where my mother was born in 1862. It's been pulled down now: there were only three thatched cottages up to the Birdham Hotel in those days. Well, he was a great smuggler and they used to row across to Portsmouth in those days to pick up their brandy or whatever, and come in under the shore, but they had to watch because the revenue men would always be watching for them, you see. They would sink the tubs down, then bring the stuff ashore. 'Course, they had a dog, and this dog was pretty cute, and he always let them know when the revenue men were about. Everybody in Bembridge helped, even down to the vicars and all the landed gentry, they all hid them in their cellars. Then some of them would get the casks and walk to Newport with the stuff.

Well then my grandfather eventually got caught by the revenue men, and in those days there wasn't a jail on the Island, so he was taken over the water to Lewes jail; but instead of serving his time there he was taken by the press gang to man a warship as a cook – and the warship he was pressed on was the one which was sent out to search for the *Bounty* after she'd mutineered. [*As the mutiny took place in 1789 and the ship which was sent out in search was itself wrecked in 1791 – while Mrs Evans states that her grandfather Tom Smith was not born until 1816 – this seems to be a clear case where a very old story has been conflated with a later one.*]

My grandmother Maria Smith [1822–1886] was also a good hand at the game, and she had a way of getting the drink away in an inflated rubber bag under her skirts. But one day they caught up with her, but they couldn't

## Chapter 5 – A Smuggling Background

Lane End Road, c.1890.

search her on the Island 'cause they had no lady policeman, so they were going to take her to Portsmouth. When they got her to Ryde Pier Head, she said she wanted to use the ladies', so they let her go and she came out thinner than she went in, all the brandy had gone! So they couldn't convict her, you see!

She was very hardworking, and in addition to the smuggling she owned a launch called the *Blanche*, which used to ply between Bembridge and Portsmouth. She was the skipper, and one uncle was the deckhand and another was the stoker [Quilly and Henley Smith]. She collected the fares from the passengers, charging them according to how wealthy they looked or otherwise!

Now, my grandfather bought all this land down Lane End, from Milverton right down to the sea, for £200. Well when he died he left each one of his eight children a portion of land plus £150, and with that they all built their own houses down through here. But I'm the only one left of the whole family now who was born and always lived there.

On a stone in Bembridge churchyard is recorded the death of my uncle Urbane, who was an apprentice on a sailing ship and was washed overboard and drowned in a storm off the Cape of Good Hope at the age of sixteen.

## My Father

My father's name was Ted Clarke: he was born in 1865 and was brought up by his grandmother in a little cottage right up under Bembridge Down – she would have been one of the Pope family. The cottage was in a field once known to most of us as Cowslip Field, but which has now ceased to exist. The only water they had for use was from a spring close by, which I see today is no longer there – I think that was due to the laying of cables up to the Culver Fort, which diverted the water supply. Well when my father was quite a boy, he was sitting in an old leather armchair and the cottage collapsed and the armchair with my father in ran backwards out the door and into the lane. After that, he went to live at Peacock Farm with old Uncle Ned Pope, and he had a very hard life with him.

My father worked as a boy helping to build the Embankment Road. He was on the last cart that brought a load to fill the last breach, and narrowly missed being drowned: the cart and horse capsized and he was thrown into the water and was just rescued in time.

Bembridge Embankment c.1890. The iron handrail carried water all the way from St Helens to replenish the steam ships plying between Bembridge and Portsmouth.
*Courtesy of Peter Chick Collection.*

He was a builder by trade and worked on many of the old houses round here. He helped build the Spithead Hotel and also The Elms. They would start at 6.30am and work through till 5pm. I've known him walk to work at Sandown, Brading, Adgestone and Nunwell. And when in those days a place was finished, there was a grand dinner or supper for the firm's employees and they would hoist the rearing flag, drinks all round – we don't hear of those customs today!

## The Lifeboat

Then again, my father was always ready to help launch the old lifeboat and believe me they *were* launchers in those days, pulling the old row boat from the old lifeboat house – away out over the third ledge at low tide was a terrible time with a nasty nor'easter blowing. And during the First World War all the young lads had gone to the war and so they called on the older men to help with the lifeboat. And I can remember as a child going down and helping all these old men put on their oilskins and sou'westers, nothing nylon in those days, and they had lifejackets made of thick cork. I often had a sixpence from Mr Couldrey, who was the secretary then.

On one occasion I remember a boat came in on the rocks and the lifeboat couldn't get in to it. So it was low tide and they walked out to it from the beach, my father was amongst them. They found four men, two had been drowned, it was bitterly cold in the winter. There was a young boy aboard that clung hold to my father and wouldn't leave go, and they carried him up to old Bill Love's house, put him on a couch by the fire. But still he held onto my father's hand, so my father had to stay with him nearly all night till he recovered and thawed out and they could force him to leave go.

Then I remember when the *Empress Queen* came in on the rocks at Forelands [*in 1916*], and they took all the troops off of there and brought off all the lifeboats and put them on the cliffs down the bottom. We had two cats came from the boat, they were Manx cats 'cause it was an Isle of Man boat. 'Course, they couldn't get it off and it broke up eventually.

Then there was the *Narragansett* which came ashore in a snowstorm [*in 1919*], terrible morning that was. So round we went, 'bout six o'clock in the morning, snowing like anything! And there was this great big boat, she was stuck right up at an angle like this, you could have walked under the bow of her! She was full of American troops, and before she'd been there long they'd thought of a song, 'The old Narragansett ain't what she used to be'. They got the troops off and billeted them all around. Lots of people did very well out of her, all the goods and chattels they got off of that.

And you used t'have lots of things washing along the shore. The first time I'd ever seen malted milk tablets, they washed in in bottles along the shore;

and there were tubs of grapes came in, bags of flour which were dry inside – which was very lucky in wartime with things so scarce. You never knew what you were going to find in those days – tubs of oranges, and all the rest of it.

I remember Major Windham who lived in Ledge House – it's since been pulled down – he was very religious, a Plymouth Brethren. Whatever the weather he would sing hymns out in the road and hold little services either in his stable or conservatory. Being children how we enjoyed it, and we used to sing that well-known Sankey hymn 'Pull for the Shore' – believe me, we did pull!

Chapter 5 – A Smuggling Background

# *Archives*

## A Special Launch

*(IW County Press archive for 7th March 1903)*

A special launch of the new lifeboat, *Queen Victoria*, took place on Tuesday last to test her capabilities in a rough sea. There was a strong south-westerly wind blowing, with a heavy sea on. The launch was a very great success. Coxswain Edmund Attrill tried the boat on all points, bringing her in under sail over the ledge among the breakers, and she acquitted herself well. Dr P. W. Hughes and Mr W. Couldrey, joint secretaries, accompanied the crew, and the launch was witnessed by a large number of persons. The crew are loud in their praise of the *Queen Victoria*.

*Queen Victoria I* Lifeboat being pulled out of boathouse.

## Bembridge Boat's Arduous Service
*(IW County Press archive for 7th March 1914)*

Mr W. Couldrey read his report as Hon. Secretary of the Bembridge lifeboat station, which stated that at about 1 a.m. on November 19th the Bembridge station received a call from the Culver signal-station stating that a steamship was apparently on fire about 12 miles S.S.E. of Whitecliff. The lifeboat went off in record time and proceeded in the direction of the burning vessel, but the farther they went the farther the vessel seemed away; she was apparently travelling faster than the lifeboat. At about 4 a.m. Coxswain J. Holbrook observed a warship coming from the direction of the burning ship and the lifeboat made for the ship and tried to speak to her by burning a white hand light, but the warship would not stop. The lifeboat sailed away again till 5 o'clock and then lost sight of the burning ship. They were now about 20 miles from the Culvers and the coxswain decided to return. On approaching the shore the crew learned that a message had just been received stating that the crew of the burning vessel had been taken off by the warship and landed at Portsmouth Harbour. The lifeboat was out for nearly nine hours.

## Bembridge Lifeboats and Lifeboatmen
*(IW County Press archive for 23rd February 1952)*

Captain R. C. Watson, RNR, of Norfolk Cottage Bembridge, who for eight years was Hon. Secretary of the Bembridge Lifeboat Committee and whose family have been associated with lifeboat work there since the establishment of the station in 1867, has written a most interesting booklet describing the chief incidents in the fine life-saving record of the Bembridge lifeboats. It is published by the IW County Press Co. at 1s 3d, and is obtainable from the lifeboat station and local booksellers.

The booklet is entitled *Annals of Bembridge Lifeboats and Lifeboatmen*, and it is a record of the chief rescues by the lifeboats during the 85 years they have operated at Bembridge (in that period 394 lives have been saved), with the author's very interesting recollections of some of the fine old characters, fishermen and others, who have so gallantly served in the crews. As examples of the calibre of these men, he mentions that the first coxswain at Bembridge, Edmund (Joey) Attrill, walked in heavy sea boots from Bembridge to Atherfield in March 1888 to assist in the rescue of the crew of the sailing ship *Sirenia*, which was wrecked on Atherfield Ledge, taking the place in one of the local lifeboats of a member of the crew who was drowned when the boat capsized; also that in November 1887,

## Chapter 5 – A Smuggling Background

in order to assist the rescue of the crew of a ship which went ashore at Luccombe, the Bembridge lifeboat was taken by road to Sandown Bay because the sea was too rough for her to round Culver Cliff. The boat was drawn by eight farm horses, and fences had to be torn down and hedges cut away at corners. After great difficulty she was launched from the beach at Sandown and rescued two men, the others having been saved by Coastguards.

In a general tribute to lifeboatmen as he knew them when a lad, Capt. Watson writes: "... under their rough, bearded exterior, and behind their coarse humour, there existed a wealth of warm-hearted, genial good nature, and a very staunch regard as to what they considered their duty to their neighbour, and as I look back over a lapse of many years, I feel convinced that some few of them possessed those particular virtues and attributes which we generally accord to the finest men of our race".

Capt. Watson has rendered the R.N.L.I. and the Bembridge station further good service by writing this little book.

# Chapter 6

# A Contented Life
## – Miss Amy Nightingale

*Amy Nightingale was born at Newbury, Berkshire, in 1894, moving with her family to Bembridge in 1899, where she lived for the rest of her life. She was 82 years of age when recorded at her home in Heathfield Road during a single visit in April 1976.*

## Family Background

My father, Tom Nightingale, was born in 1863 and married my mother, Louisa, in the year 1888. We came from Newbury in Berkshire when I was five – there were ten of us in the family but not all came to Bembridge. He came as a gardener-groom to Bembridge House in the High Street after he retired from the army: he was a landscape gardener really, trained at Sutton's. He first worked for Major Edwards, who was an army doctor, then Doctor Rostov came to Bembridge House, then when *he* left my father took on for another Major Edwards.

We never wanted for anything because we had a large allotment where the water-tower is by the windmill, he kept it cultivated for Mainwarings [*pronounced Mannerings*] at the Lodge. We were always well-fed and well-dressed, and we had pigs, we had chickens, we had a garden full of vegetables, fruits and asparagus. He was very gentlemanly, considering no education; he wouldn't sit down to tea in the same jacket he worked in the garden with.

My father was allowed to use the pony-trap at the House every Saturday to take us into Ryde – a dog-cart, two in the front and two in the back – and the horse was named 'Feb'. Father used to exercise him along the beach and I remember the horse throwing him off once in the sea, and then coming home without him! Then the little lodge at the front, that was his harness-room. 'Course, there was a light over the gate that he had to get up and light every night, then put out in the morning.

Well he left there and worked at different houses. He laid out nearly all these grounds in Bembridge, the big ones – King's Oak, Norcott, San Remo, Portland House, the Grange. And his money at the private houses was thirty shillings a week, then old Charlie Love took him on and he got two pound a week. He never earned any more, for *all* his work, attending the greenhouses 'n all, seven days a week.

And on his eightieth birthday [*in 1943*], father won the darts

## Chapter 6 – A Contented Life

Birdham Corner, looking up Foreland Road, in 1928. The occasion is the funeral of Admiral of the Fleet Sir John de Robeck.
*Courtesy of Peter Chick Collection.*

championship: he was the last player in and he wanted double something, and he got it. You never saw such a fuss as they made of him in all your life! He was a military man, he was in the Egyptian War and the Afghan War and several others, and he had a military funeral. He died the last year of the Second World War, and there were soldiers stationed at the Birdham and they all lined up and gave him the last rites. But they said they couldn't have done it to a better man.

My brother Sidney was born in 1892 and worked in Riddick's bakehouse from the age of 14 till he retired. It was an old-fashioned bakehouse with a gas jet and a coke fire at the back, not a bit modern. I used to help turn the doughnuts sometimes. PC Toomer smacked my brother's face once, thinking he was the boy that'd been playing up. And my father just went to him and said, "I'm summonsing you. My boy wasn't there". And so Toomer came up and apologised, and Dad let it drop. You didn't do things in a nasty way in those days.

## Are You Afraid?

I used to take the food up to the chickens, and I had to go across the fields to the allotments along by the Grange: we had two great big strips with a hundred chickens, three pens. And I was afraid to go through Preston's cows, and little Sid Harbour said, "Miss Nightingale, are you afraid?" So I said, "Yes". He said, "Ooh that's orright, I'll take you." So he took me through these cows with a stick, and I was really terrified of them. Then my father would slaughter the chickens in the allotment, stick it and bleed it so that the flesh was nice and white. And every Saturday morning five would be sold, people would come up and buy them. Then we caught our own rabbits coming into the allotments and that sort of thing, snare them. 'Course the kids used to take our pig up to Bembridge Farm when they wanted to mate it, y'see.

I worked down the Bembridge Hotel when the First World War was on, when all the officers were here. We used to have dances every night out on one of the aerodrome hangars. One person I remember staying there, she danced Swan Lake – [*Anna*] Pavlova, and I looked after her. And she had size three shoes, and she wanted to go up on the downs. So we had to hunt all over the place for someone to lend her a pair of size three shoes with flat heels!

One of my younger sisters Florence was called after Florence Nightingale. She worked in Walt Frampton's shoe-shop for years. He was an estate agent as well and she did all his work.

The youngest one, May, delivered Morris's milk off Mill Farm in the First War. Now her father-in-law, old Perce Watton, had the coal business here as well as a good building business, and he used to follow the footballers around. And we always used to say, if he shouted in St Helens we could hear him in Bembridge! And of course he started the Conservative Club, and then it was made a general club.

## Rollers & Royals

Well there used to be a farm at East Cliff which belonged to the big house, I've been there to fetch milk. Norris used to work there, and then they would sell eggs and milk from the big house: skimmed milk, ordinary milk, and eggs, and I think I got butter there.

Granny Woodford used to pass down our house in the High Street to the village shops, to sell her apples. Proper old-fashioned, you know, bonnet an' cape. And she'd come down with a *huge* basket of apples on her arm. She'd say, "They'll never miss one, dear!" I always ran out for an apple.

My mother was friendly with old Mrs Quilla Smith, and she used to wear five curls at the back of her hair. Never forget *her*, she was a card – and Quilly too.

Annie Butler had a huge great mangle with great big rollers. She used to take in the laundry for people – *beautiful* launderess, she was. Mrs Newark in White Cottages was a seamstress, she used to make mattresses, her work was very beautiful. And she worked right up till she was very old.

## Chapter 6 – A Contented Life

John Jones the carrier was the first Labour man here, the first man that I heard speak and talk about Labour. And I can remember the first car coming to Bembridge: it was a Rolls, at Bembridge House.

Now when I left school, I met an old lady from Shanklin, and she remembered when there was a gentleman's house in Centurions Copse, and she was one o' the maids!

Thornycrofts had a big recreation room in the grounds for the maids, and we used to go up there for dances, the village was allowed to go in. The old people were good, they also provided the village nurse.

The Queen of Spain, Princess Ena, used to come here and she would bathe from the Garland Club. Then Mrs Simpson was here that time when the Prince of Wales was [*Edward VIII*]; she had the Lodge, and the Prince of Wales and the Duke of Kent were in a yacht out on the water.

Sometimes they'd have a treasure-hunt from the Sailing Club after a dance and come knocking on your door to know if you'd got a cat – I suppose first one back with a cat got the prize. They'd knock anybody up, they used to go crazy! My father went down to the door one night, he said, "I'll give you summing, knockin' us up at this time of night!"

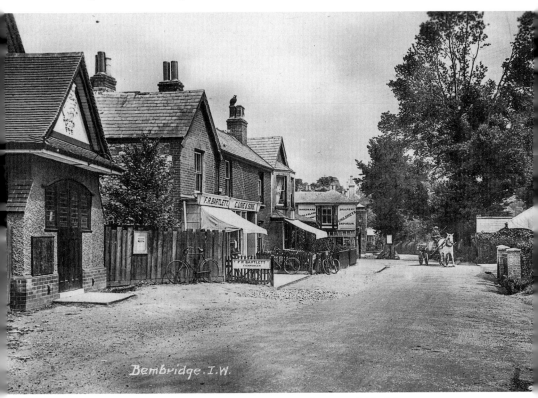

High Street, towards Sherbourne Street, 1910–20.

Mrs Mainwaring used to walk into church with an ermine cape on, very big woman; they had a private pew in the church. And it really was ermine. Then a Miss Collins and a Miss Fraser lived at Old Garth; we used to go up there to tea and bun-fights, as we used to say.

Colonel Moreton would have a big joint of meat, and when it was on the table, *hot*, he'd say if it wasn't any good or too tough, and he'd send the page-boy straight up to the butcher's with the pan, just like that! He'd say, "Take this back ter the butcher's, it's not worth eating". He was a bit of a so-'n-so, but he was good to the village.

Chapter 6 – A Contented Life

# *Features*

## My Ancestors' Entry into Bembridge
### by E. C. Wallis

*(Entry in the old WI Scrapbook)*

William Wallace, a Scot from the Lowlands of Scotland, left his native country and sailed south in his cutter *The Amity* with a small crew. He settled here in Bembridge, bought some land in the centre of the village and built the house known as Willow Cottage. The name Wallace was now changed to Wallis – it is thought that the emigration and change of name was certainly due to smuggling of some kind.

William Wallis did not return to Scotland. He and his descendants lived in Willow Cottage until some forty years ago [*now probably ninety years ago*]. They used to trade all sorts of cargoes along the coast from London to Lands End. One well known cargo was Swanage stone, which was brought up to Sandown and went into the building of a chapel.

Wallis also joined the Pilotage Service under Trinity House. In those days it was all sailing ships, so in nautical terms they used to 'beat about down Channel' and pilot the ships from off Lands End. Passengers were landed at Plymouth and other places in those early days, but later ships were met at Spithead and the Solent and all escorted into Southampton.

In the years before 1800 pilots did not wear uniforms – my great-great-grandfather used to wear a frock coat suit and silk hat to climb a rope ladder and board a ship. It must have been quite a feat in rough weather.

The story is told of his son James Wallis whose courage and skill brought *The Amity* into Bembridge Harbour when attacked by a French privateer. He was sixteen years of age at the time, all the crew having deserted the ship.

My father, the late William Wallis, was apprenticed to his grandfather John Wallis, his own father having died at an early age. His apprenticeship lasted seven years and at the end of that time he was earning the grand sum of fifteen pounds a year.

*The Amity* was replaced by *The Hornet*, another cutter which was used by my father and his brothers in the pilotage service until after the First World War. Trinity House then brought in their own steam ship pilot vessels which are still in use today. [*In fact, Trinity House is now no longer involved with local pilotage.*]

## Bembridge Brewery
*(Entry in the old WI Scrapbook)*

It was no uncommon thing when a fleet was in the St Helens Roads for an order to come in for the immediate supply of fifty bullocks, and the animals, having been hurriedly collected from the neighbouring farms, were killed and cut up in the old village slaughterhouse which used to stand next to the Row Barge Inn (now the Marine Hotel) just where Mr Hapgood's shop now is, and whilst waiting for the carcasses the crews of the various row barges tied up alongside the quay wall just opposite refreshed themselves with many a barrel of home-brewed ale, for Bembridge had its own brewery in those days, kept and owned by one Matthews which stood just where the new Village Inn now is.

## A Capital Weather-Glass...
*(IW County Press archive for 21st July 1888)*

...has been affixed to the wall of the Pilot Boat Hotel for the use of pilots and other seafaring people. This has been done in response to the numerously signed memorial to the Board of Trade, as announced in our columns some time since.

## Condition of the High Street – Letter to the Editor
*(IW County Press archive for 24th December 1887)*

Sir, – May I through the medium of your columns call attention to the disgraceful state of the road in the High Street of Bembridge. From my door to the post office, extending as far as Mr Jordan the butcher's, two of the chief places of resort, the road is always, rain or shine, one wet, pulpy mass of mud and puddles, so that one cannot avoid getting one's feet wet through each time one has occasion to go through the village. This state of things might be altered directly by putting down a few cartloads of stones. Will not anyone try and remedy this "slough of despond" and oblige the whole village by doing so.

Your obedient servant,<br>RESIDENT.<br>Bembridge,<br>December 14th, 1887.

# Chapter 7

# The Butler Family
## – Mr Harold Butler

*Harold Butler was born in 1896 in Bembridge, growing up there until he joined the Royal Navy in 1912; he spent 34 years away, returning to Bembridge in 1946 and living there for the rest of his life. He was 79 years old when recorded at his home in Manna Road during two visits in April and August 1975. Harold Butler had an extraordinarily precise memory of family and other names, as well as dates.*

## Family Background

My great-grandfather lived in Whitecliff Bay and was a renowned smuggler. I think he was called William Butler, and he had to my knowledge five sons and a daughter. The excisemen came along one day and when my great-grandmother saw them, what she did was to pick up all the clouts she had and drop them over the rum tub and carried on nursing baby.

Now then, four of my great-grandfather's sons settled in Bembridge. One of course was my grandfather, also called William. He used to keep horses and cows, and they used to graze in the fields just opposite where Portland House is now. There was another field he had out across Walls [*Road area*], he kept a white horse there which used to frighten the daylights out o' people, they thought it was a ghost. My grandmother used to go up the Grange as a sort o' cook or summing or other.

Another son was called Henry Butler. His story to me was that he went over to Portsmouth when he was sixteen years old and somebody asked him if he'd like to go 'board ship as a bell-boy. He continued going to sea, and would go round the Cape to China, and bring home loads o' tea in tea clippers. He eventually became a captain of one of those vessels. [*Henry's son, Ernie Butler, features prominently as an interviewee later in this volume.*]

Another son was Charlie Butler. For a time he lived in the old building called Old House Gardens [*in the High Street*]. He was a long-service naval man and had rows of medals. Now, he served in a ship called the *Leander* in the Crimean War, and the first two cottages at the top of Foreland Road used to be called Leander Cottages 'cos he had 'em built.

The fourth son was Mark. He went to sea with his brother Henry in the tea clippers and in latter years he took up gardening for a living.

These four settled in Bembridge, but there was another one called Sam Butler who settled in Ryde, and there's a lot of Butlers in Ryde who probably descended from him.

Then there was a daughter who answered to the name of Charlotte. She married and went off to Australia, and it was her daughter which was eventually Mayoress of Canberra and came to Britain for Queen Elizabeth's coronation. She went up to Myrtle Cottage in Hillway and visited Harry Butler.

Well then my grandfather William Butler's eldest son was called George, next came Jane, and then my father Mark was his youngest living son. I dunno of anybody else in that family.

George had a biggish family. First there was a daughter called Emily, or maybe Emma: she was married to a man named Mr Weeks, who was stationmaster at St Helens for years, then he was a gardener for the Reverend Shilton down at North Wells.

Then a son, Arthur, who also took up gardening for a livelihood: he married a woman from St Helens and had a son Lionel, and he used to live with that son in Church Row.

Then a daughter named Amy, who married a man named Gully who kept the Birdham Hotel for a time.

The next son was called George Butler [*Junior*]: he was an apprentice to Walt Frampton the cobbler, and came to live in the last house in Church Row and mended boots and shoes for soldiers in World War I; eventually he opened up a boot and shoe repair shop on the corner of Dennett Road.

Then came a daughter called Agnes, who married a butcher in Ryde: he used to come round Bembridge with a horse an' cart.

The next daughter was Alice, who married a Ryde man called Purnell, and their daughter is Mrs Moorman; Alice died in 1918 when we had that Spanish flu in the country.

Then one named Sidney, who lives at Arundel. The youngest son was Albert 'Bingo' Butler, who lives in Queens Road: he was manager of a butcher's shop in Lake.

Jane Butler married into the Caws family – she married Billy Caws, the longshore fisherman. Their eldest son was Ashford Caws [*another of our most prominent interviewees*]. Then they had a daughter called Dorothy who in 1919 married a man named Stan Jacobs – he used to ring the five minutes bell down the station, then he joined the army for about eight years. Another son was Herbert, the fisherman.

## My Parents

My father Mark Butler was born on the 15th December 1866. He used to go to school at Dame Attrill's, he paid tuppence a week, and

## Chapter 7 – The Butler Family

*Queen Victoria I* Lifeboat and crew at fundraising display, 1890s.
Joey Attrill stands in front of the lifeboat.

he used to play truant a damn sight more than what he went to school. When he was ten years or more, him and his father carted a lot of the chalk from the chalk pit to make the Embankment, which must have taken years to build. [*In fact, the Embankment was constructed between 1879 and 1880.*]

Now, Henry Weaver was proprietor of the Marine Hotel and he took my father on as a young man to be apprentice bricklayer. Then with the slump before the 1914 War building got a bit slack, so my father worked for a bit for Colonel Moreton, and he also worked down at Brambles in Lane End. During the First World War he went out on the examination vessel out here as a cook. He also used to go out in the lifeboat, which had oars in those days. Well, he was working at Brambles one day when the lifeboat was called out and he had to make a decision, "Do I go down and man the lifeboat or do I stop 'ere gardening?" And he decided to go in the lifeboat, and the pay he got for being in the lifeboat was deducted from the pay he got at the Brambles. He also helped to build the lifeboat pier around the 1920s. In his later years he worked as a gardener for Colonel Luxmore up at the Grange until he couldn't work any more. And he built Redruth (this house) almost single-handed in 1922–23.

My mother's name was Woodshaw, she was a Staffordshire girl and came down to East Cliff with the Fitzwilliams as a domestic servant. My parents were married in December 1895, when my mother was thirty-three and my father thirty. Dennett Road was opened up as a road in 1895, and I was the first one born there, in Locksleigh, in 1896. My father had Drayton Cottages built, and we moved there when I was one year old. That's why they're called by that name, because my mother came from a little place in Staffordshire called Drayton Bassett.

I left school and joined the Royal Navy on the 27th August 1912, at Ryde coastguard station. Dr Pridmore was the doctor who passed me as medically fit, and I was a special entry 'cos I was only five feet tall. I left Bembridge on the 9th September 1912 and went to Portsmouth Barracks for one night. I became a signalman in the Navy, and was eventually promoted to lieutenant on the 26th May 1939. I left the Navy on the 10th October 1946 at the age of 50, so I was away from Bembridge in the Navy for thirty-four years and a month.

## Anything To Do with Figures

My earliest memories of the village was going to school when I was three years old, and Wally Beer – who we always knew as Chinny Beer, lived in Dennett Road – he was two and a half years older than me, and he used to take me to school.

We used t'have a thing with some red, white and blue beads on it to count up, an' all that sort of thing. And we used to *sing*, "M-A-T mat, R-A-T rat, B-A-T bat, R-A-T rat"… all like that… we'd learn it, in the infants' school.

My father put me on me feet to start with, 'cos at school I was always twelve months ahead of all the other children. He always used to gimme some little sums to do, p'raps two and a three, four and a one or summing like that – eight sums, if you get 'em all right, I had a penny. And I used to stand on the rug in front o' the clock, have to tell the time; and sometimes going down Dennett Road, get halfway down the road an' all of a sudden he'd say, "Whassa time by the church now?" But I had it sort o' ground into me, so that I was always ready for anything to do with figures.

When we were very young we'd have the maypole out in school, and dance round that. Then when we got a bit older, we used to go down to the school gardens, down Northclose Road, opposite Love's yard. And then during the summer months we'd go down on the beach for swimming lessons.

Alfie Smith was considered as being one of, if not the, best schoolmasters in the Island. But:

> **Mr Smith was a very good man,**
> **He tried ter teach you all 'e can**
> **Ter read, ter write, an' arithmetic,**
> **But he don't ferget ter give you the stick.**

And you *did* get the stick in those days, I'll tell yer! And they always used to reckon, if Alfie had his whiskers cut, look owt!

## Dennett Road in the Early Days

Dennett Road was opened up in 1895, and the gardens were short, so this field known as Harvey's Butt [*now Manna Road*] was opened up as allotment grounds for the residents of Dennett Road, and it remained as allotment grounds until 1922 when Perce Watton sold it for building on. All the houses in Dennett Road had their wells and pumps – and there used to be a pump down Ducie Avenue, on the way to Fisherman's Square.

Living in Dennett Road then, top right-hand side from the High Street, was a man named Dan Austin. Next door to him was George Love, well he could play a violin – he used to get some odd coppers down the Village Inn and things like that – and he was the purser on the *Bembridge* that used to run from the harbour here. Then next door again was ol' man Beer, an ex-naval feller, I never knew him except as an old man; then Tommy Staples the painter lived next door to him. I was born in Locksleigh; then a little further along was an old man who used to ride a tricycle, name o' Freeman; and then next one was Harry Simmonds. Then there was a Harry Weaver, he was a carpenter; then Alf Weaver; then the next one was George Marsh, he was an ex-coastguardsman; and the next one was a man named Gatrell.

Now on the other side at the bottom was ol' man Frampton, who used to walk the mail from Brading to Bembridge. Now, he wouldn't have walked it if there was a railway, would he? So I think he must have walked round the downs before the railway was built. He lived in the first pair of houses built in Dennett Road. He had a son called Sid Frampton who was also a postman for years. And Framptons had the corner shop, used to sell bits o' cotton, bootlaces, darning-wools an' all sorts of different things. Well anyhow, they lived in *both* of those houses, as far as I know, Oxford Cottage and Dover Cottage.

Mr Frampton, Postman.

## Chapter 7 – The Butler Family

Then coming next to that would be a sort of a spinster lady named Miss King; further down was a man called Alf Felton; then in the next one used to be a feller in charge of the bookstall down the station. Next door was where ol' man Herbie Occimore [*i.e. Occomore*] lived, what run the carrier service over to Portsmouth – there was a feller named Chick used to go along with him when I was a boy. Well Occimore moved to Foreland Road, he was in his nineties when he's died, an' his wife was ninety-five. They had a daughter named Marjorie, she died in 1918 with that Spanish flu business. Well next door to that was a bricklayer feller name o' Billy Cotton; then George Fry, he was a gardener down at Balure. Then we lived in Drayton Cottage, as I say.

It was 1897 when ol' man Winter came from Seaview and opened up his corner shop. He bought a new bicycle for himself when he was 90! and then eventually died at 93.

## Butter, Pears and Pints

If you went down the grocer's shop, there was nothing wrapped up to speak of. You went down to get half a pound o' butter, there'd be 'arf a pound cut off and put on a bit of greaseproof paper and p'raps patted about a little bit with a little bit of a print on the top, and that was your butter, and the same with lard. And if you wanted half a pound o' currants they open up a drawer and get an old piece of paper and twist it up like a cone or something, and put your currants in there and your sultanas 'n all that just the same. Even sugar, it was always weighed up while you were there.

Down the Village Inn they used t'have a board, like, to sit on, a wooden affair – no *lounges* like they got now!

Old man named Attrill used to live in Devonshire Cottage [*in the High Street*]. Next door to PC Toomer in the same pair of cottages lived a man named Hayward, he used to be gardener down at Pitt House under a head gardener called Jim Norris. In Old Garth two old ladies lived there, Miss Collins and Miss Fraser.

Ernie Orchard lived in the cottage at the back where the Pottery is now [*i.e. in 1975*], and he was the last one to work the Windmill. He was also a coal merchant, he used to sell paraffin an' all that sort o' thing there. He was in the church choir up till he was eighty some odd.

There used to be people name of Denison lived at Balure [*in Ducie Avenue*], George Fry was a gardener down there. Chap name o' Gooseberry Woodford was a gardener for Colonel Moreton, then there was another chap there called Horton. The old lady Moreton would come up to church in one of these, like, a donkey in a wicker chair.

Eli Sillence was the head gardener down at East Cliff, and Bill Wheeler

Motor car, c.1906.

was a gardener for good many years at Tyne Hall. A man name of Collister was a gardener feller up at Thornycroft's to the best of my knowledge, and lived in that lodge where you enter. Sir John Thornycroft was the first one to have a motor car in Bembridge, as far as I can remember.

Elias Jeffery – he was my godfather – he lived in the lodge that enters Old Garth up there, he was the gardener there, and Parker was under-gardener to him.

There's a Fisherman's Square down the bottom of Ducie Avenue which the fishermen used t'use to put their boats up and so on. They go down there now to fire a gun to start racing instead of at the Sailing Club.

Nippers used to go in Neddy Pope's, there'd be like two or three of 'em, go round the back door, ask old Neddy to sell him some pears, but while he was round there talking to a nipper 'bout selling these pears and how much will they be an' that, there was a couple more up the bloody tree, pinchin' the pears! It used to be, yer know, a sort of organised affair.

Well there was a woman who used to work at North Wells who answered to the name of Ruth. And she told me herself that ol' Neddy was after her (after he lost his wife), an' uh-huh! The ol' cook answered the door and ol' Neddy was there and she says, "Well, state yer business!" – an' ol' Neddy run!

## Chapter 7 – The Butler Family

You never see a drunk these days [*Mr Butler was speaking in 1975, before the current problems associated with our town centres*]. Them days you could often see somebody a little bit tiddly, I mean what with pubs being open all day long, beer tuppence a pint – whereas today it's too weak to get drunk on and whisky's too dear to buy! Was nothing to go along the High Street and see old Ratty Blow sittin' just inside the Village Inn there ha' past ten in the morning, oh yeah! Well I know of people who got drunk time or two and slept in the ditch and all the rest of it. Get a feller like old Bill R or old Shep. Bill R never lived anywhere, far as I know: finish up with, he used to sleep in a pigsty, or anywhere where he could get a bit o' shelter, ol' Bill did! Well, Jack Bull, I mean *he* could drink a pint! But he packed it up eventually, wouldn't touch a drop of anything.

If anybody had a carpet, they used to fling the tea leaves down on the carpet, then get a stiff broom and sweep it. Then 'bout once a twelvemonth take the carpet up and stick it on the line and beat the hell out of it, an' things like that.

And then again, the *soap* wasn't like it is today, you had to get a bar of yellow soap, if you kept it long enough it'd be as hard as a brick, there was none o' these *powders* they got now.

## Fun and Games

Well there was no motor-cars to worry about, there was only the coal cart – ol' Bob Jordan or Henry Jacobs – and p'raps the milk-float, summing like that. And the roads were gravelled instead of being tarred, so you could make a big ring in the road and play marbles, and the girls would draw panels on the ground and play hopscotch or knock a wooden hoop along the road. And the boys used to go down to the blacksmith's shop and get a piece of iron what we used to call a 'scourger', for an iron hoop. Then down the bottom of Dennett Road with a tennis ball we'd play rounders, or kick a ball up and down. There was all those sort o' games that o' course children just can't *do* now, and I feel that that has got a lot to do with a certain amount of discontent among children today.

On a Sunday evening when I was a kid we always used to go down to my Aunt Jane's [*the Caws household, in the High Street*], and we generally played draughts or dominoes; this was whilst my father was in the Village Inn, then at nine o'clock he would come out and whistle, and mother an' me would trot off up Dennett Road, home!

In the early days the young chaps used to go, like, Sunday afternoons, primrosing and getting bluebells and daffydils up Centurions Copse, and up on the downs after cowslips, up the copse after nuts, all sorts of different things. But they generally used to congregate at the top of Foreland Road, p'raps quarter to six, summing like that, until the policeman come and moved them on. Then they'd all go into church.

But one o' the highlights of the village on a Sunday was to go down to the station and see the last train out. And o' course they'd go down there to see the soldiers and sailors go away, I think it was about five minutes to nine. And we *had* some soldiers and sailors in Bembridge then, 'course they wasn't always here all together. They usually used to be in the Pilot Boat, then they'd ring the five minutes bell, and you'd see 'em all come tumbling out o' the Pilot Boat, down onto station, say goodnight to their mums and sisters and what-have-you, and that was it. Seamen like Tim Gawn, Frank King, Harry Jeffery, Bert Jeffery, George Wells, Fred Beer, Dot Beer and Wally Beer, Harry Hall and Bert Hall – these two were coastguards' sons down the Point.

Where Woodland Grove is now, that was the football field, and next door to it was the cricket field, and you could go up the pathway along the allotment grounds into the football field, and go across that into the cricket

Children outside Woodford's butchers shop.

## Chapter 7 – The Butler Family

Bembridge Harbour Regatta, 1908.

field and come out on Steyne Road. Bembridge was always reckoned as having a very good football team, they always used to wear green shirts. And there was a couple o' soldiers from up at Culver Cliff in the team as a rule, then there was several Woodfords in it, Ernie Woodford – or Kingy Woodford as we called him – and Teddy Holbrook. There always used to be a saying: "Before you win the Island League, you've got to meet the boys in green".

At the Regatta a man named Freddie James was usually the Duck when they had the duck hunt. Where the pier used to be there was quite a depth of water there even at low water, and there was several yachts there, and the coastguardmen would bring a boat round from the back of the Spithead Hotel and they had to try an' catch the Duck. And he kept on diving underneath the yachts an' all that sort o' thing.

Christmas Eve, a lot of people for some unknown reason used to go to Ryde by train, but why they went to Ryde I don't know. I suppose it was one way of getting drunk or summing!

For Edward VII's coronation [*1902*] they had tables and forms all laid out in the fields of Wallsend Farm, and all us schoolkids we all went to a tea party over there, and we were all given a mug with King Henry VII and Queen

Alexandra's picture on the side of it. Those days there was horses and cows and chickens and pigs an' gawd knows what over there.

## Boats and Rockets

The old sea wall starts by the Pilot Boat Inn, goes by the Marine Hotel and right round the airport, and finishes up at the cement mill at Brading – they call it Duggers Wall. There's a little bit of a spot there which was always known as Pinnacle, and old man Herbie Occomore, who ran a wherry service between Bembridge and Portsmouth, used to land his stuff up there at Pinnacle, which of course was before the embankment was built. Afterwards he used to land it down at the Point, and the Prestons would take the stuff up from there to the Village Inn and so on.

I can remember seeing King George V going round 'ere in a snowstorm in February, 'bout 1910 or 1912, on his way to India in a ship called the *Medina*, and she had a couple o' cruisers or summing as escort of course – he was going out there to be Emperor of India. I was up against Peartree Corner and saw them going round other side of the Nab towards Dunnose Point, that way.

And I can remember the A3 submarine going down off Forelands in a snowstorm; that was about 1903 [*in fact, it is recorded as being as having been* launched *in 1903 and then sunk as the result of a collision on 2nd February 1912*].

They used to say:

**First the Nab and then the Warner,
Blockhouse Fort, an' Bonfire Corner.**

They used to fire two maroons from Foreland. My father was in the lifeboat, I suppose it would 'a bin during the First World War, and one night the lifeboat was called out, and my father wasn't there. And somebody said, "What's up wi' you, Mark? Was it too rough fer yer ter turn owt?" or summing like that, and he said he didn't know anything about it, he hadn't heard the rockets. Well very often, these rockets out at Foreland, if the wind's the wrong way, it carries the sound out to sea, and you got a job t'hear them other parts of village, partic'ly night-time. So my father suggested they should fire these rockets somewhere handier. And it was eventually decided to fire two rockets from Weaver's yard, and that's the ones you hear go off with a terrific *bang*! Well my father was the instigator of that. And I don't know anywhere else in the United Kingdom that fires four rockets to get a lifeboat out.

*Chapter 7 – The Butler Family*

# *Obituaries*

## Death of an Old Inhabitant
*(IW County Press archive for 21st December 1901)*

A well-known and much-respected inhabitant passed away on Monday last in the person of Mr William Jacobs, in his 87th year. Deceased was for years a carrier between Bembridge and Ryde, and he latterly carried on a business as a coal merchant. He had a wonderful physique for a man of his years, walking as upright and assisting in his business as actively as a man in his prime.

## Mr Harry Weaver – Obituary
*(IW County Press archive for 13th November 1943)*

We regret to announce the death of Mr Harry Weaver at Two-Ways, Foreland Road, Bembridge, where for over half a century he had been prominent in village life. His passing removes a highly respected East Wight resident, one who unobtrusively devoted much of a long life to the welfare of Bembridge, where for over 40 years he was parish clerk and overseer…

Born in July 1861, he was the eldest son of the late Mr Henry Weaver, and a grandson of Thomas Weaver, who fought at Waterloo, and subsequently settled in Bembridge, where he lived in the small stone cottage still standing in High Street and named after the famous battle. His father for many years conducted the Marine Hotel at The Point, and founded a successful builders' business practically a century ago. On his father's death Harry Weaver succeeded to the management of the hotelier's establishment, and with his brothers, the late Mr Alfred Weaver and the late Mr Percy Weaver, conducted the builders' business… He was one of the oldest and most loyal members of the Parish Church. For nearly half a century until 1926 he sang in the choir.

# Chapter 8

# Shh! Don't Say Another Word!
## – Mrs Ivy Bryant (Part 2)

**Tuffley's Grocery Shop**

When I left school, I went into my grandfather's shop. There weren't any visitors then except in the season as we called it, it was only about six weeks and we really had to work to make a living. We used to have to weigh up everything, we had to get up early in the morning, five o'clock often, and start weighing up sugar and so on, nothing in packets then. Open up at eight o'clock. And then at night you used to have to do the booking.

We delivered by pony and trap, my mother would drive a dog-cart for people's orders – there was a low dog-cart and there was a high dog-cart, and she'd drive both. You had to give credit in those days, and often these people that came from London, the nobility and so on, they'd have their six weeks and you wouldn't get a *penny*, p'raps, until they went, and sometimes you even had to wait till the next year for it! But you couldn't do anything about it. Yet you had to live on what you made in the summer, through the winter.

I remember we used to have a raffle at Christmas, we'd have it down in the stables, which were at the back of the shop. But the policeman had to be there to see fair play! That was late at night after we'd closed, and in those days we didn't close till eight o'clock every night, Saturday night ten o'clock. Sundays we never opened. We had an hour's lunch break, but we didn't used to shut the shop then, we had an assistant and he'd have to stay. All the shops opened all through the dinner-time.

A lot of the shops in Ryde would deliver out here so we had competition, you see, and we had to work hard, I can tell you. Our supplies used to come from Newport: we would deal with wholesalers such as Jordan & Stanley's and Upward & Rich. And then o' course a lot of stuff would come over from Portsmouth in old Occomore's boat, and a man called Jacobs with a horse an' cart would meet this boat and bring the things up.

You know how the shops send out notices in envelopes not stuck down? Well my brother – he could only have been about ten – he was sent out with these to go round to all the houses in the village. But he wanted to go to a

## Chapter 8 – Shh! Don't Say Another Word!

football match that afternoon, so he went and put them all in the postbox! And ol' Frampton brought all these back to my mother. You see, if Frampton had delivered them they would all have had to be paid for – it would've only been a penny, I s'pose, but that would've upset some of them, so he was very good and brought them back. And my brother was sent out with them a second time!

Then there was the oil episode. Well there was a family in Sherbourne Street and two of the girls 'hadn't got all their ha'pence', as we used to say. And there was a son who used to come over and do odd jobs for us at the shop, 'cause we sold oil then and he would fill the people's oil cans. I was in the office and I heard the most awful language going on, went out and there's poor ol' Daniel with his finger pushed up the spout of the big oil tank, and he couldn't move it because he couldn't get the tap to turn off. And there he was using the most *dreadful* language, and he could use language, ol' Dan'l! Ah-ha-ha!

That reminds me of another occasion. Jim Smith came in the shop one day, he was telegraph boy, the son of gardener Smith in Foreland Road. We always used to have telegraph boys in Bembridge; telegrams were only sixpence each in those days, there'd be a lot of them sent. Anyway, he'd come in the shop for sweets, 'specially butter-nougats, and I would serve him sometimes. And he came in one day – I'm gonna say a wicked word – he wanted "two penn'orth o' bugger-nougats"! 'Course, I laughed, I couldna help it, then afterwards he'd always come in and ask for "two-penn'orth or quarter of a pound of B-nougats".

## Up and Down the High Street

Now in the High Street there was nothing but a gate and fields where the hairdresser and library are now [*i.e. in 1975 – currently the fish shop*]. The other shops on that side used to be just a row of little cottages along there. Mr Couldrey at the Emporium made one of the cottages into a storeroom, and down the garden he used to keep fowls. Then Freddie Searle had a cobbler's shop along there – he was in the choir for donkey's years – before it became Warne's the greengrocers. Next came Jordan's the butchers, and his sisters the two Miss Jordans lived in Laurel Cottage next door. Mr Jordan himself lived round in Foreland Road.

There was a pair of cottages along there that lay quite far back, and the village policeman used to live in one when I was a kid. First it was a Mr Toomer, oh he was a scream, he was there for *years*. And every day he used to have to walk half-way to Sandown and meet the Sandown man half-way, to see if there was any trouble or anything. There was never much trouble in the village then, though.

High Street, towards Village Hall.

Then after him it was Shotter. 'Course, they had no telephone in those days – fancy, the police with no telephone! We had one in the shop and Shotter, I remember, used to come over and use our telephone for any of his calls – if there'd been any body washed up or something like that, there often was in those days. I remember once he came in, took off his helmet and there was this photograph inside it, and he said, "Have you ever seen that man about?" So I said, "No, I don't know him". So he said, "Well we've just found his body in the woods up at Howgate". He was telephoning the news of him, s'pose he'd shot himself or something. I always remember thinking, "Oh, fancy showing me that!"

The old boy in Woodbine Cottage was a pilot, David Newman, now *he* was an old Bembridger. And there used to be a nice old gentleman living at Willow Cottage: he was very interested in animals and he used to give us sort of little tracts and papers about animals. Another pilot lived in Rose Cottage, William Wallis, again a very old Bembridge family. Of course, the actor David Niven later lived at Rose Cottage for a time. There were three Wallis brothers who were pilots in Bembridge: one lived at Middleton House in Foreland Road, and the other one lived at Ducie View in Sherbourne Street.

Where Burden's wine shop is now in the High Street, that used to belong to a Miss Mursell, mostly a sweet shop. At one time before that, it was a wine and spirit shop as it is now. Next door in Waterloo Cottage lived the two

## Chapter 8 – Shh! Don't Say Another Word!

Miss Jordans, Sarah and Amy, aunts of the two Miss Jordans who lived in Laurel Cottage. So they were sisters of Jordan the butcher – a bit ancient, as you can imagine. They were quite good dressmakers.

Then next door, that used to be a private school, Alton House, run by Miss Bailey and Miss Jameson. Then Miss Ivy Winter had it as a sweet shop, I believe – belonging to the Winter family that were greengrocers on the corner of Dennett Road. That was Mr E. Winter, they came from Shanklin here and opened that shop in the 1890s. He got on very well with the shop anyway, 'cos he bought some land up in Steyne Road and put up that row of five houses, one for each of his children – the names were connected with his children's names: Erndene, Ivybank, Rosedene, Violet, and Olivene.

Coming across the road where Wreaf Woodford's butcher's shop is now [*still trading as W. W. Woodford in 2023*], was a shop belonging to the *old* Prestons. Dark and miserable! Sort of dried fish, red herrings and a few odd things. And this salt-fish, horrible long bits hanging down like this, all dried up an' – oh it used to look *dreadful!* I suppose John Cox was coming out here from Ryde about the same time, he had a fishmonger's there, 'cause you couldn't fancy anything out of that old shop. John Cox used to come out two or three times a week with a horse and cart; I suppose he'd stop where he had regular customers, or you'd have to catch him.

Where the war memorial is now on the corner of Church Road, a Mr Woodford had a butcher's shop there, but not related to Wreaford Woodford who afterwards came to have the shop next door.

Now the glebe land belonging to the Church was supposed not to be built on. There was nothing on it at one time and we used to have it for all sorts of things: flower shows, dancing in the evening. Well then they wanted to make a road through and get it for a car park, but the glebe land wasn't to be sold. But then the telephone people came along and they let them have the exchange there. Well then the White House got a bit of land and built a garage there, then they built those bungalows. So now you see it's just used for building. It belonged to the Ecclesiastical Society and they weren't *supposed* to sell it.

And Church Row – one of those houses used to be an almshouse belonging to the Church, they let it out to poor people, widows and so on. Well, there used to be poor families in Bembridge then, but I don't think there are any now. You see, it was only labourers, fishermen and tradespeople, they didn't make much money in those days.

Next you had the old school playground, and then Mr Ashford Mursell's baker's shop. He was the father of the Miss Mursell that kept the sweetshop on the other side of the road down a bit further. They had a bakehouse there and sold groceries as well. Then Jack Riddick took it over and built on a big bakery, and they would make cakes and tarts an' all that sort of thing,

High Street and Village Inn, 1870s.

and they were provision merchants as well. The chemist shop up there was built for him along with Lacey's shop, there was nothing there before – well, Dennett Road wasn't even built then.

And the Olde Village Inn used to be quite different and yet the outside seems to be the same. It was kept by a Mrs Rebecca Woodnutt and her son in those days, she was a big, buxom woman. They used to have a little side window where the people would go up and drink from the street, or get a bottle of anything without going into the pub.

There were two Miss Jefferys where the pottery studio is now, they were very good dressmakers, they used to make my frocks, but there were other dressmakers in the village too; either that or you had to go to Ryde or Portsmouth for clothes. The fashion was all long skirts in those days. *Now you can't get anything done in the village.* Anyway, their father John Jeffery used to work up at the mill for my grandfather. And his brother, the other Jeffery, was gardener up at Bembridge Lodge at one time. The first people I remember at the Lodge were name of Mainwaring – 'Mannering' we used to pronounce it. She was a biggish woman and she used to sing at concerts.

## Fish and Ships

The Forelands fishermen were considered quite different to the Bembridge fishermen. The Bembridge ones were Caws, Mursells… The Caws often

## Chapter 8 – Shh! Don't Say Another Word!

used to call on us when they were going down: would we like some winkles? And then they'd bring them up on the way up. And Mr Bannister, who lived on the corner where Lloyds Bank is now [*High Street / Sherbourne Street*] – he didn't marry till quite late in life, they were engaged for years. Well then they went down Swains Road to live, and he used to fish off Forelands and he was going out fishing by himself till he was quite old, over 80. And Nita got so worried about him, she said to the doctor, "Well what about him going out?" Doctor says, "Let him go! If he goes that way, well it'll be the way he'd *like* to go". But he did die in his bed. 'Course, there was no retiring in those days, you just kept on as long as you could.

I can tell you a story with a little bit o' swearing in it if that's alright. There was a Pewey Mursell, a fisherman, who lived in No. 2 Sherbourne Cottages and his speech wasn't very good. He used to go round selling fish, shellfish and that sort of thing. And he called on this Mrs Hoare, who lived at Holmleigh down the bottom of Pump Lane, and she asked for some prawns. So he gave her the prawns and she went to pay him, but she only had a sovereign. So he said, "Haven't got any change for that, madame, I'll go over the road and get some". So she said, "Oh, I don't know whether I can trust you". So he said, "Give me back my buddy pawns! If you can't trust me with your buddy sovereign, I can't trust you with my buddy pawns!" Ah-ha-ha-ha! That's a *real* old tale of the village.

We never knew whether the *Bembridge* and the *Island Queen* [*passenger ferries*] were going from the Harbour or Under Tyne, and if they went from Under Tyne you had to go down the Ducie and right along. There was a fisherman's hut and a little sort of harbour there, and you were rowed out to the boats, whichever one it was. I suppose twenty to thirty would travel over at a time.

Bembridge used to be quite a place where the pilots lived. It was quite handy; they had a pilot boat that would go out and meet the liners by the Nab as they came in and went out from Southampton to New York. In the old days it used to be a sailing boat.

On one occasion I was just going home to my lunch and there were several men looking over the gate [*by Jordan's fields*], in what is the village centre now: in those days there were just fields all round and you could see the liners going round. So of course I had to go and see what they were looking at, and it was the *Titanic* going out, from Southampton. And I said, "Oh wouldn't I love to be on that boat!" It was on her maiden voyage, well she only had the one. And about a week afterwards I was going down Foreland Road and I met one of these men, and he said to me, "Aren't you glad you weren't on that ship?" So I said, "Why, what's happened?" He said, "Well, she's gone ter the bottom," so of course I was very pleased to know that I *wasn't* on it.

Passenger Steamer 'Island Queen' and the Spithead Hotel
(before the addition of the upper windows), c.1880.

## Foreland Road and Beyond

The post office was originally at the corner of Foreland Road, and the three Miss Osbornes used to run it. There used to be about three deliveries a day then, including two or three on Saturdays. I could write a letter and catch the midday post: it would get to London that night and I could get a letter back next morning! When you think of today! Then the post office was open on Sunday mornings, and we children would call there on our way to Sunday School to collect the letters – there was no delivery on Sundays but you could collect them. Our boyfriends used to write to us and the letters often arrived on Sundays. And at seven o'clock every night the mail van would fetch the mail, you could tell the time by him. The mail van was a horse and carriage, of course – you'd have thought it would've gone by train, wouldn't you? Old Mr Frampton was the postman, and at one time he used to have to walk from Brading with the mail.

Then at one time the Osbornes also had the bakehouse and paint-shop at the top of Foreland Road – these were a different family from the Osborns

## Chapter 8 – Shh! Don't Say Another Word!

Osborne's Stationers and Post Office with the Misses Osborne, c.1900.

in Sherbourne Street, by the way, though both were bakers. Mr Walter Osborne was the father, and he's listed here [*in Hill's Commercial Directory*] as:-

**family grocer, provision dealer, warehouseman, baker, agent for W & A Gilbey, wine importers and distillers, house and estate agent, ornamental painter, plumber, glazier, oil colour and varnish merchant.**

I suppose he did all this from these couple of shops! Then Ernest Osborne took over from his father, well *he* ran the baker's shop and he also sold wines and spirits. We used to get the most lovely lard cakes, a penny each, and buns, a ha'penny each, which we used to take on the beach and have picnics and that sort of thing. His sisters, the three Miss Osbornes – Grace, Annie, and Jessie – kept the post office next door. And then I remember at one time they changed over and Ernest's shop went onto the corner, they tried that for a while and then they moved back again. And even the library was on the corner once, but we always called that Post Office Corner.

Next door, I remember that as the Osborne bakehouse, and little Mr Bastiani, who worked for Mr Osborne, baked the bread for the baker's shop round the corner. And it was one of the old-fashioned bakeries, you had to light the fire inside the oven and then scrape it all out and then cook the bread in the hot oven. He had a door that was half an' half, you know, it had the top-half open like a stable-door, and we used to love to go and hang over the half-door for the lovely smell of the bread and talk to him. Bastiani would go out from there with one of these little handcarts to take the bread round the village. He lived at what we used to call Newtown, by Steyne Cross.

So then you had Osborne's paint-shop, a long building reaching right along where the rest of those shops are now in Foreland Road. It was *called* the paint-shop, but it wasn't a shop as such, more a kind of store or workshop where they kept all their paints and stuff, and sold them from there. Then o' course Ernest did quite a bit of decorating on his own – he'd close the baker's shop while he was out decorating, or Mrs Osborne would take over.

Now opposite, there's a room there which was used as a mission hall, but now they let it out to different societies. There was a lot of controversy over that as to who it belonged to, and it wasn't to be used for anything else but religious things. And then Mrs Collins who lived at Willow Cottage, I think she rented it for about a shilling a year, something like that.

Now Herbert Occomore the harbour master built the post office [*in Foreland Road*] for his son, who was also Herbert. Because the son was with Thornycroft's at Hampton, and his father wanted him to come back to Bembridge. Now the postmaster's grandfather, *that* Mr Occomore, he was the one who used to run the boats over to Portsmouth to pick up stuff, as a carrier.

There was the thatched cottage in Foreland Road where Miss Sybil Noble lived, the cottage that burnt down. She was an actress, very good in the village for theatricals and that sort of thing.

I remember Inver House being built as a private house for some people by the name of Goodall, that was in the 1900s. Jerry Goodall was an Island man who went away then came back, and they lived at Providence House at the top o' Ducie Avenue. He was brother to the Goodalls who lived down by the Wesleyan Chapel. Mrs Henry Goodall was always wandering about in white sandshoes, she was quite a character!

There was quite a lot of grass in Foreland Road in those days, not like now, and our boys used to go and play football in the road. And then Swains Road I can remember as fields with a stile at each end.

The Birdham was two houses before it became a hotel, but for some years it was only halfway built up, evidently the builders went bankrupt or something. All those Lane End shops were fields then, of course. Then Arthur Weaver's workshop came a bit later. St Luke's Chapel was the cemetery chapel, *that* was there and the cemetery, but they were sort of, in the middle of nowhere then.

## Chapter 8 – Shh! Don't Say Another Word!

And there was only just a *pathway* out to Forelands, I can remember when it was just a little hamlet, with only the Crab and Lobster and a little cluster of fishermen's cottages roundabout, with the coastguard station. The fishermen used to have their lobster pots and catch prawns – they would sell great big prawns a shilling a hundred in those days! Attrills used to catch those chiefly; that tall, lanky one we used to call Spider Attrill would come round house-to-house with them.

Then the Lane End people were considered different again: they were 'Lane End', they weren't 'Bembridge'! it was a separate hamlet. And of course, Hillway and Peacock Hill were *quite* separate. In the wintertime, there were only what you might call the village people that really lived here, like the farms and the tradespeople and the fishermen. And then a few of these bigger houses like the Moretons and Thornycrofts.

## Farms and Coal

Farmer Way used to have Foreland Farm when I was very young, because I would go down there to play with his three girls. And opposite the Lifeboat House in those days there was a sheepwash, a deep sort of ditch where old Farmer Way used to dip his sheep, and we'd go down and watch him. That was before they built the seawall at Lane End. Well, then Prestons were at Foreland Farm after that.

Now Farmer Morris's wife at Stanwell Farm, she used to come to the dances, *he* never joined in anything in the village. But it was a long way to walk, she'd walk in and then walk all that way home by herself, two o'clock in the morning! Well then one of the Humphray brothers took over after Mr Morris.

Jordan's Farm used to be roughly between Foreland Road and what is now Meadow Drive, he didn't have a *big* farm, but he had several fields and some cowsheds, in fact I think some of them were made into garages over there belonging to the houses. That was Tom Jordan, and he was the butcher too of course. Then they had horses and carts for the coal merchant side of the business, which his brother John ran from the yard behind the butcher's shop. John Jordan lived down Darts Cottage with the other brother Bob, who used to help John with the coal-bags. These three were the sons of the previous Tom Jordan, who was churchwarden for a long time.

Steyne Farm belonged to Sir John Thornycroft, and it was run by his bailiff Dunster – that's another place we used to go for parties when we were quite young. I remember old Sir John Thornycroft had a gamekeeper, Albert Mead. I know he went after our boys, they used to go down under Lynchens there, all Thornycroft's land, you see. It was partly wooded then, he looked after all that, and some of the men would go down there shooting – duck,

I suppose. And the boys would be up to mischief down round the harbour, bird-nesting or fishing an' all that sort of thing. But Albert Mead was quite a character amongst the boys, they were frightened of him!

Bembridge Farm belonged to the Dennetts before the Taylors went there. We would go up and get mushrooms from the field which is now the airfield. Wallsend Farm ran along where several shops are now up in the High Street; it belonged to Kingswell when we were children, then Prestons took it over after old Kingswell died. He would let us use one field as the football field, and another one as the cricket field, roughly where Heathfield Road is now.

Well Harold Watson once told me that his people came to Swains Farm, which was by the crossroads of Swains Road and Swains Lane. I can just remember the old stone ruins.

The coal used to come down from Newcastle on the *Allerwash* and the *Ellington*. Then when we were teenagers [*in the 1900s*], one of the managers' sons and his friends would come down on the *Allerwash* and stay with Dick Mursell the fisherman in Mitten Road. And we got quite friendly with them, one's name was Mason and another Harry Hodgson – took me out sailing once, I shall never forget it. Oh yes he could sail a boat, but I was petrified! They came down every year for a few years just for the trip down, they'd go in at the wharf, where Ways were [*St Helens Quay*]. Mr Way lived at St Helens Mill, and he used to call on us at Tuffley's shop for

Cottages at 'Newtown' (Steyne Road), 1900s.

corn and wheat orders, oats and so on, ears of wheat out of their shucks. Nearly everybody would keep fowls in those days and they'd come in and buy it.

Now there was an Alf Wilson the photographer who married Polly Osborn, who had the bakehouse in Sherbourne Street, and he lived there. He used to go round with a camera, he took it on as a sort of sideline. He had the old box-camera on a tripod with a black cloth over, took photographs of weddings and things.

Then there was the Nursing Association, started by Lady Thornycroft. The village nurse lived up Newtown [*i.e. Steyne crossroads*].

## Fun and Games

Of course, we used to have real regattas in those days, they're *nothing* today, only for the sailing people. The whole village used to take part *then*, and we had two regattas, the village regatta or Bembridge Regatta, that was great fun, it was quite a day of the year. Then there was Lane End Regatta, that wasn't until several years later, but that was very interesting too.

With the Bembridge Regatta, they had all the sea and shore sports down at the Point, then after tea they had sports in the Love Lane fields, and also the field at the top of Ducie Avenue. Down at the Point they'd have greasy pole: a pole was rigged up from the pier and it was smothered with grease, and the men had to crawl to the end and fetch something in. 'Course, they nearly all fell off into the sea! There was a man named James who was very good at it. Then there was Harry Laughrin, he was good at sports too, and a great dancer. And they also had what they called a duck hunt.

They ran about with bangers an' all sorts of things. Bangers were pigs' bladders or 'bladders of lard' as they were called. We used to sell them in the shop, they were supposed to be the best lard going, more expensive than any other. Then the lard was taken out and the bladder was blown up and attached to the end of a stick, and they went about banging people, all that sort of thing. Oh, it was great fun! And they had these strings of paper on the end of a stick, waving those about.

The Point coastguards under Mr Petty always did all the hanging of the Chinese lanterns down Ducie Avenue, and then they used to have a band down Ducie and there'd be dancing, oh it was a great day!

I remember the sports in Love Lane, one of Earl Fitzwilliam's fields, to celebrate Queen Victoria's Diamond Jubilee. That was in 1897, when I should have been seven. It was the first time I ever saw anything like ice-cream, in those days they called it okey-pokey, and we were *dared* to have any because it was supposed to have been made in Ryde in a very poor part and it wasn't the done thing.

Bembridge Harbour Regatta, 1908.

My mother and my eldest brother went over to Osborne to see Queen Victoria lying in state in 1901, and I know I was very upset because I couldn't go. I should think there must have been a wagonette laid on from Bembridge, 'cos there weren't coaches in those days. We must have had a school holiday then and the shops must have been closed, otherwise my mother and brother couldn't both have gone.

For King Edward's coronation in 1902, we had a do up in the old football fields. I can remember there being races and things in the afternoon, and dancing in the evening.

Voting day used to be another great day. Everybody would have their colours up and the candidate would come to Bembridge and visit all around. I think we went to vote in the schools then. And it wasn't *always* Conservative in Bembridge. Godfrey Baring and Seely were both Liberals on the Island, and William Couldrey was a strong Liberal in the village. They'd go all round the village with a horse and cart at election-time, all the Moretons and so on.

Then during the Boer War we had a couple of holidays for the Relief of

## Chapter 8 – Shh! Don't Say Another Word!

Mafeking and the Relief of Ladysmith. One came through and it wasn't true, but we'd already got the holiday!

We used t'have our Sunday School treats at Tyne Hall and East Cliff, we'd have tea and games and that sort of thing. East Cliff would be long after Fitzwilliams' time. Eli Sillence was head of the Sunday School. We'd also have sports all down this field here, Jordan's field it was called then, before these houses were built [*i.e. Meadow Drive*].

We'd have entertainments, singing, recitations, little plays, and somebody'd talk to us and so on. In the evening there was Band of Hope and Good Templars – that was a temperance society more for grown-ups – and they were held in the schoolroom. And the Church of England Temperance Society was also held in the school, we kids all belonged to that. All these things, they used to have the meeting about once a fortnight, or some once a week.

Later on there was a new hall built between the Grange and Bembridge House by the Reverend Nelson Palmer, where we had roller-skating, entertainments, concerts, dances, plays and pantomimes. Mrs Palmer was an actress and she used to train us for these different things. We'd have three or four balls a year for charities, they were real do's. We had lovely times, jolly good eats, and generally they got a good band together from the village. Everybody helped to make it a good evening.

We were at the rehearsal of a play, and all my brother Wallace had to do was let the curtain down, and he let it down an' knocked the Reverend Palmer's wig off! Mrs Palmer said, "Nelson, you silly man, why didn't you get out of the way?" Then he picked up the wig and put it on the wrong way round. 'Course everybody roared! it was a joke in the village for a long time. And then we took one play to Sandown and he only had three words to say, and when it was his turn to come on, he was down below looking at the fire engine!

I remember one ball, there was quite a big crowd there, when the lifeboat gun went, about midnight, and we were left with very few men as most of them went off to help. I believe it was the night of the Ryde Lifeboat tragedy, when several of the crew were drowned. That was about 1907.

That hall was taken down later, by the way, and it's now at Seaview, it only lasted here a few years. Yes, we had dances there, also in the church room, and we *have* had them down at the Garland Club. They also had a very good boys' club after the church room was built, in 1910, and it went very well until the War came.

Indoors, some people would play the piano, have singsongs and that sort of thing. We'd play cards and games – happy families, ludo, snakes and ladders, and we'd p'raps go out to tea with somebody or have somebody to tea.

Unveiling the Palmer Memorial, Bembridge Point, August 11th 1910.

There was great rivalry between Bembridge and St Helens in those days amongst the young people in sport and so on. We both had a hockey team, that was about 1906, and we used to play in one of Thornycroft's fields up by the mill. Didn't last very long but we thoroughly enjoyed it while we were at it.

On the Ducie shore there were a couple of wooden bathing-machines that belonged to an old man called Joe Bond, and he used to have tents on the beach. If the tide was a bit far out, the bathing-machines would be pulled down to the edge of the water, and the ladies would go in there to undress and dress, so that they shouldn't go down in their bathing-costumes – not like they do today, undress on the beach! He was retired when he did that, but he had been chief boatman for the Point Coastguards, under Mr Weeks; it was when he retired from that that he came up into the village and lived at no.1 Sherbourne Cottages. Well then at the Garland Club, which was a club for the 'Upper Ten' in those days, the ladies used to wear black bathing-costumes with black stockings and black shoes to go in the water.

I remember the Matthews family, in my youth, they had a tent next to ours on the beach. We all used to gang up together, sort of thing, the Matthews boys Stanley and Willy, our boys, and the Smith girls. The father, Jeremiah Matthews, was secretary to the Missions to Seamen. They had a cottage down next to the old chapel that they used to come to every summer. He was a biggish man with a long beard, and he used to bathe a lot and dive off the diving-board that was in front of our tents. Their mother would come in the shop sometimes and say, "Oh I hear our boys came to supper with you last night," and the boys had never been near us, they'd been out with some o' the girls, you know – lads, they were proper lads! One of the daughters, Mary, was a very good singer, she was with the Carl Rosa Opera Company; and she married a well-known cricketer, Gillingham. *Old* Jeremiah Matthews lived in Ducie Avenue, but that was before our time.

## I'll Buy You A Watch One Day!

I heard a very funny story about Neddy Pope that used to live at Peacock Farm. They say he kept a few cows but he never fed them at home, he would take them all round feeding on the grass, you know, on the road verges an' that sort of thing. And he was supposed to have quite a bit of money and he used to keep it all in the house. And somebody said to him, "You oughta put that money in the bank, Neddy, it's not safe you know". Little while afterwards they met him one day and they said, "What did you do with that money?" "I put it in the bank." "Which bank?" He says, "I dug a hole in the bank an' I put it in there!" Ha-ha-ha!

I can remember him saying t'me, "**Shhh! Don't say another word! I'll buy you a watch one day!**" That was when he used to come up to the mill at haymaking time, we would take their teas down, you know. I don't know why, it was a favourite saying of his. I never had the watch! I think he'd say it to everybody. Then when we were still at school a little gang of us would go up to Neddy Pope's on Sunday afternoons, and we'd buy a pennyworth of pears and a ha'porth of skimmed milk, and we did get a *handful* of pears for it.

There was Ratty Blow the chimney-sweep, he used to run after us, we would call out after him. And then there was another old man that lived up the High Street, Billy Butler. I suppose us kids used to sort of call after them, you know, or be a bit scared of them or something, then they'd make out they were running after you.

Old Mother Wednesday was an Italian who used to come round the village on Wednesdays with a barrel-organ and a monkey. She'd push this great thing out from Ryde, I expect she played as she came through Nettlestone and St Helens. She'd walk round the streets playing and people would give her money. I must have been about seven or eight then [*1897–8*]. Well our housekeeper who used to look after us was called Sarah, and she would heat farthings and ha'pennies up, and then we would get up in the top window and throw them out. And this Ol' Mother Wednesday, sometimes she had a man with her, and they would scramble round in the dusty road for these coins an' then swear like anything when they picked them up! Hot! And there *was* dust in those days 'cos there were no proper made roads. And they'd shake their fists at us!

Old Tom S pushed this tank of oil right round the village to sell it, and he was very conscientious. One day he owed some people up Longlands a ha'penny and he didn't have change, so he said "I'll bring it back," and they said, "Don't bother". Well that's halfway to Sandown. 'T any rate, that night he went right up to Longlands to take that ha'penny back! Yes, but that was Tom all over.

Another time, I suppose I was only about seven and I was looking in the glass and titivating myself up, I suppose, and Sarah said, "You needn't do that, you'll never be as good-looking as your mother!" She was ever so strict with us children – but she was kind. She used to take us up to Hillway Chapel on Wednesday evenings, and old Griffin an' old Jeffery that lived up in Glover's Cottages at Peacock Hill, they used to run the services up there and they'd keep shouting out, "Praise the Lord! Praise the Lord! Alleluya! Alleluya!" It amused us kids. Real Nonconformist Chapel, for those days. But ol' Jeffery's wife and daughter would come down Sunday evenings to church, so they were obviously of different religion!

# Chapter 9

# Poaching, Piloting and Driving Bullocks
## – Mr Ashford Caws (Part 2)

### Up and Down the High Street

David Newman used to live in Woodbine Cottage, he was harbour pilot, and then Louis Newman the son, he took it over for a bit, but 'e couldn't do't, I suppose. Now they was bifore Occomore, before *my* time, so I should say that was in the old harbour before the Embankment was built.

Now Caldicot Smith lived in Mulberry Cottage, he was a retired naval architect. He used to come in 'ere [*Caws Tea Gardens*] for a prawn tea sometimes in the summer, and bread an' butter. But he'd have a teapot out there, with a cup, and e'd have to put a bottle o' beer in that teapot, yer see! That's right.

They had that Mulberry Cottage pulled down once and Walt Frampton got some money out o' the government to have that done up for the fire station. There used to be a mulberry tree there on the corner.

People by the name of Osbirn [*Osborn*] used to live in the back o' Clematis Cottage before Miss Mursell took that over as a sweet shop. Then front part was put on for the shop. They had a son Wally Osbirn, he did a little bit o' butchering, well 'e didn't have much, 'bout one mutton chop! He had a shop in the back there, just round the side.

Charlie Butler used to live in the old cottage where Smith's the chemist and Lacey's is now [*i.e. in 1975*], 'twas a fairish long bungalow. He was a retired Crimean veteran, always wear his medals when he went out dressed up.

I can remember Farmer Way had Wallsend Farm first, he's the same one who had Foreland Farm. All the fields at the back 'ere, what's built on now, they all belonged to Way's, they used to keep cows up there. Then afterwards John Jordan took it over and he used to go round with milk on a yoke – the buckets wouldn't touch yer legs then. I don't think they had any cows when he had the farm, I think they used to get their milk from Taylor's up Bembridge Farm. And Jordan was a coal merchant an' all.

Now Alfred Attrill, Dame Attrill's brother, had that house built next door to the school, Devonshire House. Then when he died, the son Charlie Attrill come an' lived there. He used to work down Cowes on the shipyard, and he used to walk from here to Cowes on a Monday mornin'! Then walk back at the end o' the week. But he worked over Portsmouth dockyard first, and he told me his job over there was making oars, he had to make one pair a day, and that's what he's supposed to do! Now that was when they used to make spoon oars, not straight oars.

Tabuteaus used to live in Woodlands, they was independent, yer see. Then next to Woodlands was the White Cottages. One of 'em was Polly Attrill – she was very religious, always used t'have tracts stuck out in her garden. Mrs Newark used to live in next White Cottage and she had two daughters. Then my grandfather Billy Butler lived in the upper one.

Watton the builder lived up at Lynchens Cottage – that's why 'tis they says 'over Lynchens', yer see.

Rothschilds came to live in Bembridge House, and Nightingales come with 'em, and they used to look after horses for them.

In them days all the High Street down to Mursell's all belonged to the Lodge, 'twas all fields, no houses at all, not till you got down to Mursell's. Harry Chick used to go round from there with a handcart, wi' bread in it. Mrs Thomas from down Tyne Hall used to go in Mursell's shop and buy cakes, then she used to give us lardy cakes if we went over there. She was always very good.

Lammy Etheridge an' Joey, they used to go down and sweep the High Street, and some people used to come down there curling.

When Queen Victoria died [*in 1901*], I can remember dad took some people out in the boat to watch the procession go by down through the line.

## Pubs and Poaching

Well now Frank Mursell was a man could get a pub anywhere: he had the Marine twice and the Crab once. And some relation of his before that once had the Village Inn. Well Frank used to do funny things to draw customers, yer know. He used to be out in his garden putting his broad beans in, stickin' up a stick to each one, yer see. When he's down the Crab, on a Sunday morning he could see 'bout twelve chaps stood outside there, so he drawed off twelve pints o' beer. So when they went in they said, "Aw, we'll 'ave a drop o' whisky" – but they had their pint afterwards, so he won all the time, yer know! They used to come some blessed games, I tell yer that! And he used to do that, and go fishin' besides, his wife 'ud look after the pub while he was out.

The first one I can remember in the Village Inn was a man named Parkes, his daughter Sally Parkes was a schoolteacher. It was two separate places once, if you can make out – one part for letting and one for the pub. And when it

# Chapter 9 – Poaching, Piloting and Driving Bullocks

High Street around 1910, showing Yew Cottage and St Helens View, the two cottages where the Caws family lived, next to the Village Inn.

used to brew its own beer, bifore Occimore [*Occomore*] did his carrying, they used t'have a dog who'd keep watch, see nobody didn't come round!

The Glanvilles used to lodge at the Village Inn in the summer. Trevor and Geoffrey, they's only little boys 'bout so high, they used to come round: "Fishermen home yet?" And ol' Sir Hercules Langrishe used to be living there sometimes. The son used to cut capers with a bicycle, go out on the road. He'd put a hank'chief, shove it down in the road and go and lean owt over an' pick it up with his mouth, 'e did!

And I've heard Rainbow Preston an' Tim H–– was gonna foight outside Village Inn once! Rainbow lived down under Newtown Hill, he used to work on Bembridge Farm, and his brother Ed was a bit of a under-gardener up Thornycroft's.

There used to be a girl and her mother down Mrs Knight's down Ducie Cottage. The mother would do the cooking and the gal would do the housework. Anyhow, the gal used to go down the Pilot Boat to get a jug o' beer every night for her mother's supper, and one of the reg'lars had somethin' to say t'er. She took hold of his glass o' beer and threw it right in his face! She says, "You say 'f yer like, I'll put another one in yer face!" I bet he never said nothin' else *t'her*! No fear!

Ol' Devon was a bit of a rough character, used to drink a good drop and quarrel with people. He done a bit o' gardening about, sort o' odd jobbin'. Well I heard there was a bit of a fight on down the Crab one night, with one or two soldiers. An' Devon see these soldiers coming down the road an' he says, "Get owt the guns missus an' bring owt the barrel". An' a policeman was there, I think that was Toomer – "There," he says, "you throw 'em away an' I'll shoot 'em down!"

Albert Mead was gamekeeper for Thornycroft, he was always after we bloody boys! But we never done him any blessed harm, I s'pose. We used to go up the road an' down over Lynchens, down the big copse after hazel nuts, what blessed boys *would* be after, 'bout ten or dozen of us was down there. I think 'twas on a Sunday, Charlie Attrill's there an' oh a lot o' boys down there. And o' course, somebody's, "Look out, Albert's comin'!" And we head through the blessed wire an' up over Lynchens. And o' course he'd come up 'n down the road and come down that way to try to ketch us! Couple of us we nipped in an' up through into Lodge gardens. But he didn't come that way, he went after a few boys what went out 'long Point there. He was a bit proper o' strict one, anybody was poachin'.

Truman was poacher. Some relation was out 'ere one day – I says, "Well 'e ain't a True Man unless 'e can ketch a rabbit!" An' o' course these chaps *larfed*. Well he used to come in in the evening, "Wan' a rabbit t'morrow, missus?" Only charged yer sixpence fer rabbit, that's all. "Well, one or two?" Whatever we wanted, p'raps "two". "Orright." You'd *'ave* 'em right enough!

## Piloting Tales

There used to be three pilots in Bembridge once, Josiah Caws, Bill Wallis, and Ted Wallis. Bill Wallis lived down Rose Cottage, then afterwards had the Willows built down Lane End. Ted Wallis lived down Foreland Road, he had Milverton House built and was a great big feller. They used t'have a pilot boat called the *Hornet*. Then there was Harry Wallis, 'e could play a violin priddy well if you could keep 'n on his feet, but if he had a drop o' drink he'd wanna lay down!

Then Josiah Caws had two sons, Perce and Ted, but they was colour-blind, they couldn't go piloting but they was the crewmen for the boat, yer see. When the steamers come in, they used to go and put their father or the Wallises aboard. And then Charlie Caws, another son o' Josiah, he was a pilot but he worked on the other boat, the *Edginora* – *she* used to do piloting, they used to take turns, I think. I's only a boy then. I told one of 'em I liked monkey nuts once. He said, "I'll bring yer a bagful," and brought me a mailbag full o' monkey nuts orf one o' boats. Blimey, I got sick o' them things!

George Bannister told me 'bout before the Embankment was built, he'd get five shillings from the pilots for rowin' 'em up to Brading from Under

## Chapter 9 – Poaching, Piloting and Driving Bullocks

Tyne. The London pilots brought the steamers down the Channel, and then someone landed 'em down Under Tyne, then they'd be rowed up to Brading station fer five bob – 'cos the train come through there to Ryde, yer see.

And he used to tell me 'bout the Spithead Hotel was built on a pond, 'cos he used to *paddle* in there! That's why when it's a very high tide, that gets flooded down the basement, y'know. And the sewerage used to come up in there years ago, they had it down the harbour – but now they pumps that all down Lane End, don't they?

Ev Love an' Judd Bartlett, they had a boat called the *Undine*, they used to take the pilots out o' the P&O boats what's going down the Channel and go orf an' land 'em round by Brading, yer see – again, that's 'fore the Embankment was built. Me an' Herb Occimore started doing that once, and then we got stopped afterwards – we land 'em out o' Dutch boats what come down there, they used to give us a pound to land 'em. We had to go and larnch a boat Under Tyne and get 'em orf against the Leg Buoy somewhere, and put 'em ashore down Under Tyne somewhere.

Now ol' Walt Caws was a pilot, he used to go ter Hamburg and bring the big liners down, I think. He had a house built 'long Mitten Road.

And Robert Newman was ol' pilot. He used to come down shore putting a line out to get fer fish, 'e did. That's after he retired, he's getting on. He lived out 'long Point somewhere, close to the Marine.

Then there was Bill Mursell, Joe Mursell and Bob Mursell. They went off trying to get jobs out of steamers, 'cos years ago there used to be a lot o' steamers anchored off 'ere. Tain't like 'tis nowadays y'know, *now* they can get all their weather-forecasting but they never used to. You'd see 'bout thirty anchored orf 'ere sometimes, and they'd all go orf 'bout teatime, but next morning they'd be all back again.

Ol' Tom Occimore and his son Herbert run two sailing boats from Bembridge Harbour to Portsmouth, they used to bring over all the goods. Herbert 'ud be in one, and the ol' chap and another feller in the other one. Anything that was comin' to the Isle of Wight, they'd bring over. One boat was called the *Agnes*, it brought all the beer from Long's Brewery, cases o' beer, bottled beer, tubs o' beer, and any parcels there was to come 'ere they'd bring it over. George Attrill worked with 'im. Down a pub in Seaview – they called it 'Simmy Trinders' then – that was the only place where they'd bring a thirty-six gallon over. And they had to land that small boat, y'know. Ol' Tom Occimore was a Salvation Army man.

Occimore's going over Portsmouth once, his wife had been poulticing him, but he's goin' over wi' blessed poultices on! And then he's sent back home. Then Dick Mursell went over afterwards. Dick bin up round and got orders an' all. Then Occimore come down an' says, "Well, all ready?" Dick says, "Now, 'ave you had your dinner?" He says, "Yes." Well Dick says,

# An Oral History of Bembridge – Isle of Wight

Station Road, Bembridge, c.1906.

"I'm gonna 'ave *mine* now then, you'll 'ave to wait." Ol' man had had *his* blessed dinner, 'e didn't care whether… Oh dear!

Now his son Herb Occimore took over the pilot's, well I used to go out with him sometimes. We used to go off and put in aboard the steamer an' then tour in, yer see. The *Ellington* come in wi' coal – 'course, sometimes it couldn't get in, then he had to go to Cowes, all depends on whether 'e had enough water in.

Now one time the *Ellington* was comin' in wi' coal, and there's a fresh breeze east'ly. Well we was going up the Quay to see if to take her in, and Herb says, "What d'yer think of 'er, son?" I says, "Not much, fresh breeze east'ly." "Aw," he says, "the skipper warnts ter get away." "Yes, orright fer 'im with a blessed great steamboat!" So comin' down the Harbour, he turned her to come round at Duver Point there, and then before he could pick her up again, she was goin' over towards ol' Church! And he shouts down to me from the bridge, "Look owt son, look owt! We're over the top o' the buoy!" He says, "I dunno which way it's comin' *owt*!" I thought, "Oh God, I hope 'e don't come out *my* blessed side – would nearly smash the small boat in half!" But anyhow, he happened to go out the other side.

## Chapter 9 – Poaching, Piloting and Driving Bullocks

Herb says, "Oh we shall drag over into the bay, I expect." Well there was two S'n Helens men workin' on her, one was Reg Williams. We drove up into Ol' Church Bay, halfway out 'long there yer see. So Herb says, "Come 'longside son, be careful what yer doin', y'know, bit of a swell there. Better get a bit of wire away. Coupla chaps 'll come down in the boat with yer." So we took a lot o' wire in, and anchor, then two of us rowed away while Reg Williams was playin' over the wire. And got right out to 't. An' I says, "You gotta turn rownd that stock, Reg!" [*A stock is a crossbar at the top of the anchor.*] He says, "That don't matter, she'll pull in home." So 'course when they hove on the wire, she didn't hold, nothing to stop her, so she had to stay there till next day.

The best of Herb Occimore, during the Second War he used to borry our dinghy sometimes. P'raps he'd get an order, he'd get a chance to take a steamer in, he'd take 'em up Southampton or wherever they went, well up so far yer see. And he used to tie the dinghy on orf there and we had to go 'n get it. Well he'd always give yer ten bob.

Well, a boat called the *Marden* used to bring granite chippings for the roads, unloads up the Quay for putting on the roads. I didn't like towing out with *her*, because she had a big rubbing streak round 'er, and if she fell on top o' yer boat you had ter bloomin' watch your step. [*A strake = a course of planking or plating on a vessel's hull.*] Herb used to go out with her. The chap on the *Marden*, she's come from the Channel Island, he had a box somehow, so he says t'Herb my brother, "Would yer mind takin' this over the railway station?" – 'fore he got up the Quay, 'cos it cost 'em summat to come across up there. So Herb didn't know what was in the box when he went, but he says afterwards, "You could smell the scent in there!" Smugglin', see. He took it up, never heard nothin' about it! And Herb Occimore says, "Never do that again son, never take one o' them on," he said, "or you'll get us into trouble."

Kempson, what wrote *The Cruise of the Green Finch*, well he come ashore one day an' he said, "Am I right t'anchor orf there?" An' I said, "Yeah, you'll be orroight there," but I didn't know how much *rope* he had out on his anchor, I didn't ask 'n that. And next morning when he come down, his boat had drove down on a blessed ledge down there! He never had enough rope ter anchor the boat yer see! He was some religious bloke, he used to be singin' orf there.

I know how they built the S'n Helens Fort rocks orf there. Them big rocks what's round there, they brought them there in barges from somewhere an' tipped them over. That was bifore *my* time.

Charlie Attrill was the architect o' the seawall down Lane End, but that was gonna be for a fort down there, where the huts are. And Lloyd was the foreman of the works.

## The Trouble with Bullocks

Ol' Charlie Lacey had Stone Farm, and then George Lacey used to work for him. He used to bring the cows up this meadow just over 'ere then [*abutting the High Street*]. Ol' man couldn't bear the boys to get and start swingin' up on the gate. He shift 'em orf! Then Jordans took that farm over when the ol' man died.

Longlands Farm used to belong to Taylors – man named Bartlett used to look after that. Me an' Dad went up there after some bullocks once for Jordan. Well I didn't have much sense them days, I'd 'a sooner come behind. He says, "You keep *ahead*, they might wanna bolt back" – 'course, 'twas quite true. And we hadn't got down so very far along the road 'fore there was this ol' man Bartlett shouting out, "Another one comin'!" Beggar had jumped over the gate! Ha! So, we had to go back with every blessed bull and sort 'em out again, it's true. They used to pole-axe 'em down Jordan's, down the slaughterhouse, they didn't shoot 'em like they do now. But Louis Jones, well he's a pretty safe head he was. Then Pudgy Bear used to work down there.

Driving the cattle through the High Street to Jordan's Fields, around 1900.

## Chapter 9 – Poaching, Piloting and Driving Bullocks

Steyne Farm – buliding the hayrick.

Now Jordan 'ud gimme half-a-crown p'raps to go down and get a coupla bullocks from down Ryde. Now I'd sooner go down Ryde and get 'em, come along quiet as yer like, you wouldn' believe how quiet they come along from Ryde – or sheep. They reckon they bin seasick comin' over from Portsmouth and they come along quite *easy*. Being along Christmas they always used to buy a coupla big bullocks, used t'have great horns out 'ere!

Now me an' dad went down Boscombe Shute [*most likely the former name of Marshcombe Shute*] to get a couple, and the ol' keeper there he says, "Oh, quiet as a lamb!" Yes, so they was while *he* was there, but when we got rownd the down we couldn't get 'em by the chalkpit! Dad says, "Look owt fer that little cow up over that down!" And bloomin' thing went up over there an' back over where they come from. And we had to go back over there and get 'em *again*! Dad says, "Now don't let 'em go up over that down!" The farmer lived up Yaverland, he just kept a few bullocks there.

Then another time when brother Herb was there, blessed went right down through Steyne Copse, they went! I throwed a stone an' hit one in the hoof and he quieted down then, come quiet as yer like afterwards. They used t' be devils up round that way, I didn't like goin' up round there, they's a bit too wild! Wreaf nearly had it out in the road 'ere once, if he hadna' bin able to jump over that little hedge round the other bit o' garden there to come in 'ere [*Yew Cottage*], or else the bullock would've had him, 'e would!

There's several lots o' people bin up Steyne Farm: Guy Dunster, and then Emery, they looked after it for ol' Sir John [*Thornycroft*]. Bill Pope used to work up there one time, he lived in Thatch Cottage, Steyne Cross. Nippers used to go there for skimmed milk. Wally Beer used t'have to go up and get some. And instead of going up there, he used to buy two penn'orth o' milk orf o' Lacey's man and then water it down out of a tap!

Neddy Pope had Peacock Farm, and he always had a dog, he reckoned his dawg wouldn't ketch a rabbit, but *I* knew he would! He said, "Ain't much doin', can't nearly afford one boot at a time!" Boys used to go up there for two penn'orth o' pears, y'know. You'd get a capful fer tuppence, they generally went up round there on a Sunday. That was fallen pears.

## More Village Characters and Occupations

I had a wart once right there on the nail. Well I was down Barber Potts's one day, and ol' Tom Crockford, he was a dry old character, 'e says, "What's yer got there then, mate?" An' he just put his hand there, "Agh," he says, "'e won't be there long." Never took no more notice of 'n, I went down there few months afterwards – he says, "How's that wart?" 'Course 'e was gorn!

Well Frank Love was gonna have his hair cut, and they started talkin' about rats, somehow. "Aw," says Crockford (he was a carter), "down Foreland Farm there's rats big enough ter go in harness!" But Barber Potts couldn't cut his hair though, he says, "You'll 'ave ter go out an' come in another day, I can't cut yer hair", he keep on laughing.

There only used to be one postman in Bembridge at one time, he used to walk from Brading rownd the Downs – bifore *my* time – and deliver the letters round Bembridge. Then he used to go and work down Freddie Searle's snobbin' [*mending boots and shoes*], and then he used to carry the letters back night-time.

Bob Stickland was gardener down Hillgrove and he lived up Newtown Corner, he'd do any work for Colonel Moreton. He built that big breakwater down S'n Helens Quay, I don't know who he had t'help him, needed blessed giants ter lift the stones! How they could get 'em up there I'm damned if *I* know!

George Hobbs made bricks in a field up Glover's Farm, then afterwards at Howgate brick kiln. A lot o' people 'ud only earn about fifteen shillings to a pound a week, them days. *I've* known a blessed bricklayers about 'ere only get sixpence an hour – and lose wet time! And labourers only got fourpence! Once when the harbour was froze over – 'course they couldn't done any work – they prayed for 'em in Church, for to get some finer weather so they could work.

## Chapter 9 – Poaching, Piloting and Driving Bullocks

Ol' George Watton used t'have a good building trade, he lived up Clifton Lodge [*in the High Street*]. He used t'employ two carters an' all the bricklayers. Now Loves done the carpentering, and they worked in together. And then after the ol' man died, Loves went on their own after that, they become different parts then.

Well I used to go down East Cliff, that was when I was a boy, and bring up sackfuls o' chips, throw them on the barrow, three or four sackfuls. Walt Sillence couldn't half wield a axe – you wanted some chips for firewood, he'd cut 'em out for yer. Then in the winter Dad an' Uncle Henry [*Butler*], they'd go down East Cliff cuttin' out piles from any o' the trees there to drive in for breakwaters down the shore. But they had to drive 'em in with a betel hammer years ago – dig out and then hammer 'em down as far as they could, I s'pose.

Tom S couldn't learn a bit at school, but you tried cheat him out of a farthin', you wouldn't do that! No blessed fear!

Walt Butler used to live in Leander, Foreland Road, and he used to do snobbing from a shed by the side. And in the summer he was purser on one o' the passenger boats, and George Love 'ud be purser on the other one, he lived up the top o' Dennett Road.

Ol' Muncher Granger lived at Flint Cottage, he used to just row people cross ferry or somethin' or other. And he used to be skipper o' the ol' mud-dredger the *Fanny Grab*. His daughter Mrs Willard, she used to look after the Sailing Club years ago, with her daughter Nora.

Jubilee Jim [*Woodford*] lived down the Point, he'd do any odd job he could pick up. 'Course he was getting old when *I* knowed him. He used to tidy up the footpaths, and they used to be *tidied up* years ago, not like they are now! He always had to be careful what he smoked, y'know – 'e says, "I ain't got much baccy!"

Before Hapgood's had their shop down Point, that was a butcher's shop owned by Flux for a time. I can remember when they had pigs down over Point Hill there.

Joe Bond was a featherbed sailor [*coastguard*], then later he had two bathing machines down shore.

There was more swimming gals coming 'long shore in the morning than there is swimmers about nowadays – to bathe, there was! Seemed to be all the fashion years ago. And ol' Beckridge used to be about there, they called 'n Bubbly Joe, he used to bathe winter and summer. He lived down Foreland Road, they called 'n Bubbly 'cos he used to blow his cheeks out, you seen 'em do't, ain'tcher? And he used to make little paper boats, all different things, and he give 'em to youngsters goin' along the street.

Ol' Merryweather was ploughing somewhere, and a man if he's ploughin' he talk to his horses yer see, 'e'd say, "Bither, woot!" They know's what that means, that means, "Stop it". Now Peter Adams he's sayin' "Bither, woot" over the hedge, and Merryweather got over hedge and he took hold of Peter be the beard an' he says, "You say that once more, I'll bash yer head in fer you!" He would have, too! I think Peter Adams used to work on the pleasure steamers in the summer, and he had pigs at the bottom o' Lynchens. He'd go round the big houses and get the wash [*pigswill*], down Pitt House an' that.

Tom Warne used to be the road sweeper. He had a greengrocer's shop down where they got the tea-place now [*Fox's Restaurant*].

Tom Nightingale was soldier, he had lots of war medals for North-West India.

Jack Gouge was a gardener for Miss Dick down Lane End, and his brother Bob used to drive horse an' cart for Preston's, here at Wallsend.

Ol' Goodall used t'have a blunderbuss, muzzle-loader, that's what he used to fire for the starting an' finishing gun down Under Tyne. He used to wear an eyeglass.

Granny Woodford lived in that little house going down Newtown Hill. She'd see two or three boys goin' round wi' a message or summing – "You boys are after my apples!" And you had ter look owt 'n scoot out pretty fast too, she's out then after yer!

Corny Orchard had the Harbour Gardens, that was bifore Winter had 'em, then Burden come there.

George Wratten was gardener down Norcott for Westmacotts, what had workshop over the Duver. He produced the Howgate Wonder cooking apple, y'know.

Dutch Rose was just ordinary sort of a navvy, do anything, mainly tree-felling. Priddy strong man. Mrs Rose was the cook for Palmers up the Grange.

Dickie Deacon from Brading used to come round with horse 'n cart selling vegetables. He fell owt with Teddy Holbrook over football, and they set about one another in Foreland Road!

Henry Jacobs was a coal merchant, he used to go round wi' coal, when 'twas eighteen shillings a ton. They warnts one pound sixty a hundredweight now. God alive! Dear oh dear! He kept his coal in a bit of shed just 'fore you gets out to go up Folly Hill. There used to be three or four ol' barracks there y'know, years ago.

Cap'n Rich Churchill lived down Foreland Road, but he come from down Bug Alley really, 'e warn't no gentry, I tell yer that.

Flynn was Chief Point Coastguard, and the son Archie Flynn was in the army.

Damp used to build boats down Point, not very big boats, only size of our pot-boats.

John Snow was a wheelwright and undertaker, and his father was a

## Chapter 9 – Poaching, Piloting and Driving Bullocks

wheelwright too, lived down over Newtown Hill. And John was the agent for Hampshire Friendly Society after Alf Weaver died. He used t'have his offices in next door, he had the front room.

Albert Pocock used to be a verger over the Church. And he used to go painting with ol' Walt Osborne that had the paint-shop in Foreland Road. There was him an' – well they used to call him Jack Mac-Man but his name was MacMahon, 'e lived up Brading. They only had two speeds – dead slow or stop!

John Blow was chimney-sweep. You'd know if you called 'n Ratty! He caught Fred Butler, nearly twist his ear orf! oh dear!

Jim Sheath used to work for the Sailing Club, help fit the club boats an' that out. He lived down over Point Hill.

Billy Cotton was a bricklayer for Wattons, he lived in Dennett Road too. Had a daughter Rose Cotton, she had a lodger in, painter I think he was. She says, "'Ow d'yer like yer eggs done?" He says, "Two at a time!" They used t'have a lot o' painters comin' over for Weavers years ago, y'know.

Trooper Weeks must 'a bin in the Boer War, then he was down on the tollgate, down round the bank. He lived up Dennett Road too, Alf Weeks his proper name.

The butler from up the Lodge, he'd ride very fast on a bicycle, sort o' racing, with head right down, an' he run into Upward an' Rich's, 'course they used to come round with a van, two horses, well he run right into the centre o' that just down on the Memorial corner. Well there used to be a house there on the corner, a Dr Hughes lived there then, an' they took him into the doctor's, but he died yer see.

Pocock used t'have a bootmaker's shop at the top o' point Hill, over where the White House is. There used to be a chap there worked for him, they called 'n Dorothy Dean – I dunno why they called 'n that – he used to come out from Newchurch. Pretty fast walker, they reckoned he'd have a pint o' beer in the Village Inn at ten o'clock an' he'd be over to his own pub to ketch one at eleven!

Tommy Staples worked for Love's first and then he worked for hisself. His father was the gardener up Tabuteau's at Woodlands – and after he died, Timmy Attrill took that over after he finished down the Ladies' Golf Links.

Harry Simmonds – the weather was always too wet fer 'im or else too dry! oh dear! I think he was helping-gardener over the Vicarage, but a chap name George Woodford worked there bifore 'n.

'Course, they used to call Foreland Road 'Shady Lane'. And where you goes across Egerton Road, well they used to call that 'Brumbles'. But you didn't go that way at it, you had to go down an' over a stile there, and then Charlie Preston built that road there. And Charlie Preston was Lord o' the Manor – I don't quite know how *that* happened!

Ol' Beer the blacksmith up Hillway, he was the one who made those big iron gates up towards the Lodge there.

Thornycroft's was the first motor car I can remember, the H99, I believe that was a Rolls.

Jack Pittis was a tinsmith in the Navy, he lived up Newtown. His father was a Coastguard. Ol' Toomer [*the policeman*] hit 'n once with a stick down Point somewhere and cut his legs open.

Young used to work down East Cliff and they give him two shillings rise. He said he didn't know what to do with the two shillings 'cos he had all the rest worked owt!

I remember 'em *talkin'* about a lot o' smuggling, but damned if I see any done! Ha! bifore my time!

## Mischief and Violins

There's chaps used to go about 'ere playing tink-the-spider, they'd put a brass button on people's windows yer see, and get across the road and keep letting it go into the winder. The boys tried to go 'n play a game with [*brother*] Herb when he's living next door. Instead of Perce Weaver goin' out round by the path, he got over the Village Inn wall and went round that way. Well Herb hit 'n across the behind with a withy. "Agh!" says Perce Weaver, "you ain't never played before?" Herb says, "Yes I *played* before, but I never bin caught!" he says, "Caught *you*! Yer gonna get that thing owt of it!" Perce Weaver didn't forget it either!

Then the boys used to put ol' parcel down the road y'know, see some ol' lady comin' along, and when she's gonna pick it up, give 'm a jerk! "Yer devils!" Then playing marbles in the road – had *all* the blessed road for marbles.

Blessed boys used t'have pea-shooters and fire at the windows, y'know. Young Dodds, the Coastguard's boy from Foreland, he used to bring a pocketful o' peas for boys t'have pea-shooters, he did, from down Foreland Farm.

I see a man the other night throwing those boomerangs up in the air – d'you know, I seen a man do that *seventy* years ago down Under Tyne. And it come back again to his feet.

They used to go down t'all the pubs y'know, there'd be George Bannister an' Harry Love, Ned Rooke, used to go round wi' their violins and go in the pub an' strike up a tune, get a little crowd there and you'd get a singsong then. There'd be George Attrill – 'Oh Take Me Home Again Kathleen' he used to sing.

Then there was Arthur Sothcott – they always used to call 'n Daniel, he was engineer of the *Lord Kitchener* – he used to sing a very good song, 'The

## Chapter 9 – Poaching, Piloting and Driving Bullocks

Ship That Never Returned'. And they used to say, "Don't roll 'er, Dan'l, don't roll 'er!" He used to roll it a bit, I think. There was Ned Rooke, he'd sing, 'Two Little Girls in Blue, Love'. Adams used to sing, 'Half a pint, gill pot, put in a little drop more; here's good luck to the pint pot' [*The Barley Mow Song*] – an' he'd go all right up. In the Bembridge Hotel when Norton was down there, he used to sing, 'Hang my heart on a weepin' willow tree' [*There's a Tavern in the Town*].

Couple o' farm chaps used to come in Village Inn from up Bembridge Farm, and they never got much money, beer was 'bout tuppence a pint, but they only had 'bout a shilling a week to *spend*, so they couldn't afford beer. And they used to be in there spinnin' yarns, and Freddie James he was, "Go on, 'ave another drink!" "Yes orright." So they said, "We're winnin' all the time, y'know." 'Course, they were getting free beer without payin' for it. I knowed a carter from Foreland Farm – they only used to get about sixteen shillings during the week – and his wife gave him a shilling when he got paid, and that was for six pints on a Saturday an' two pints on a Sunday!

# *Interludes*
## The Christmas Boys

Bembridge Christmas Boys, c.1906. *Courtesy of Jan Field*.

*Mummers' plays were traditional folk plays performed in towns and villages all round the country until the outbreak of the First World War – most expired, some continued, and others have since been revived. The Island, and Bembridge in particular, were no exception to this pattern, and the plays were popularly known as the Christmas Boys. They involved a cast of all-male characters, some wearing disguises or spectacular costumes whilst often speaking in local dialect, and indulging in vaunting boasts, mock sword-fights, and knockabout comedy. A champion is killed and then promptly restored to life again by a quack doctor. Four of the interviewees remembered seeing the plays, with one even taking part.*

## Chapter 9 – Poaching, Piloting and Driving Bullocks

# Harold Butler

We used t'have in those days what they called the Christmas Boys. There was about eight of 'em altogether, and they had their different parts to play, one of course was Father Christmas, one used to be King George – George Butler usually played the King George feller. Old Father Christmas would say:

> **Here am I, Ol' Father Chrismus**
> **With roast beef, plum puddin', an' mince pies,**
> **An' who likes that better than all my boys an' I?**

And there was another feller name o' Neapy Warne who was Ol' Mean, always dressed up as a woman with a broom, used to come in with this broom and say:

> **Here am I, Ol' Mean**
> **Hardly worthy to be seen,**
> **Sweep, sweep, all I foind I keep.**

That was *his* part, like.

Well then they used to go round from pub to pub, then 'course they would go to the different houses – like for example, if Colonel Moreton was giving a Christmas party down there, or anybody else, the thing to do was to invite the Christmas Boys along; and then p'raps another evening it'd be the choirboys, another evening the choir-*men*, go round singing carols.

# Frank Brooks

At Christmas there was about seven or eight of us, we used to go round as the Christmas Boys. There was Old Mean, the Doctor, Father Christmas, King George, and I know I was the Valiant Soldier. Always used to amuse me, when the Old Mother Mean fell down, you found she had trousers on and hobnail boots and that sort o' thing! I was only about 12 or 13.

## Arthur Orchard

Now the Christmas Boys – there used to be Ol' Mean, then:

**Here comes I, little Johnny Jack
With a wife an' family on me back**

– he used t'have a doll on his back, me brother Frank took that part. Then there was the Soldier, the Doctor, they used to do very well round the big houses.

## Ivy Bryant

I can remember one Christmas, when we were living at Burton House down Swains Road, going from the shop [*Tuffley's*] with a clothes-basket full of all the Christmas things that were left over that we had to use up at home, you see. Carol singers used to come round, of course, and they would often be invited into the house and have a mince pie or drink or something. And then there used to be Christmas Boys, they were dressed up and they would do a little sort of play. They'd come indoors and do it, house to house, collected money for it of course.

## Musical Programme at a Unionist Meeting in Bembridge
*(IW County Press archive for 5th March 1892)*

During the evening a musical programme was carried out. Mr F. Searle sang 'Old England for ever', Mr F. Weaver 'Killaloe', and Mr N. Newman 'Six o'clock in the Bay'. Madame Pusterle gave a magnificent rendering of 'Sally'… The audience insisted on an encore and she gave 'This Day a Stag must Die' with electrical effect. Messrs Weaver, Searle and Jordan contributed the trio 'Ye Mariners of England'. Another treat was in store for the audience as Mrs Palmer, who has won honour in the dramatic profession, made her debut before a Bembridge audience by reciting 'The Story of a Miniature'… Mr A. Pocock was loudly applauded for his song 'The Muddle Puddle Porter'. The Chairman's amusing little recitation of 'The Reason Why' created much merriment.

*Chapter 9 – Poaching, Piloting and Driving Bullocks*

# Church of England Temperance Society (Bembridge)

*(IW County Press archive for 20th December 1884)*

On Monday evening last an entertainment was given in the Boys' School by members and friends of the above society to a crowded and appreciative audience. The programme consisted of the following songs: 'Millie's faith' – Mrs H. Caws; 'Tom Bowling' – Mr A. Smith; 'Grandma's advice' – Miss Matthews; 'The British lion' – Mr Bashana; and a duet by Mrs W. L. Tuffley and Miss Matthews. Next followed an interesting dialogue entitled "How we cured a drunken husband", the different parts of which were well rendered by the following: Joe Drinkall (a drunkard) – Mr Charles Love; Sarah Drinkall (his wife) – Mrs W. L. Tuffley; John Plane (Joe's workmate) – Mr Alfred Smith; Ann Plane (John's wife) – Miss Matthews; Pat Sawyer (Joe's workmate) – Mr Bashana; Clara Thornton (a servant) – Mrs H. Caws. The seven double-burner Duplex lamps recently purchased by voluntary contributions were used, and added much to the cheerful appearance of the room. The singing of the National Anthem brought an enjoyable evening to a close.

# Chapter 10

# Granny Pryke the Smuggler and Other Stories
## – Mrs Celia Blackman

*Mrs Blackman was born Celia Adams in Bembridge in 1897. She was 79 years old when recorded at her home 'Ducie View' in Sherbourne Street during two visits in May 1976. Her memory was acute and her delivery forceful and direct.*

Early Motor Bus outside Couldrey's Emporium in Sherbourne Street.
(Note gate and tree by Jordan's Fields which later became the site of the Council Chamber and Fire Station.)

## Chapter 10 – Granny Pryke the Smuggler and Other Stories

# A Tin Can of Tea

My father, Peter Adams, was born in Shanklin in 1857. He must have come here about 1880 to help reclaim the harbour. My mother was born in 1851: she was an overner, she came from Southampton but was Irish, really – O'Brien. Well, my brother Tom was born in Shanklin, and the day that my mother came here, she walked from Brading to Bembridge with him (my father had already come on over to start work). And it was wintertime, and they got lost on the marshes 'cause it was so dark, and they knelt down and prayed, and they managed to find themselves up by the Windmill. I know I *cried* when she told me, as a child.

My mother and father first lived in what used to be called Benfleet Cottages in Pump Lane, those have been made into one house now – Pump Lane Cottage. Well after Benfleet they moved to some houses down the bottom of Folly Hill which was called The Barracks – I don't know why it was called The Barracks, I don't think ever the army was there. Well my brother Gilbert was born down there. And Folly Hill was called Ticklebelly Alley in the 14–18 War, because the troops were supposed to take their girls down there, ah ha ha! There's two curves down there and you're out of sight, oh yes!

Well then they moved from there to One Perth Cottages [*in Sherbourne Street*]. I was born there in 1897 – my mother was forty-six when she had me. I was the last of eight boys and two girls. And d'you know what I was brought up on? (my mother couldn't feed me) – tea-biscuits, the old-fashioned type. They were quite big and quite thick, and mother used to roll and roll those biscuits till they were very fine, and that's what I used t'have as food, done with milk.

So we lived there till I was about fifteen, when we moved into this house [*Ducie View, also in Sherbourne Street*]. Well as I say, my father worked on the reclaiming of the harbour, and down by the Spithead Hotel there's layers an' layers of chalk there, 'cause I used to go and get chalk for my mother to clean the front doorstep. Then after that he worked on the *Allerwash* in the harbour; then for Watton & Son on buildings at Longlands and Brading, he'd walk there and back. I know he used to take a tin can with his tea in and a top of a cottage loaf, and he'd cut a cone out and put the butter in. And he had a red nammet handkerchief that he used to take his food in and cheese. D'you know, anyone would think that us youngsters never had anything, we'd nearly fight over the cold tea that was left in his tin can! And we used ter sit *goggle-eyed* to see if he would leave us any of his dinner! Oh dear!

But he was often out of work, and my mother used to take in laundry. Oh I can see her now doing the long frocks of babies with a goffering iron: it's like a pair of scissors and there's some string whipped round it, then there are these two round bits of iron and you put them in the fire an' make them hot, then you'd do all the frills round.

My mother had a lot of very funny sayings. She'd say, "Like old Ology's horse" – what it meant, I don't know! And like, if she saw a man walking along the road and he'd braced his trousers up too high, she'd say, "Oh, you can see *that* feller got up in the dark!", 'cause he couldn't see where he was doing his buttons up. And then if she saw anyone in bright clothes she'd say, "Cor, look at that dress. Whatever colour is it? *dandy grey russet!*" And I can hear her now, tittering. She told the boys but she never told me what it meant, well apparently it referred to the rectum of a dormouse, which is all colours!

[*In fact, 'dandy grey russet' is an old slang term for 'a dirty brown', the colour of the Devil's nutting bag according to Grose's Dictionary of 1811, so Mrs Blackman's mother was spot-on with its meaning if not necessarily its origin.*]

When I was young, I used to speak a bit of dialect. "What time d'yer get up 'smarnen?" "Arf adder five, you." "Di'n yer 'ear the scoops a-rattlin'?" [*What time did you get up this morning? Half past five, you. Didn't you hear the milk pans rattling?*]

## Telling Tales

I tell you another thing we did at school. We had other teachers come in, and one came from Sandown – aw, he was a *devil!* He'd come with a book and he'd look at your exercise book and if you had a little blot or anything, he'd *catch* you this way an' that way with that book, he'd nearly stun you, he really did! Well d'you know, I didn't know if I was over in the vicarage front garden, my head hit the next girl next door, Evelyn Sothcott, and when *she* came to she was blinking, she didn't know where she was!

And one day Fred Butler says, "I'm going ter bring some cobbler's wax" – his father was a cobbler – he said, "I'm gonna try an' get it softened a bit without Dad seeing. Skinny Taylor takes us in botany this afternoon, an' I'm gonna smear it on the chair. An' I'll do something that he'll get up an' clowt me, an' I bet that chair won't come away from his backside!" 'Course, then in the lesson Fred Butler did something, and Skinny Taylor got up and this chair was stuck to his backside! 'Course, *me*, I couldn't laugh quietly, I sniggered away through my nose. And he had on a new suit, and it took all the pile off the material. Well we were all kept in for a week over this, but no-one split, no-one split.

I never liked people telling tales. And there's another story. We went up to Brading to learn cookery. Well there was a girl called Melanie C, she'd been expelled from goodness knows how many schools. Well I was thirteen or fourteen and top girl of the school but I was always one for a skylark. And Melanie C came over in the train and she said, "You're the monitor and top girl of the school, you ought ter know better, Celia Adams, than play around". So I said, "Well you go an' shut yer mouth" – you see, being polite – I said, "I'll biff yer one, if you don't mind yer own business!" Well then the train was moving out of Bembridge Station – well you know how sometimes children have a fit of the giggles, and I was standing by this carriage door and Hilda Hayward gave me a shove, and the blessed door wasn't shut. And as it was just going round by the Sailing Club cottages I went clean out, and I went down over the bank but I managed to grab the wire or I would've gone in the pond! The guard saw me and stopped the train, and I clambered up. So when we got to Brading, d'you know, that Melanie C, she hardly let us get in, she went straight to Miss Williams. So Miss Williams called me out, she said, "Er, Celia Adams, what I hear from Melanie C, is it true that you fell out of the train? You've been misbehaving, I understand. Oh well," she said, "you will *not* do any cooking today" – 'course I liked cooking – "you will just sit on the seat and you will write". And as I went to sit down – they were seats that topped like that – and the darned seat tipped back, which didn't make me feel any better with Melanie C!

Well we would go up on Bembridge Down and have our lunch. But I never had any lunch that day, my goodness, didn't I belt her! If Bertha Newman hadn't pulled me off 'er, I think I might have killed her! I do, I was in the most filthy temper! I banged her, I punched her, I kicked her! 'Course, I copped it then, going back to the cookery school that afternoon. Miss Williams tackled me: "It's not at all ladylike, Celia Adams, is it?" I said, "No, Miss Williams, but I'd do it again. That's one thing that I do detest, is for people to tell tales". I was really a terrible girl that day, there was no lady about me.

## An Open Bible on her Lap

Well when my family lived at Benfleet Cottages, my grandmother lived there too, Mrs Pryke, who used to smuggle. She used to go out to Sands Head, where the shingle bank is down Point, or over to the Old Church at St Helens, and meet the boats coming over from France. She had a marvellous velvet cloak, a most lovely blue my mother said, which had five hundred pockets in! What she used to get was no odds to anyone, I don't think, from bottles to – allsorts. And she had a carrier boat that went to and fro to Portsmouth, I can't say what she used to carry. And down at Benfleet they had very big cavities in the chimneys, where things used to be hidden. There was also a passage sort of underground where they were able to get down to the shore.

Well granny was a notorious person really. She must have been born about 1817 in Yarmouth; her father was a smuggler and sea captain, Captain Webb. She was married *five times* in Yarmouth Church and outlived them all, then she came to Bembridge on the smuggling racket, I expect. She was Mrs Pryke by then, but she soon saw *him* off! And when she used to meet these boats coming in at the Old Church [*at St Helens*], there'd be some didoes going on there.

Then after Benfleet she lived in the almshouses in the High Street, and lived till she was 91 [*1908*]. She was an old so-'n-so! My elder brother was a nature's boy, very fond of flowers an' that, and of course in those days there wasn't a lot of money. So in the springtime he used to get up early in the morning and go out and pick bunches of primroses, he wasn't made to do it. Then he'd go and sell them and bring the money home. One morning he had a couple o' bunches of primroses over, so he said he'd take them up to grandmother, which he did. Do you know what she did? She threw them on the fire! He *never* forgot it, he never went and visited her anymore, not even when he grew up.

When I was coming up to twelve, I had to go and tidy her room every day, get her tea in et cetera, get her coal in. She was ninety, you see. And she was *supposed* to be religious, she would sit in her window with an open bible on her lap. But my mother would sometimes give me a ha'penny for twenty-four aniseed balls, and if granny saw me go in to Winter's she'd tap the window and I knew I must go up t'her, or else she'd tell my father you see, and I'd get into trouble. So she'd say, "Where did you get that ha'penny from?" An' I said, "My mother gave it to me". "Pity your mother hasn't got something else to do with her ha'pennies than give 'em ter you ter go an' buy sweets! Never brings yer *granny* any sweets, do you?" *That* was the sort of person she was.

And yet she was supposed to be against drink. I went to Waterloo Cottage, and old Miss Sarah Jordan lived there, and she started talking about this old lady that lived in the almshouse. 'Course, my ears flapped! I never said a *word*. But it was – oh the disturbance she'd created one evening on a wooden platform somewhere in the village, shouting out against drink! An' o' course it was my grandmother. But I kept very, very quiet. But she was a blessed hypocrite, she used ter drink alright, she was *smuggling* the stuff!

Then she used to attend the Wesleyan Chapel, and every year they would have sort of a tea-party and bunfight. And I always had to go with grandmother. She would wear her Paisley shawl and her little tiddly bonnet and elastic sideboots propping her toes turning up, you know. And when I used to go up to the almshouse to do her rooms, she would have a lady from Sandown come and see her, a Mrs Salter. And they used to hold forth in this room, and she told me to kneel down and pray with them. I wouldn't do it;

# Chapter 10 – Granny Pryke the Smuggler and Other Stories

and my mother said, "Yes, an' you did right". But if anyone ever came in to see her, there she was reading this bible.

The best of it was, when she died, my father arranged with Weavers to bury her, but she'd already paid for her funeral, coffin an' everything 'fore she died with Havelock Perry at Cowes, he was a 42nd cousin of hers. She's buried at Northwood Cemetery on top of her smuggler father. During the War there was a bomb dropped in that cemetery, and some of the things went sky-high. I know I made a remark: "Oh I wonder if Granny Pryke went up!"

## More Smuggling

The smugglers had a tunnel up through Howe Chine into the field where they used to hide the kegs of brandy till they could get it away. The boys would go up there, you see – Peeping Toms!

Then the vicar here, Canon Le Mesurier, that built the vicarage, he was in with the smugglers. Well, out on the Glebe land here there's a mound made of the spare stone or granite – they've got lovely sort of weeping trees, and when they come out in the spring they're really beautiful. And I learnt from my parents that they used to hide the kegs of brandy underneath that mound. Someday when it's disturbed, if they ever build out there, they might find a keg of brandy!

Then another place they used to hide the kegs of brandy was down over Lynchens, along by what they once called Sandy Walk, in a boggy place. I know where the boggy place is because when I was a girl I went gathering flowers with PC Toomer's girls, and we got in this bog. I didn't lose *my* boots, thank goodness, but Emmy Toomer lost hers, she had to go home in all these muddy stockings! We went in right over our knees.

When my father worked on the reclaiming of the harbour, it said on the papers he had, that from the bottom of Folly Hill up to Duckers Wall there was to be a path wide enough to take a wagon and horses. Then of course when Major Savile came here and had his house built, he took a bit of the path and put an iron fence along; then the Reverend Francis took a bit too. So that closed Sandy Walk.

I remember old Mrs Quilly Smith, she had long corkscrew curls. And on one occasion Mr Osborn was delivering bread to Granny Jeffery, and he found her cutting her corns with a carving-knife!

Then there used to be two men up under Hillway, Merryweather and Youngie, or Bunny Young they used to call him. They used to go poaching for rabbits. And one or the other would call down to mother if she wanted a rabbit, they'd be sixpence each in those days. And old Merryweather would come to the back door an' he'd say, "Mrs Adams, I cotched this one 'smarnen".

Then he'd talk about Bunny Young – well they used to fight, these two men, and I suppose Bunny Young had won, you see – and Merryweather would say, "I'm goin' ter fight 'im agin an' I'm goin' ter be the king o' kings!" Top dog, I suppose!

*Chapter 10 – Granny Pryke the Smuggler and Other Stories*

# *Press Cutting*
## Tales of Bembridge Smuggling
*(Adapted from a newspaper cutting in the old WI Scrapbook)*

Patrons of the Crab and Lobster, c.1860s.

Eight men would sit playing cards round a table at the Crab and Lobster Inn at Forelands. When darkness had fallen, four would walk out and the others carry on playing. To the innocent bystander the men leaving would appear to be tired of any game. But not so, for in a small fishing boat they would soon be playing a far more dangerous game – that of smuggling.

This was among the stories told to a County Press reporter by Mrs E. M. Bunce of Cowes about the exploits of her grandfather, Mr Aquila William 'Quilly' Smith, a well known Bembridge smuggler in the nineteenth century. Mrs Bunce expressed the opinion that in those days there was just as much smuggling in the East Wight as in the West, and along the Southern coast of the Island.

The four men would row across to France, and within twenty-four hours they would be back for another game of cards at the Crab – with a curt word that the job was done. They always had to think quickly in order to dodge the 'gobbies', as the Excise men were called. Shore helpers, awaiting the return of the smugglers, used to take a collie dog called Nelson along the cliff-top, and he would invariably stiffen his tail and give a quiet growl if there were Customs men below. The valuable wines, brandy and lace they brought ashore would often be taken through Lane End Copse to a hiding place, and in order to cover up their footprints the smugglers would drive sheep over their trail.

At Bembridge an old pedlar called 'Clockie' used to make the rounds at night, distributing the smuggled goods to those who had ordered them. Sometimes the illicit spirits were sent across to clients on the mainland, and her grandmother helped in this by carrying the liquor in pigs' bladders under her skirt or in a 'Jimmy John', a large bottle dressed up as a baby. She had a few near escapes from the revenue officers.

On one occasion Mrs Bunce's grandfather was arrested by preventive officers when hiding a cargo at Wallsend Farm, and was sent to prison for illicit trading in spirits. But alongside his smuggling activities Quilly Smith and his brother ran a passenger launch between Bembridge and Portsmouth.

# Chapter 11

# The View From Hillway
## – Mr William Langworthy

*Mr Langworthy was born at Howe Copse, Hillway, in Bembridge in 1905 and lived all of his life there; it was in fact at Howe Copse that I recorded him, aged 78, during two sessions in November 1983 and March 1984. His wife Nita (née Bannister) was also present and acted as a memory prompt, but she also provided a short contribution of her own which, owing to its conciseness, is presented here in the first two paragraphs; all the rest of this transcription belongs to William.*

## Mrs Nita Langworthy

I was born in what's now Lloyds Bank [*on the corner of High Street and Sherbourne Street*]. My father George Bannister was born down in the cottage next to the Crab & Lobster. He used to work for the Waterlows, looked after their boat. [*Mr Waterlow had 'Fuzzie Freeze' built as a home, since expanded into Warners holiday camp and currently Bembridge Coast Hotel.*] My grandfather William Bannister came onto the Island as footman up at Nunwell, and he used to go out waiting a lot to several big houses.

My mother come here to service down in Ducie Avenue, and the first job

Ducie Avenue, seen from the top of Bembridge Hotel Road, c.1905.

she had to do was to go up Langworthy's and get a chicken – then I ended up marrying his son! And she was courting my dad at the time, and they used t'have to go down Pump Lane to get water, well o' course Dad would be about there waiting, y'see. And when she was wanted at the house, the other maids would go and strike matches, shine a light or something, and back my mother used to come!

## William Langworthy – Family Background

I was born on 22nd of June 1905, on the same bit o' ground we're on now, and I've never slept a night orf of it 'cept for three weeks in Ryde Hospital in 1979.

My father, also William, was known as Ol' Devon, he came here on the reclaimin' of the harbour on the 30th of March 1878. The *Eurydice* went down on the 24th of March, on the Sunday, and he came here on the following Saturday, that's about the time the harbour job started. He was one o' the workmen there, shovelling the chalk and unloading the barges; I believe there was barges of chalk coming over from the other side, it didn't all come from the Island, no. He actually belonged to Devonshire but he came here from Cheltenham. He had a paper, the *Labourer's News* or something, and there was an advert in there for three hundred good labourers wanted. He came here for sixpence an hour; I think it was a toss-up between going up to the Manchester Ship Canal which was being cut at the time, but only fourpence ha'penny was being offered there, so that's how he came 'ere! A lot of 'em came but there wasn't many stayed – he stayed, and old Albert Mead stayed: he became gamekeeper for Thornycroft's – and old Tom Keeping stayed, yeah! And o' course they picked up a lot of local labourers. I've heard my father say when they first came here, you'd hear the old women say, "Here – comes – some – more – o' – them – overners, – come – over – ter – take – our – men's – jobs – away!" Ha-ha! 'Course now it's *all* overners, isn't it?

I think the blokes working there that unloaded the barges made a little more money. There were several barges used to come across, but two I've heard my father mention: one was *Zulu* and the other was *The Longest Day*, and *The Longest Day* was a terrible awkward barge to shovel out, none of 'em liked getting in there. Well they were watching these barges come across one day, and all of a sudden, "Well where's that other one gorn?" *The Longest Day* had gone down comin' across! I suppose the blokes on there was *saved*, I dunno 'bout that.

Well this place was a copse, and my father took the copse about 1892, grubbed it out and turned it into a market garden. Had the old corrugated iron place built and lived there – that's where I was born, it's still in the

## Chapter 11 – The View From Hillway

garden but derelict now. As he got his crops, he had a pony and van and used to go round Bembridge selling his vegetables. Well then Winter started here with a shop and from then on he started selling to Winter y'see, and then to a few camps that was comin' here and so on. Then I followed on from him, I used to supply the school up 'ere [*Bembridge School*]. I never had to go anywhere else to work! Up this way 'twas *very* quiet, all we used to see was the milkman, the postman and the baker.

My mother was a Clarke, born in Peacock Hill. Old Clarke came onto the Island as gamekeeper in 1860, and he went up to Peacock Hill to live. At that time o' course the Island was all *agog*, Queen Victoria was on the throne, there was all the high-class sort o' people coming on the Island; and the proprietor of the Pier Hotel at Ryde – which was at the foot of Union Street, it was pulled down – he'd taken all the shooting around here for his guests and he employed a gamekeeper to look after it. Well my grandfather on me mother's side, he came up here from Somerset in 1860, lived at Peacock Hill, and three or four of the children were born there. Old Clarke's wife was a *real* Bembridger, she'd lived in the old cottage that was right up under the down, where she was born – she was Ned Pope's sister. The Popes had been connected with Bembridge for a very long time.

And I used t'have a great-aunt that was very old, 'course she was one o' them that was born up in this cottage. She was only a girl at the time and she heard a lot of feet marching along the lane outside, thought it was the French comin' an' hid herself in under a hen coop! So that's going back a bit t'have the fear of the French, isn't it?

## Shh! Massy, Mate!

There used to be an old drover come, I believe he came from Horringford, and he used to drive a couple o' bullocks rownd the downs and so many sheep; and he would be driving the bullocks and his two dogs would be in front driving the sheep.

As you go along the footpath to Whitecliff Bay, you'll see four stones in the path there, that was the gateway to old Trilly's Cottage; before that it was Praines Cottage. Well Praine was the coastguard, but Trilly Attrill that was there *after* Praine, he lived there and I believe he was an old smuggler. So first orf there was a coastguard's cottage, and then we come an old smuggler's cottage afterwards! I 'spec that must've been just about a hundred year ago that was pulled down [*1880s*] – I think most of the bricks that come from it is in this place, in brick drains in the garden. The stone doorstep of the other old house where I was born is one of the flagstones that was in Trilly's Cottage, yeah! In *my* time up to the last War there'd bin a grape-vine growing there.

There was *supposed* t'have been an old smuggler's cottage, more or less a mud hut, standing somewhere where the old house of Bembridge School stands. Then what I know as Granny Squibb's Lane up by the School, well my father could talk about Granny Squibb. I believe her cottage was only about one room parted with a sheet or somethin'. Well they call it Jenny Streets Lane officially – Jenny Street lived there before Granny Squibb. I *have* seen a painting of the cottage with old Johnny Street stood outside with a smock on.

As for Mollie Downer, the Butlers reckoned she was a witch, but the Pope side of the family – those old uncles and aunts I was telling yer about – they said she was a very respectable woman. I think she was a little better class, y'know! [*See following chapter.*]

Remember that snow we had in '62–63, well that's the deepest snow ever *I've* seen. My father-in-law was up here living with us at the time, he was an old man by then an' he says, "What's it like this mornen'?" I says, "Well, tidy drop o' snow abowt!" He looked out the window an' says, "Ugh! There ain't s'much as there was in '81!" Do you know, that weekend in the County Press it said that the Isle of Wight had had the biggest snowfall it had had for many years, but not so deep as 1881! Ha-ha-ha!

I can remember the old house that was down the bottom o' the airport there, well it was more of a barn in my time but it *had* been lived in. I've heard the tale that Charlie Blow was born down there 'when Bushes was into beans'. Bushes is the name of that field immediately opposite Stanwell Farm; the crops used to be rotated, and I believe that's how some of the old-fashioned people that wasn't very educated used to remember the age of their children!

Ol' Ned Pope was a great-uncle of mine, he was a real character! He had about ten brothers and sisters, and his father was Samuel Pope, who was a farm labourer at Bembridge Farm. Well Ned had one cow at Peacock Hill, and I've heard my father say Ned used to reckon that cow would bring him in 'arf-a-crown a week. And he worked down the harbour on the reclaimin' job, drove a horse 'n cart and earned another 'arf-

Bembridge Harbour frozen over during the winter of 1962-3, giving some idea of how it must have looked in the great snowstorm of 1881.
*Courtesy of Peter Chick Collection.*

## Chapter 11 – The View From Hillway

crown a week – well ol' Ned was quite wealthy to what some of 'em was! I can remember him bringing me down a penny once and it was wrapped up in four or five pieces of paper, I s'pose so's he wouldn't lose it! ha-ha! Eventually he ended up with a few cows, fed 'em along the road verges. He'd carry a sack of straw and a stick, and the sack of straw was to kneel down on, he used t'come down on one knee! And at night they say he'd put 'em in *anybody's* field, y'know! That field that he used to have for hay there I should think it was about three acres; he didn't cut it himself, he'd have it cut for 'n, but he carried every bit of it on his back into the farm, I s'pose so he didn't have to pay out for carting!

And if his wife put two or three logs o' wood on the fire, he'd pull two of 'em *orf*, he wouldn' only burn one at a toim! ha-ha! I've heard say that old Ned picked a sackful of pears up there, walked to Brading with 'em, he couldn't get his price at Brading, so he come back on to S'n Helens, couldn't sell them there, so he walked back to Bembridge and sold 'em to Tom Warne down the village!

And he used t'say, "**Shh! Massy, mate!**" oh, that was a great expression of Ned Pope's, I dunno what it meant, yeah! "When I lets go the rudder o' this ol' ship, she'll run agrownd!" That's what he was getting out of it up there.

[*'Massy' had two possible meanings: either 'massive, of great bulk', or, more likely in Ned Pope's case, taken from the old phrase 'Lawks-a-massy' (Lord have mercy), which Ned Pope no doubt heard and picked up the phrase from this context.*]

I've heard a tale about Young the cowman. Bill Pope and Jim Mundell, they used to walk up to the Anglers in Brading of a Sunday night, through Centurions Copse and across the marshes; and they saw Youngie sitting on the bank of the river there with a stick an' a bit o' string hanging down in the river, and they started to go across to 'n. Presently Youngie sings owt, "Don't let yer shadder fall on the water, mates, or they'll go upstream like hell!" Well, Bill Pope said they made a detour and came back round behind Youngie. "Well what sort o' fish d'yer catch 'ere, Youngie?" "*Oh, big 'uns, mayet, big 'uns!*" Ha-ha-ha!

Well, Farmer Morris's brother lived up Hill Farm and looked after that, and his daughter used to bring the milk over to Stanwell Farm every mornen' for 'em to go round with. So old Farmer Morris out Stanwell says to this daughter, "You tell your father that I thinks he's *lazy*". Er, so she goes back and tells old Mike Morris what he'd said; well next mornen' before she leaves Hill Farm wi' the milk, ol' Mike Morris says, "You tell your uncle that I bain't as lazy as what I be goin' ter be!"

I don't know how much truth there is in this, but the blacksmith also pulled out teeth. Well he'd got too old and beyond it, and old John Snow took it over, the wheelwright. Anyhow, Joey Attrill's supposed t'have had the toothache come on, so he went up to John Snow t'have this tooth pulled

# An Oral History of Bembridge – Isle of Wight

Hillway c. 1870. John Snow's builders yard. The Snow family were carpenters and undertakers; they also made wagons, for which the Callaways made the wheels across the road.

out. Goes into carpenter's shop there: "Well sit down on that tressle then, Joey". So Joey sat down on the tressle, John got hold of the tooth with his pinchers and pulls Joey rownd the shop *five* times, and says, "Well we can't get 'e owt, Joey, 'e'll have ter bide in there!" So that was that, and Joey used t'say, "If ever that tooth come on t'ache again, I always tell 'n I'll take him up ter see John Snow an' he'll stop aching at once!" ha-ha-ha!

Somebody met Joey one morning: "Cold this mornen', Mr Attrill!" "Yes," he says, "'tis." "Well I 'spect it'll go good yer know," they said, "kill some o' the slugs an' vermin in the grownd". "Yes," Joey says, "but 'twill kill you first! They can get down owt 'f it where you can't!" ha-ha!!

## That be Wuts!

Just between the chemist's shop and the butcher's shop [*as they were in 1984*] was the old blacksmith's shop where they used to shoe the horses there.

## Chapter 11 – The View From Hillway

Man called Perkins had that and a chap called Harry Atkey was the blacksmith there.

Where the war memorial is, that was a butcher's shop called Swiss Cottage, and behind that was his slaughterhouse. And that was right close to the school: well, when we were in there Wednesday afternoons having lessons, we'd hear the pigs squealin' where he was killing 'em in there. Then 'course eventually Woodford had the new butcher's shop put up in what we used to call Gypsy Field. And in those days the butchers would have a trunk of a tree for a block, didn't they? I s'pose that wouldn't be called hygienic now. And they had a bundle o' withies to hit the flies and wasps with. And Tom Jordan was *always* smoking a cigarette.

Then on that same corner by the school there was always a ring in the middle of the road where we used to play marbles; p'raps it'd be the time o' the year for peg-tops and we'd be out there spinning our tops. Well then 'course the school bell would go if we were playing marbles, and they used t'say, "Pick up stakes an' run!" and you picked up what marbles you could an' orf to school, bell had gorn!

Prestons' old shop in Church Row had one room – for selling kippers and sweets. And if the sweets was stuck in the bottle, old Jimmy Preston would break a bit orf a kipper box and shove in the bottle to break the sweets off the sides!

I've heard the tale, my father was working for the doctor that was about here at the time, and apparently old Governess Attrill had died. And some bloke came to the doctor's and said, "Gov'ness Attrill is dead, sir, an' she warnts 'er death certificate!"

Bill Mursell used to do ferrying across the harbour to S'n Helens and I daresay at the same time Attrills was bringing people across from S'n Helens to Bembridge. They used to keep their oars down there by the Spithead Hotel, in a big box they locked up – 'W. Mursell & Son, Ferryman' was painted on it.

I've heard my uncle say that they was building the Spithead Hotel, and these pilots used to come down there by the harbour. And they wore pilot jackets as they were called, and half-boots black and shiny, more or less a pilot's uniform. And he had another chap who was working with him, Jarge [*George*] he called 'n. Jarge came from Ventnor, they didn't have no pilots there. And Jarge says, "Well whatever be they fellers then, Ted?" "Ooh, tha's pilots, Jarge." "Well, I never seen no fellers like them afore!"

Isn't there a difference in the pilots today to these old pilots that we're talking about? The modern pilot is a real educated bloke. I heard two pilots talking some while ago, they were referring to white buoys, sounded so proper, whereas you go back and think about old Ev Love, "Well I'm buggered, Judd, we've turned the tiller the wrong way!"

Outside the Spithead Hotel c.1880.

Bernie Woodnutt used to be the landlord at the Old Village Inn down 'ere, and him an' Perce Watton went over to a match between Southampton and Portsmouth. Perce was for Southampton and Bernie was for Portsmouth. Anyhow, the match started and Portsmouth scored a goal. 'Course, Bernie started to cheer, and I was told he had a bowler hat on. Perce brought his hand down across Bernie's hat: "You *bloody* traitor!" ha-ha-ha!

They used to go in Barber Potts' shop more for a yarn than anything. Barber would be cutting somebody's hair, and the local policeman Shotter would be in there poring over this draughtboard, then he'd move. "Your turn now, barber!" Barber 'ud put his scissors down, go over and study the draughtboard, move, now go back and cut this bloke's hair – I've heard 'em say, anyhow! Things was priddy *slow* in them days, weren't they?

There was an old Granny Parker lived in th' almshouses. Well she was a real celebrity, her husband used to be shepherd at Bembridge Farm, and when I was a little kid she lived in one o' the little old thatched cottages down Hillway. Well anyhow when she got old she shifted from there to the almshouses. She was a real old Dorset woman, proper ol' countrywoman. We were kids going to school, and that field up Mill Copse there was into oats at the time. Well we used to pick off a handful of oats and Granny would be at the gate down there. "Look, we got some wheat 'ere, Gran!" **"That – bain't – no – wheat –** *that – be – wuts***!"** We only did it to hear her say "Wuts"! [*Oats*] They reckoned she'd have a youngster in and go out setting rabbit-wires in the afternoon, but I expect that's a bit stretched, y'know!

## Chapter 11 – The View From Hillway

George Fry was gardener down at Denison's, Balure. He was disposed to exaggerate things. Somebody said, "Oh, you got a well there then, Mr Fry." "Yes," George says, "that well must be 'arf full of sovereigns an' gold watches! When I used to wear a cardigan, bendin' over, dippin' owt water, I'd either drop a gold watch or a sovereign down there!" ha-ha!

You've heard that East Cliff burnt down, once. Well they rebuilt it, and Daddy Acre got a job there. And Sir Ralph Gore, one of the nobs about here, went t'have a look round. He says, "Well where's the front door goin' ter be?" Daddy Acre says, "Rownd the back!" Ha-ha-ha!

Old Tom Cole was a proper old-fashioned winemaker down Lane End, he used to keep it in a brandy tub. Well there was Ike Lane and Claude Ash, Tom showed 'em up to his shed one day, he went indoors to get something and ol' Tom swore that they got to work with this wine. They ended up sitting in the ditch with the water running over 'em! "Well serves 'em right," Tom says. Ha-ha! Tom Cole's wine was pretty strong stuff!

Tim H–– was noted for his rum sayings. He was reputed to have sawed the same branch off the tree he was sitting on! Somebody asked him how his wife was, well he's supposed to've said, "Well I'm very sorry ter say, sir, she's enjoyin' very bad health!"

Old Rainbow Preston used to put a lot of time in the pubs, and he would sleep along these roads on the verges. Well they said the drink would get him in the end, and so it did – he died at 94! Rainbow 'ud go out in the garden an' it'd be pouring with rain, and he'd come in and sit over the fire. If you looked in there, you couldn't see acrorss the room for steam, Rainbow was dryin' owt, ha-ha-ha!

I saw Rainbow one day – it was before these roads 'long 'ere were tarred – and Hillway Shute was pretty rough, all loose stones. I said to ol' Rainbow, "It's priddy rough up 'ere, Rainbow!" "Yes," he says, " if I happen ter step on one o' these rollin' stones, it makes me hiss an' snarl like a billy goat crackin' hammers!" I never heard such an expression in my life! And when they was digging out the sewer in Howgate Lane, Rainbow was coming up from the Crab and fell down in the sewer trench! Somebody heard some groanin' an' moanin', and there he was in the trench – they pulled him owt of it!

# Chapter 12

# Mollie Downer 'The Witch' and the Smugglers

*There are two main prose accounts of Mollie Downer's life, inevitably giving rather different interpretations of her character and deeds. The first appeared at a date close to her own demise in* The Isle of Wight Miscellany, *published by Ebenezer Hartnall in 1844 – shared online from his unique Isle of Wight collection by the late Dr Alan Champion of Ventnor. It relates the history of Mollie Downer, 'the last of the witches' at Bembridge, Isle of Wight. Hartnall stated that his account was based 'on the oral tradition', indicating that even in 1844 historical fact had become intertwined with folk tradition.*

*The subject's name has appeared as both Mollie and Molly, and as Mollie is often the older form of the name, I have used that throughout. The following is my adaptation of the original text.*

## The Last of the Witches

In a dilapidated cottage known as 'Witches Hatch', at the bottom of Hillway not far from Bembridge farmhouse, for many years resided Mollie Downer, a spinster who had the local reputation of being a witch. Mollie was the illegitimate child of a clergyman from Niton who at his death left her an annual pittance barely sufficient to support life. In youth and middle age she possessed none of the personal attributes of a witch. Her person was tall and not ungraceful, her features well defined, her hair fair, and her large blue eyes full of animation and expression, and until well past her prime she was remarkably neat and bright in her apparel and fond of the company of others. However, her chastity was unimpeachable; and when her lifelong female friend embarked on a series of adulterous affairs, Mollie's virtue was so shocked that she renounced the world and the flesh – but apparently not the devil, at least so it was rumoured throughout the neighbourhood.

Her home was a dilapidated, rather isolated cottage. She was rarely seen abroad, and admission to her dwelling was vouchsafed to very few. Anyone entering immediately encountered the squalor within, with spiders' webs given free rein.

A few neighbours supplied her with provisions and deposited these on a broken stool beside the door, on which Mollie also placed money in payment,

## Chapter 12 – Mollie Downer 'The Witch' and the Smugglers

but on no account were they allowed to enter. One charitable lady attempted to win over the recluse by supplying her with a series of religious tracts, which she placed in a cavity of the fence wall, where Mollie duly replaced them after reading; but it was extremely rare that even *this* favoured visitor was allowed an audience with her.

Mollie was by repute a charmer, with the power to remove and heal many minor ailments without using any visible means. Even the village schoolmaster had implicit faith in her powers of healing.

The neighbourhood were in no doubt, however, that Mollie was a genuine witch, though positive evidence of the fact was nowhere to be had, and the old custom of subjecting suspected persons to the 'infallible' ordeal in such cases had long since fallen into disuse. The circumstantial evidence of her having made a compact with the devil rested principally on the fact that in her chimney were suspended several bottles supposed to contain harmful compounds and maleficent potions for accomplishing the ends of witchcraft. In addition, it was claimed that she had in her possession fourteen dolls, to which she was extraordinarily attentive, dressing and undressing them and thrusting innumerable pins into them, which according to the neighbours represented those many ill-starred individuals who had incurred her curses.

One such victim was Harriet, a young girl who had unfeelingly mocked her, whereupon Mollie put a curse upon her to the effect that if ever any good fortune were likely to befall her, she might die before possession of it. Not long afterwards Harriet was afflicted with a paralysis depriving her of speech and partially also her faculties; this lasted until her death which by a remarkable coincidence occurred the same day she was bequeathed her a legacy of twenty pounds, no inconsiderable sum for the time. The sequence of events is lost to us but it is quite possible that if this coincidence occurred early on, it might have been the template for accusations of witchcraft directed towards Mollie.

The manner of Mollie's death was very much in accordance with her character. The lady who supplied her with books, calling one day to reclaim the last loan and leave another, found they had been removed from their usual spot but not replaced. She approached the house and tried knocking. Receiving no reply and sensing something might be amiss, she called together some of the neighbours, but their attempts to arouse Mollie being futile, they finally forced open the door and found her lying dead on the floor in the back room. The doors and windows were all fastened on the inside and nothing exhibited the least signs of violence. She lay on the ground with her clothes adjusted neatly around her, her hands crossed as is sometimes done when a body is laid out, her eyes and mouth tightly shut, and no visible sign of a death struggle about her, as if she had died peacefully in her bed.

It was thought that Mollie possessed some secret hoard but none was discovered, and to appease the curiosity of the neighbours the local minister had the body taken out from the coffin and stripped to ascertain whether money or anything of value was concealed there, but the search was fruitless. Out of a superstitious fear Mollie was then reclothed, re-coffined and buried without rites in Brading churchyard, where no memorial points out her resting place.

## Smuggling at Whitecliff Bay

A very different, though overlapping, account of Mollie Downer is presented in an article which appeared in the IW County Press for the 6th October 1962, as a result of an interview with Mr Harry Butler, then living at Myrtle Bank, Hillway, which stands immediately behind the foundations of Witches Hatch. (Harry Butler was the brother of Ernest Butler, whose oral memories follow in the next chapter, but is not to be confused with Harold Butler in a preceding chapter.) In this version, Mollie was a leading spirit of the local smuggler gangs who operated in Whitecliff Bay – and it is a well-established fact that one way of frightening off prying eyes from smuggling activities was to claim supernatural or witchcraft associations around them. On the one hand, Mr Butler's narrative is well over a century after Mollie's decease, allowing plenty of time for folklore to accrue, whereas Hartnall was much closer in time to the events and does not hint at any smuggling. On the other,

Myrtle Bank, Hillway – site of the former Witches Hatch, c.1880s.

## Chapter 12 – Mollie Downer 'The Witch' and the Smugglers

Hartnall was not living in the area and might not have *known* anything about any smuggling that occurred, whereas Mr Butler's family had long lived in the locality, been directly involved with the smuggling gangs, and had personally known Mollie. Furthermore, Mr Butler has the correct details about Mollie bequeathing her possessions to the Revd Henry Thompson, but which Hartnall seems oblivious of. The following account is based largely on the County Press interview, supplemented by some additional typed notes left by Harry Butler.

According to the story as handed down to him by his parents as well as records claimed to be in his possession, Mollie Downer was the last of her line of the Downer family who made their home in Bembridge in 1558. Born in 1764, Mollie was believed to be one of the leading lights in the local smuggling gang, though at the same time was held in great awe by her neighbours who avoided her as much as possible, claiming that she could cast spells and bewitch or unwitch at will. Her cottage, named Witches Hatch, was a long, low, thatched building with leaded window lights and a quaintly shaped chimney.

During the period 1806–1817 excise officers were trying to stamp out the smuggling which was rife in many parts of the Island. Before long Mollie came under suspicion, and in 1822 Lieut. Ross was determined to interview her, suspecting she was the leading spirit of the gang. But calling on her at Witches Cottage he was not only unable to prove anything but was confronted by Mollie: "Begone, or you may soon find yourself in Davy Jones' locker! You have indeed a stout heart to call at old Mollie's cottage!"

In her latter years local feeling against Mollie had grown so strong that her only visitor was Sir Henry Thompson, 3rd Baronet, the first vicar of Bembridge, who called on her occasionally in his clerical capacity. Then on visiting Witches Hatch on the evening of May 10th 1835, the vicar discovered Mollie lying dead in the kitchen attired in her burial robes. Evidently fearing her end approaching, she had as far as possible prepared herself for burial. On the table nearby lay her will, in which she had bequeathed all her possessions to the vicar (a copy of which still exists in the County Record Office, under Mollie's birth name Mary Downer).

Mr Butler's grandfather William Butler was one of the bearers at her funeral, at which it was suggested that they should be given an extra glass of ale 'to keep them hurry with the witch'. Mollie was buried in Brading in a grave alongside that of Little Jane, the service being conducted by a curate named Young. According to Mr Butler, her grave was marked by a small headstone bearing the inscription 'Mollie Downer the Witchcraft', which was still in position in 1933 but had since disappeared.

We can only conjecture to what extent the Revd Thompson might have been embarrassed by having inherited Mollie's worldly goods, but following her funeral he promptly ordered her cottage and its contents to be burned to the ground, giving as his reason that he did not wish anyone to be able to say they possessed anything which had belonged to 'Mollie the Witchcraft'.

The plot of land on which the cottage had stood lay derelict for forty-five years until purchased in 1880 by Mr Butler's father, Captain Henry Butler, who built Myrtle Bank in the following year. The foundations of Mollie's cottage were still traceable in the garden of Myrtle Bank. One stone bore the date 1764, the year of Mollie's birth.

## The Butler Family

Mr Butler's family settled in Bembridge in 1521 and are reputed to be the oldest surviving Bembridge family. In 1526 Henry Butler built Smugglers' Cottage on the gentle slope of the down overlooking Whitecliff Bay, where the family continued to live for the next three centuries. The cottage was well named, as the early Butlers were notorious smugglers and wreckers. The cottage was on the north-east corner of the down; and on the south side, where the white chalk cliffs rise to about 300 feet, a narrow path leads down to a cave which has been known for centuries as the Hermit's Hole. The Butlers would hang lights in the cave to act as a decoy to lure ships on to the sharp rocks below, where they could plunder the wrecks at will.

They also made frequent trips to the Cherbourg peninsula in their small ketch, always returning heavily laden with brandy, which would be landed in Whitecliff Bay. They cut a pathway through the rocks to facilitate working at low water, where they would be out of view of the coast watchers at Forelands and Praines Cottage.

On one occasion the smugglers were surprised by excise officers led by Lieut. Ross, who raided the cottage at a time when there was a cask of brandy on the premises. They ransacked the cottage but failed to find any brandy, which was hidden beneath the voluminous skirts of Mr Butler's great-grandmother Hannah, who remained seated on the cask and calmly continued to nurse her baby. This was the same period in 1822 when Lieut. Ross paid his unproductive visit to Mollie Downer.

But clever and daring as the smugglers were, the net was tightening and eventually the government issued a writ confiscating Smugglers' Cottage and ordering its demolition. Mr Butler alleged that the shape of the old cottage garden could still be traced and mint could still be found growing there (in 1962).

But if the Butlers broke the law, they also served their country nobly and almost every generation provided a sailor or soldier, many of whom died in battle. Two members of the family fought against the Spanish Armada in 1588; Howard Butler served as a lad with Nelson's fleet at Trafalgar in 1805;

## Chapter 12 – Mollie Downer 'The Witch' and the Smugglers

while Lieut. Charles Butler served in HMS *Leander* during the Crimean War. Captain Henry Butler, who built Myrtle Bank, was in the West Indies in charge of Lady Exshaw's yacht *Elmina* in 1902 when Mount Pelée erupted and caused the loss of 50,000 lives.

Following the County Press article in October 1962, Mr Butler received a letter from a distant relative, Mr H.G. Jones of Dartford, Kent, pointing out that Hannah Butler – who nursed the baby while seated on the cask of brandy – was his great grandmother as well as Mr Butler's. As a small boy Mr Jones, who was born at Shanklin in 1894, listened to his father's stories of 'Granfer' Butler's expeditions to Cherbourg and other French ports for brandy. The stories confirmed the details given in the County Press article.

His father told him that at the bottom of the garden of Smugglers' Cottage on the downs was a large pigsty. The men would bring the kegs up the cliff and through a tunnel to the pigsty where they were stowed under the floor until such time as a buyer could be found. The brandy usually found a market in Newport, and in the dead of night a four-horse wagon would be loaded with the kegs under a covering of hay and driven post-haste through the quiet country lanes to the buyer's secret store.

Mr Jones added that as boys he and his brother often chatted with an old man who used to spend most of his time with the longshoremen at Shanklin. Alfred Downer, known locally as 'Old Alfie', would often speak of his forebears, one of whom was Mollie the Witch, and their association with the Butlers in their smuggling exploits – thereby confirming the key details from Harry Butler's account, including especially the connection between Mollie and the smugglers (but contradicting the claim that Mollie was the last of her line of the Downer family). Mr Downer would point to Whitecliff and say, "Just round the corner's where they did their business, boys."

# Chapter 13

# Early Days Around Peacock Hill
## – Mr Ernest Butler (Part 1)

*Ernie Butler was born in 1890 at Peacock Hill and spent most of his life in Bembridge except for a short break at East Cowes. He was 84 years old when I recorded him at his home Glengower, Forelands, during April and July 1975.*

## Family Background

Well halfway between Howe Chine and the School, or nearer the School than the other way, there was an old house there which eventually went over the cliff. That was Praines Cottage, or Trilly's Mansion as they used to call it, but there was no-one there, not when *I* knew it. He was a smuggler I dare say, same as the rest of 'em, nearly everybody was at *that* time. Well my Dad said, they only made roads where smugglers used to go by the paths!

My great-grandfather used t'have Smuggler's Cottage up at Whitecliff Bay on the foot o' the downs – see, there's a stile there and just to the right o' the stile there was a footpath running down along the bottom o' the down, and there was the ol' cottage there. And over the other side of Culver Cliff the smugglers used ter use Hermit's Hole, they used to pull the tubs up and hide 'em in there. Anyhow, the Excise people caught up wi' them eventually, and the old lady was sit on the tub feedin' the baby, and they got away with it then, but after that they caught up wi' them and confiscated the house and knocked it down. Well, Dad used to take us up there, and a few years ago you could see the old stone foundations an' that there.

My father's name was Henry Butler and he went to sea when he was thirteen. My mother was Emily Hayles, she originated from Ashey. Dad never went to school much, but he was a beautiful writer. Goodness knows what he done. He was put on board a schooner off Brading Cement Mills when he was thirteen, and he went to sea all his life.

Some years after the Witch's Cottage was burned down, my dad bought that little bit o' land and put that bungalow up, the one that's Myrtle Bank. Because Brading Harbour was still open at the time and he was master of a fairly big yacht that used to lay up in the Harbour 'ere called the *Oenone*, it's a funny name I know. An' he had that bungalow built in 1880 so he

## Chapter 13 – Early Days Around Peacock Hill

could walk straight across out by Centurion's Copse: she lay up there, place called Whiteoak they called it then – there's a old water-pumping station there now. And mother and dad lived aboard this yacht there one winter when they were first married, while they built that bungalow. She was a private yacht, she belonged to someone b' the name of Schenley. Then o' course when the summer come and the people wanted her, they went back in the bungalow. Then my father used to go cruising with 'em, anywhere, Mediterranean, somewhere or other. I can show yer a reference that was wrote about him saying what a excellent man he was, sober and honest, excellent navigator, an' all the rest.

*Mr Schenley's reference:*

**Warsash House Fareham South Hants.**

**Henry Butler has again had charge of my vessel *Goddess* for the last 12 months. We have been up to the Faroes and down to Albania. I can recommend him to go anywhere in the world, an excellent pilot, *strictly sober*, honest and obliging.**

**G. A. Schenley. May 4th, 1894.**

And in 1868, he joined the tea clipper in Liverpool, square-rigged ship, from Liverpool to Shanghai and back which took nine months and eighteen days for a round trip. As I say, he went to sea right up to 'e was about seventy, yer see. Never seen much of 'n! Sometimes he was away for a twelvemonth, maybe sixteen months. First Sunday he was home from a voyage or being at sea, he always went to Church on Sunday mornin' and o' course he used to meet a lot o' friends like the Thornycrofts, and Ismays, and Suttons, and Colonel Moreton and Cap'n De Bully [*Du Boulay*], all that lot. He used to say to mother, "I expect I'll be a bit late home ter dinner, because yer know what 'tis, first Sunday I goes down there, everyone wants to know where I've bin."

An' another thing, mother'd never know when dad was comin' home, he'd come anywhen p'raps. 'Tisn't like now when you have wireless and things like that. He'd come in wi' the door with his kitbag and, "Any oranges today, lady?" I never knew him go in a pub 'ere, or anything.

It was dad's brother Charles who served in the *Leander* in the Crimean War – and this other brother Sam which lived in Ryde, he went through the Crimean too. Then his brother Mark was mate in the ol' *Bembridge* that used to run across to Portsmouth Harbour. And when dad was at sea, Mark always come up home to see mother. I remember him now saying, "'Ello Emily, yer alright?" "Yes I'm alright , thank you." "Now, anythin' I can do or anythin' yer wants?" He was a good sort.

Dad's sister Charlotte, she married a chap name o' Jacobs, and went t'Australia in 1860 in a boat called the *Tantivy*. It took three months to get there, one little 'un toddlin' along with her hand and another one in her arms, and her belongings in a red bundle handkerchief. They went out under the emigration scheme – o' course, they never had no money. Well they went up country, they cleared the ground, there was the trees all round, and they built a log cabin and started a market garden there. And there was a little village place close to where they were called Rosebery – well d'you know, he got on and they farmed a thousand acres when he died. All business suspended in the town, banks an' everything closed when he died. Then one o' their daughters married a chap from Scotland which was out there, and they was Mayor and Mayoress of Brisbane. They came over 'ere for Queen Elizabeth's Coronation and they visited my brother Harry at Myrtle Bank.

Well then there was three boys in the family: Charlie, Harry, and me. My oldest brother Charlie was killed in the '14 War. And I had two sisters, one's Emily an' one's Alice, well Alice never married and Harry never married, they lived up Myrtle Bank till *they* died out, y'see. I was the youngest born at Myrtle Bank, an' I'm the last one left. I s'pose I was *alright* in them days, being the youngest one! My elder sister Emily was sort of apprenticed to dressmaking with Miss Jefferys in the village. Then she went away, she was lady's maid to a French lady, travelled the world with her.

Now my Uncle Bill [*Billy Butler*], he used t'have a few cows an' a horse an' cart, one time. That's what *he* done. He used t'have them just opposite Portland House there [*in the High Street*], and he had two or three cows 'e used to keep just by the Mill there, on the way to Newtown.

## Schooldays

My mother was taking me to the village down Woodclose Lane [*now known as Common Wood Lane*] when I was a little nipper first going to school, we was comin' along there when out over the hedge jumped a great bull right in front of us. And my mother had a umbrella in her hand and she went up and opened this umbrella and walked to the bull, like that, an' 'e turned tail an' run, mate!

And we always kept a dog, and if the dog barked in the night my mother'd get up – dad was away at sea – and go right round the garden. She was fearless. But that dog 'ud tell her if there was anybody there, yeah.

Now when my uncle Mark – he was mate in the ol' *Bembridge* – when he used to come to visit my mother, 'e used to say to me, "Come down t'morrow mornin'," he says, "Take yer across all day, all day in the boat tomorrow." I used to go to an' fro, I'd be a nipper like, running about on the boat.

## Chapter 13 – Early Days Around Peacock Hill

Passenger Steamer 'Bembridge' – under steam!

I had to walk to school every day from the duck pond, through the lower part o' the copse, up over Melons Hill as they used to call it, by the Windmill, an' down there. And it wasn't very good in the winter, I can tell yer! And nearly always there was a bull what Thornycroft had in that lower field there, he got out an' 'e was waiting for yer when yer got down the bottom, you had t'run back, up through that path an' away! Oh dear! Then sometimes I'd meet the Smiths from up Hillway, they used to meet me at the bottom o' the path be the chapel there – Alf Smith, and Charlie Smith, an' Ethel Smith.

The older boys, sixth and seventh standard, used t'have an hour once a week on the schoolmaster's garden, on the allotment. We planted potaters or seeds or anything, see. The allotments used to be where Perce Watton afterwards built the social club in Queens Road. Then another hour we used to go out measuring fields. All round the village, different fields – down East Cliff, all round there, an' Tyne Hall, well I suppose Alfie Smith the master asked if they could go down and measure. We used to go and measure it up and then go back and work it out, see.

Now, chap that we used to call Daddy Acre, he was a case 'e was! K-O-W for cow! Ah-ha! Alfie used t'have him out, he give him eight cuts on his hands, an' he only turn round and laugh at 'n! Like leather 'e was! Alfie used to tan him with the cane but never a tear, mate, he just laugh at 'n, yes he would, just laugh!

There's a Italian feller used to come round, hurly-gurly with a monkey up the top. Outside o' Miss Mursell's sweet-shop Daddy up with a stone,

The Organ Grinder outside 'Shorelands', Point Hill, 1930s.

hit this monkey in the head and knocked him off the barrel. Out comes this Italian and chased 'm round, he couldn't *catch* 'im, mate! Daddy waited for him next time he come round, he used to come 'bout once a week. He used to play the organ there, see, and then he'd go in the shop and they used to give him a copper or two – and anybody else there, he had a little bag thing they used to pop a copper or two in. Well anyhow while he was in the shop, Daddy went down there and turn the handle the wrong way an' handle come orf, he throw 'm down the road! Ha! Oh dear! Case that one! If there was anything to be done owt, Daddy was in 't right enough!

He was tough as leather, mate! I dunno *why* he was called Daddy Acre, that was all he went by, ever I knowed 'n! But when he got a bit older, he good chap in a boat, I ain't sayin' nothin' 'bout that. They used to get hold of Daddy and rub his ears like that, an' give 'm the stick! "Now catch us!" He used to chase us round everywhere!

Then when we went to school, I always had a boat down on the duck pond, model sailing-boat what eldest brother give me. Always playing about down *there*. In the summer 'course I was always down the shore with Bert Baker, Whitecliff Bay or Forelands. Bert finished up Cox'n o' the lifeboat for some years. Biggish family he come from, they all lived in that little Isabel Cottage [*at Forelands*] at the time.

Had to go to Chapel Sunday mornings, and Sunday night. I didn't mind it at the time, there was nowhere else to go, nothing much else to do! Mr

# Chapter 13 – Early Days Around Peacock Hill

Couldrey used to go to Chapel reg'lar, morning an' night, well he had Hillway Chapel put up.

Some o' the boys used to send somebody into Alf Mursell's for a penn'orth o' leather-me-owt or summing like that, y'know! Huh! Or else wanted some pittance-milk or summing or other! Ol' Ashford used to say, "I'll give yer leather-me-owt!" He used to draw a stick acrorss them! Oh dear! They never bought nothin'! He used to bake Bembridge Buns there, and Riddick after him. They were beautiful! Tuppence they were. Ashford Mursell had a little grocer's shop there as well as the baker's. You went in the shop an' it was baker's on the left, and groceries the other side.

## Early Days Around Peacock Hill

Well one time all the farms round there, Longlands and Peacock and Glovers, they all come in Bembridge Farm. All those fields right round the downs there, an' all up over the downs, was all come in Taylor's. They used to turn cattle up on the top there to feed. Yer see, one time Sir Egerton Hamond-Graeme owned *all* the land, and Taylors rented Bembridge Farm from 'n. Then he gave all the farmers a chance of buying up a piece of it, so finish up with even Taylor's got split up. Ol' Ned Pope bought Peacock Farm, Stanwell bought theirs, Calloway bought Longlands, and ol' Charlie Preston bought Foreland Farm. Glovers Farm came under Taylor's as far back as *I* can remember, somebody must've had it before. They only put cattle in there and things like that, nobody worked it 'specially for 'm.

Now Ben Jeffery lived in one o' Glovers Cottages, then Mark Griffin, he lived in the other when I was a boy. Years before that, Ben Jeffery went to sea with my father, he was 'long with him for *several* years, Ben was. Then he finished at sea, I s'pose, and took on the job at the farm. Reuben Jeffery, Ben's brother, used to live at the bottom of Hillway, and his son Harry Jeffery was the biggest sailor I ever seen in me life, 'e was! Now there was a big walnut-tree by Stanwell Farm, and Mark Griffin was going up the hill with a wagon, and he slipped orf o' the footboards or summing – he must 'a bin sitting on the footboard there, and the wagon run over him, killed 'n.

Then after that the Warnes come there [*to Glovers Cottages*]; Mr Warne worked on Bembridge Farm all his life as general farm labourer. Then just down the road on the same side was Shepherd Parker; he had some o' the sheep up on the downs and some in the different fields. They used to *plough* all the fields round there then, well they had turnips and this an' that, then they'd turn the sheep out into the turnip fields. And when I was a nipper they used to put beasts up on the down – bullocks! Well after Parker died, his son Joe Parker bought a horse an' cart and done a bit o'

Stanwell Farm, Hillway, c.1880.

haulage work in the village – anybody want any gravel or dirt or anything shifted, he was the chap to do't. Well then the other shepherd that came there was a chap come up from Dorset, name Holdaway, and he lived there till he died.

On the other side of the road, there's a cottage there where Mr Young the cowman at Bembridge Farm used to live. Good-tempered bloke, never any trouble t'anybody. Now Young 'ud start work at six o'clock, go down and get the cows in, milk 'em, come home to breakfast, go back and clean out the stables an' things like that. Then in the afternoon about three o'clock he'd get the cows in again for afternoon milk. In the winter he'd have to go back and get 'em in the stables and give 'em some food an' that. But o' course summertime they never got 'em in night-time.

Merryweather lived close by, and he worked at the farm too. He was in the Army, and stationed in India for years, and he married an Indian woman and brought her back. Two girls and a boy, Bill.

Now Farmer Morris, he went to Stanwell Farm the day that I was born, Christmas Eve 1890 – so my mother said. They were married and then went there to live that day. He eventually took over the Mill Farm as well. Then Ted married Morris's niece and worked it for him, while Morris was up at Stanwell, see. As a boy I used to go and get the cows in for Morris or turn 'em out in the field, go round and collect the eggs, help with the hay, anything like that for 'm.

Then I used to go over Bembridge Farm when they used to thresh the corn, that was Taylor's father and grandfather before 'm. I can remember Mrs

## Chapter 13 – Early Days Around Peacock Hill

Taylor taking the children down to school down there in the little pony trap. They used t'have eight horses and ploughs an' that. And they used to take the corn to Newport, yer see. Load up a wagon overnight, with four horses, and that was a day's journey to Newport an' back, with the corn.

People b' the name o' Calloway used t'have Longlands Farm at one time. He married a local girl, name o' Sarah Snow. Then James from Sandown took it over for a long time, they used to be haulage contractors, any amount of horses they had, used to do all the government contracting, take all the ammunition to the different forts and all the government stores. Then when they finished, Monck from Yaverland had it. There was ol' feller used to work there that lived in Longlands Cottage, and when I was goin' to Sandown as apprentice I used to call the ol' bloke every morning as I went along. I used to ride me bike along there, an' I started work at Sandown at six o'clock yer know, then. Called him 'bout twenty to six, go and hammer the door! I used to get up 'bout five o'clock. Mother was always up and had me breakfast for me to take – eight o'clock breakfast at the workshop – an' dinner as well. She used to get up 'bout four o'clock, mother did. Ol' Morris used to say, "I can never be up bifore yer mother!"

The carters and ploughmen on the farm were up, start work six o'clock, out in the fields ploughin', or general work about the farm when the weather was bad. Two horses on a plough yer see, or harrowing, or whatever it might be.

There was a village blacksmith's down the bottom of Hillway there, there's several had it, a man b' the name o' Beer had it, and there was a man b' the name o' Callaway had it. They used to do shoein' horses, and farm horses, and put the iron tyres on the wheels. I used to go up there and blow the bellows when I's a nipper.

Then go in John Snow's and have a look round the carts and wagons and one thing 'n other. He was the wheelwright, 'e made the wagons and carts and gates for the farms all round 'ere. Ol' Smith, father o' the Smith nippers, he was a carpenter, 'e used t'help Snows quite a lot on the wagons and carts and one thing 'n 'nother.

And several more boys that lived up there, we used to go in John Snow's shed of a evening and play 'Hook 'em' – he had three rubber rings, and throw 'em on the hooks. Darts wasn't thought of then, I don't think! P'raps I'd see one o' the Smiths and say, "Well we'll 'ave a game of 'Ook 'em t'night!" "Orright!" And then two or three of us 'ud go in there, see! It was a big shed, where Nightingale's got a shop or two, that's built back now. That become a nasty corner there, several bad accidents – well when Snows died the Council knocked that shed down and cut a bit off the corner, made it easy corner there, see.

Dad used to say if he was home anywhen, "Now be sure and get a little pig in the spring, feed him up an' have 'im killed in October. We used t'have

Hillway, c.1875. The Blacksmith's Shop, where the Callaways made the wheels for the wagons built by the Snow family just opposite.

half of 'im smoked an' half in the tub. We always had a bit o' meat then. 'Course there was a lot o' farm-labouring chaps living there *then*, they all kept pigs. Well John Snow used to smoke the hams an' that for us with oak dust [*oak sawdust*], and the side, and that was bacon. Oh I can see my mother goin' in the larder now with a knife and cutting out a rasher 'bout half an inch thick, out o' the side o' the bacon! Then we had some pickled in the tub, have salt pork or anything yer see. We kept fowls and things like that, cat an' dog, that's all.

We had big garden, apples and plums and vegetables, and great big fig tree we had there. Any amount o' trees. Well me older brothers, they done most o' the gardening you know, but I used to have t'help 'em when I was a nipper.

Then Annie Butler, Billy Butler's daughter, she used to come up prac'lly every Sunday afternoon if it was fine enough, have a cup o' tea an' that. Because it appears that she acted as sort o' midwife to my mother with all the children, like.

When I's a nipper we used t'have a man come round from Sandown b' the name of Starks, he used to come round for Hibbards of Sandown, they

## Chapter 13 – Early Days Around Peacock Hill

had a grocer's shop down Avenue Road. And mother used to give him order beginning of the week and he'd come round 'bout Friday or Saturday with it, and that's it. Anything else we wanted, 'course we had to go to Bembridge for.

I just remember the remains of Wolverton Farm just to the left of the airfield, it was dialect [*derelict*] even *then*.

I used t'have to go through Centurions Copse to get the medicine if my mother was bad, or any of us, if there was a doctor wanted, or medicine. Dr Lucas used to come round in a little trap, he had a coachman used to drive him round – an ol' feller with a high hat on an' everything, you know. Well then, he'd say, "Now you come to my surgery tonight at such a time and there'll be some medicine there for yer." You had to go in there and wait while he mixed up some medicine for yer. I dunno what he put in it! You had to pay then, he'd send in a bill.

I was going through Steyne Copse one night, it was pitch black all through there, it was all growed in yer know with trees an' that, and there was somethin' in there just moving about in the bushes. I knew it couldn't be any person, I didn't know *what* it was. It didn't ruffle me a bit, I just scuffed around like this, found a nice stone, picked up the stone and waited till the next movement. Then I throwed the stone – a white horse!

I know the first motorbike I saw, that was Tom Thornycroft, 'e darn near run me over on the road in Steyne Copse. He was tearing about on this motorbike, anyhow.

Before we was married we had bicycles with 'cetylene gas lamps. You used to get the 'cetylene stuff in tins, and you put it in an' then you add water in the top. And you could just turn it on, and drip, drip, drip… made the gas, y'see. Beautiful light it give yer.

The Coastguard Cottages was over there 'long where Ledge House is now [*at Forelands*]. Then there was a little ol' thatched hut for the Coastguards on the edge of the cliff, that went over cliff. The Foreland Coastguards at that time used t'have to walk along the cliff every night to look out for smuggling; they had to meet the Point ones, and they had to meet the Sandown ones halfway between Forelands and Sandown. There wasn't any Coastguards up Culver, not till 'bout 1900s. I've heard that the Coastguards had a fight with some smugglers up Culver and one o' the Coastguards was over cliff. That was before my time.

There's another thing, when I's a nipper, they put the big wireless pole up Culver, that was 'bout 1900. It was a big pole, 189 feet he was. Dismantled it bifore the last War. They used to say, well that controls the fleet in the Mediterranean an' all that, well o' course it would. We couldn't make that out at the time, it was something *very* special. Then they built those houses up there to take the Coastguards who looked after it, and they had a big signal station there.

Bembridge Coastguards c.1906.

Chief Officer up there was Goddard, yeah. He had two girls, they used to go to Bembridge school [*i.e. the village school*]. What's called 'Bembridge School' now wasn't a school *then*, that was a dialect [*derelict*] hotel really, Whitecliff Bay Hotel, I can just remember when the people moved out o' there. It was dialect for years, and then a man b' the name of Whitehouse bought it, he was Lloyd George's Secretary, one time. Built the lot of it for the School.

I remember the big bonfire up Culver for Queen Victoria's Diamond Jubilee [*in 1897*] 'cos I was up there! I was seven then. Goodness knows, they carted stuff up there for weeks I s'pose, there's a *terrific* bonfire, big as a house! Barrels o' paraffin, tar, everything you could think of. There's a barrel o' tar went rollin' down over cliff, all blazin', all alight. It's one o' those things that you never forget, innit?

## A Life in Boats

Well at 14 I was apprenticed to a boatbuilder at Sandown, Arthur Taylor, and stayed there for over five years. 'Cos I wanted to go to sea all the time. I went

## Chapter 13 – Early Days Around Peacock Hill

to work be train from down Point first goin' orf, then in 1922 I got one o' the ol' Douglas motorbikes, handles up 'ere y'know, belt-driven; then it got to other motorbikes.

When I was nineteen [*in 1910*], I went to Cowes for 'bout four years, worked in Cornubia Yard for a man b' the name of Joe White. Built a 90-ton yacht there called *Amarella IV*. Then I went to S.E. Saunders at East Cowes, who was building the lifeboats, I was there about three years or more, I s'pose.

We were married while I was there – in Bembridge Church 'course, we went to school together. Well then, the wife was took ill and Doctor Hay, the port doctor, he says, "D'you know," 'e says, "I should get away from 'ere [*East Cowes*] if I was you. It don't suit her 'ere." 'Course, *then* it was all mud and one thing 'n another. So anyhow, packed it in, we come back to Bembridge to live, and I went back to Sandown to work, to same place. We lived over in that Anchorage for a time, up Steyne Road, four or five houses there that belonged to Wally Osbirn [*Osborn*]. Then we lived at The Haven up Howgate, then we come down 'ere to Glengower.

After a couple o' years at Sandown I became pier master at Shanklin pier, I was there thirty-two years, left when I was nearly sixty-seven, in 1957. 'Course, we had all the steamers from Brighton, Eastbourne, Hastings, Bournemouth, Swanage, Weymouth, Portsmouth, Southsea, and Southampton, yeah. Used to be *Brighton Queen* used to come down, the *Glengower* and the *Waverley* – that's three Brighton boats that run trips to Shanklin. Now that's why we named this house the Glengower, there y'are, I liked the skipper of 'er, Cap'n Fields his name was. I was the marine manager there, check orf the passengers an' everything.

Eventually I came back down 'ere to the kiosk on Forelands beach, which my wife used to run, yer see. We run it together for some years. We'd bin married sixty-two years when my wife died in January [*1975, a few months before the recordings*].

Have you seen that little boat that's hanging up over the Pilot Boat? Well that was my boy's cradle, padded out an' that, and on a rocker. And you could just put yer foot on it like that... An' I'll tell you where we saw that – we went aboard the Earl of Crawford's yacht called the *Valhalla* at Cowes, and there was one there. And my wife said, "Well there we are, there's an idea, now make one..." Well so I did! Now how did it come to be down the Pilot Boat? Well Mr Vernet was bailiff and chauffeur to Lord Herschell, who come to have that house what's Warner's now, after Mr Waterlow did [*Fuzzie Freeze*]. Herschell was a big noise in the Marconi, and Lady Herschell come from the Shetland Islands. Now Lord Herschell died, and Lady Herschell wanted this cradle for a baby that was a friend o' the family's, anyhow. And I wouldn't sell that to her. Well then, they sold up and went away. Vernet, he was a Frenchman, took over Pilot Boat. He knew I had this cradle and

Pilot Boat Inn and Station Road c.1890s.

he kept on tormentin' me to let him have it. So eventually I says, "Orright, take it then!" Ah-ha – just like that! That was it. And it hangs there now [*or it did*]. Mr Vernet was a clever engineer and he drove all the crowned heads of Europe.

# Chapter 14

# On the Home Front
## – Mrs Elsie Hibbert

*Elsie Hibbert was the daughter of Alfie Smith the schoolmaster, who features so prominently in this volume. She was born in Bembridge in 1890 and lived there until 1909 aged nineteen, when she moved to Sussex. She never moved back to the Island but would continue to visit Bembridge over the years and especially her old friend Ivy Bryant, contributing to a couple of the recording sessions with Mrs Bryant in April 1975, aged 85. Her memories of the early days in Bembridge are acute, especially on the domestic front.*

## Family and Schooldays

My father Alfred Smith came here about 1880 as headmaster of the boys' school, then some years after it became a mixed school and he took over the whole lot. My mother's maiden name was Mary Louisa Duckett, she came from Cookham in Berkshire, and dad came from Marlow in Buckinghamshire. He didn't live in the house that was provided: a very

Couldrey's Emporium, Sherbourne Street, c.1900.

small row of cottages, one was supposed to be for the headteacher, but we never lived in it. We lived in Sherbourne House in the High Street, where I was born. It was a house adjoining the shops and it had a shop underneath it, which was originally the post office; then the post office went into the next half, which belonged to the same people, Osbornes, and then they moved back again.

Now, my brothers and sisters. Connie was born in 1884, Ethel in '86, Dorothy in October '88, and I was born in March 1890. Then comes Dick in December '92, Eric in '94, Madge '96, Joyce '98, and then Norah in 1901 or 2, she was always known as Babe. She and Babe Newman were both baptised in coronation year: Babe Newman was called Corona, after the coronation. I lived in Bembridge till I was nineteen, but I've not lived here since then, I went to Cooksbridge in Sussex. Connie was always at home with my mother and father, she didn't go out to work at all and she stayed in Bembridge until my father retired in about 1920, he was here for forty years anyway. Eric and Dorothy were the only two who stayed living in Bembridge after they were married: Dorothy's husband came to live in Bembridge, his name was Ernest Lucas. Eric was in the Royal Naval Air Service during the First World War, and then he came back as a carpenter for Love's and then he went on for Weaver's.

Well as I say, my father first lived in Sherbourne House when he came to Bembridge, which is where I was born. Then we moved to Number 3 The Cedars, Foreland Road, then a year or two after that when my grandfather died and left my father a certain amount of money, he built a pair of houses a few doors down called Thameslea and Quarryville. We lived in Thameslea and the Tuffleys lived in Quarryville.

My father used to get ten bob a week for being organist and choirmaster. And in those days it was a hand manual for pumping to get the air in the organ, and somebody had to be behind the organ, sitting up on a big stool, pull this handle up and down and watch the tell-tale thing when it was nearly out, start pulling up again. Many a time I've gone up there and manhandled this thing, 'cos I couldn't sing very well as I'd had double pneumonia as a baby, and most of my family were good singers and they were in the church choir. But I used t'have to go up for church practice if the regular boy wasn't able to go, and use this thing. I also used to do it sometimes on a Saturday morning for a certain lady in the town who wanted to learn to play the organ because she'd fallen in love with the curate! That was Margaret Moreton, the daughter of Colonel Moreton of Hill Grove. Fourpence an hour she would pay me.

My dad also taught piano- and organ-playing at home, so we'd have quite a number of his pupils come up for lessons. Every week Belle Way from Foreland Farm, the eldest daughter there, she used to come to us for a lesson.

## Chapter 14 – On the Home Front

And my dad was one of those people who can't see in the dark, so one of us always had to go with him with a lantern to take her home, you couldn't let her walk home alone from our house, down through which was all fields. Of course, there were no street-lamps in those days. When we were children, if you went out in the winter you took a bicycle-lamp or a lantern with you.

My father would go down to Tyne Hall 'cos Merton Thomas was very musical like him. Mertie was quite small, a very dapper little man and a great favourite with the ladies!

A Miss Drew was the governess in charge of the girls' school, and we always called her Gubby Drew. We were with Miss Matthews, the infant mistress under Gubby Drew. We were favourites, we got on alright with her. Of course, we were only there while we were infants; soon as we were about seven, by that time dad had taken over as headmaster of the mixed school. We'd get into trouble with dad because we always used to talk, we weren't allowed to speak in those days in school. If you were caught talking, you got the cane, never mind whether you were the headmaster's daughter or not! You weren't treated any differently from the rest of them. You had to forget he was your father whenever you got inside the school, he wouldn't have any favouritism at all.

But he used to teach us all sorts of different things. For one thing, he'd teach us gardening: in those days very few schools had school gardens. Then very few had human anatomy and physiology like we had, and first aid. We had a very lurid poster he used to put up, showing all the different parts of the body, with all different pictures on it, and one of them was all red, blood. And Alf Jordan, the son of Tom Jordan the butcher, immediately fainted away at the sight of the red, which was supposed to be blood. And when we got him round again, I remember my father saying, "I don't know what you think *you're* going ter do with yourself afterwards. You'll not be any good to your father in the butcher's shop if you're goin' ter faint at the sight of blood!" It was a whole front of the man, you could see all the innards. Drec'ly he saw that go up, my father would say, "Outside!"

I remember when my brother Eric first started school. He had long, dark curls, a *beautiful* head of hair, and my mother was absolutely heartbroken because my dad wouldn't let him go to school with hair like that, he had to have it all cut short. 'Course, these days it would've been alright, wouldn't it?

Mrs Grueber at the Ducie – if you went to school 'never absent never late' for a year, she would have us round there for tea, and give us apples. And I had a medal for five years' perfect attendance. She was one of the school managers, and her husband was some big pot at the British Museum, in the coins department.

Bembridge Station turntable.

When we were at school at Sandown, we used t'have to catch a train at three minutes past eight. We'd go *tearing* down that hill, schoolbag on our shoulders, just about get it by the skin of your teeth. Usually hear somebody shout, "*Train's in!*" The train would come in just before eight o'clock, and the little engine had to get unhitched, go onto a turntable to get back on the other line and then hitch up on the front of the train again. And when the train was in, you'd just got time while it did this. And more than once, they've stopped the train and brought us back for a gentleman who owned a big estate here, I forget his name.

## Skirts and Shirts

When we were eighteen we had skirts right down to our ankles, and we had to put brush braid round the bottoms to prevent the edges of the hem wearing out on the roads. We used to put our hair up 'cos we had long hair then. When I was seventeen and first apprenticed at the Shanklin Parochial Girls School, the first time I went in with this long frock and m' hair up, one of the mistresses said, "You'll have more influence with the children now you're grown up and not just a child. I'm glad to see it". We first put our hair up to go to a dance, tied up in a bun – that was a great occasion, like society debutantes coming out! Before that, we always had it back, with a big black bow.

My mother always made all our clothes, she'd been a dressmaker before she was married, and she used to make for *all nine* of us! Little Lord Fauntleroy suits for my brothers – little velvety suits with white shirts and frills all down. I was well in my teens before I bought anything ready-made, we made our

## Chapter 14 – On the Home Front

own underclothes by hand too. And my mother was in hospital one year and she made us two Red Riding Hood dolls, all by hand. We used to do a lot of that at school – needlework these days, they just seem to do sort of oddments and fancy work. To make the garments, our parents had to provide the material and we used to take it to school and make it there in the needlework lesson.

There weren't pyjamas in those days, they were all nightshirts for the men and nightdresses for the women.

Men used to wear waistcoats with their suits, of course. And a Norfolk coat for any sporty business, that was a loose coat with a belt at the back. Then knickerbockers with a strap on their knees for cycling and so on. And straw boaters! Boys didn't go into long trousers till they were leaving school, almost.

Shirts used t'have stiff, starchy collars – no soft collars in those days – or white rubber collars that you used to wipe off, for schoolboys. The men's collars had to be ironed wet so as to make them stiffen up. You had a buttonhole in the neckband of your shirt, with a stud to hold the collar to the shirt.

## Food and Water

My mother used to make no end of jams when the fruit was about, hundreds of pounds every year, and jellies and so on. 'Cos my dad always grew quite a lot of fruit, that was his hobby. He had a big garden at Thameslea, where he used to grow strawberries, raspberries, plums, pears, and *crowds* of different apples. He'd got one apple tree where he grafted different kinds on the stump, and he got seven different apples growing on the same tree! He had something to do with originating the Howgate Wonder apple, and then one of the gardeners down Howgate brought it out, sort of thing. We grew practically all our own vegetables, too.

Then the copper used to be used for boiling Christmas puddings. We'd have a row of them along the shelf in the kitchen. For every birthday we'd have a Christmas pudding, about a dozen per year.

Dinners and teas used to be much the same as today. We never spent much on cakes 'cos my mother used to make them. For supper we usually had bread and cheese, somewhere round about eight o'clock. And always on a Thursday night after choir practice during the winter we had lovely boiled onions with biscuits and cheese, you see, something hot for when they came in. My dad and three of my sisters and both my brothers were all in the choir.

When we first went down to Burton House in Swains Road we had gaslight downstairs, and my mother couldn't afford t'have gas taken upstairs so we had to have candles to go to bed with. And there was no gas heating in the home, so you had to get up in time to light a fire or use a Beatrice stove – that was a very well-known little oil stove, you could get one with a single flame or a double flame and you used it to boil kettles an' that.

We had to take turns in pumping water, we'd each stand on the table in the scullery and pump for a hundred pumps. There was a runaway pipe down from the tank into the scullery sink, had to keep on pumping till the water ran into that pipe, then we knew the tank was full and we didn't have to pump any more till the next day! Our hot water tank was in a cupboard at the side of the kitchen, with an airing tank above it, they don't put those in kitchens these days. All the cooking was done in the kitchen but the washing-up, the sinks, the mangle – if you had one – were kept out in the scullery. You couldn't sit out in the scullery, it was all stone floor.

In the bedrooms we had marble-top washstands, earthenware bowls, tall jugs, and a jar at the side for your toothbrush. And we had to wash in cold water – either that or you'd have to go downstairs to boil a kettle and fetch some hot water up. For our weekly bath you'd have it in front of the kitchen fire, in a big tin bath. And all that water had to be carried away to the 'slops' every day: you had a slop-pail which had to be taken down to the scullery and then the water thrown down the sink.

Well, we used to sit in our dining room, down in Swains, and we could see the liners go round then because there was *nothing* all round. I think ours was the first house that was built there. The dining room was really the living room, it used t'have a dozen chairs to the table to sit round it, play games, sit reading, all sorts of different things 'ud be going on at the same time. We had a big bookcase in the hall, with a hallstand. Then we had a big cupboard under the stairs, with hooks with our names on, and we used to hang our hats and coats in there, and all sorts of things.

Then we had a tank room up top, where my father stored lots of music. People used to take sheet music when they went out to parties in those days, nearly everyone would sing or recite something.

## A Lovely Six Weeks!

When my sister Joyce was about four, she and Stuart Hapgood, the son of the tailor, both got scarlet fever at the same time. How they got it nobody knew, there wasn't another case in the village at all. And we had to be segregated, nobody was allowed to go into Hapgood's house, and nobody was allowed to come into our house. My dad being the headmaster had to turn out and go down to Tyne Hall with Merton Thomas. And my sister Ethel was teaching then, she went to Bill Wheeler, Merton Thomas's gardener. My brother Dick was a bit delicate, so he went to live with Petty's, the retired coastguard officer at the Point. The rest of us stayed at home, we weren't allowed to go to school. People come down the road and cross over ostentatiously and walk down the other side, they wouldn't come down past our house!

We had our mother's sister, Aunt Tops, living with us then – she was Aunt Tops to all the village – she nursed my sister, and the rest of us weren't allowed to go upstairs. We had to turn the sitting room into a bedroom and all of us slept downstairs. She had a curtain inside and outside my sister's door which had to be kept soaking with carbolic: we had to take the meals halfway up the stairs and then go down and knock on the lower stair. Then we had to go into the downstairs rooms while Aunt Tops would come halfway down and fetch their meals from the stairs. And all their plates an' everything had to be put in a bowl of carbolic in the bathroom, which luckily was next door to the sick room. Never saw such a *fuss* as there was in your life, and nowadays they think nothing of scarlet fever!

We had a lovely time during that six weeks! My mother had an ulcer on her leg, she'd knocked it after my brother was born and it never healed. And every now and then she'd get an awful lot of inflammation in it, well she had to be kept in bed while she was like that. So we had to wait on her as well as the others upstairs. I was about twelve at the time, because my sister Babe was in a high chair, and we got porridge for breakfast one morning, and when my sister Con was bringing it in, Babe dabbed her hand into this boiling porridge and she had all blistered fingers, she was only a tiny kid in a high chair. What with mum's leg and then that...!

Then as soon as they came out of that bedroom, the very next week, my aunt had got a little tiny sore on her finger, didn't take any notice of it, just washed it and left it – and put on some new gloves, and in two days her hand was all swollen up. And without any anaesthetic, the doctor – two slits at the front and three at the back, and she stuck that out, she wouldn't have an anaesthetic. Doctor Gordon did that. In the end, that finger had to be taken off, it was poisoned you see, but by slicing it as he did and fomenting it two or three times a day as we did, we kept it down for a time. We had a *lovely* time that year! 1902, it was. Then I remember there was one epidemic of German measles: we had it, and the Jacobs girls had it, so they came up and slept in our bedrooms 'cos Will Jacobs was very ill with typhoid, down the Point.

## More Chores and A Lot of Dust

We children all had our own jobs to do. We didn't do very much during school hours because my eldest sister, soon as she was old enough to leave school, was kept at home. But Saturdays each of us had a certain amount of work to do before we were allowed out to play. When I was about eight or nine I, s'pose, one of my jobs was to wash up the breakfast things, and I used to do it on the kitchen table, with a big tray to drain them in. But my brother Dick was a perfect *demon*, and he wouldn't get up. And Saturday after Saturday he made me late getting out 'cos I had to wait till he'd had his breakfast, to wash up his things. And one morning he came down and he was sitting the other side of the table, I'd just put his breakfast on one corner, and he was sitting there jeering at me about keeping me in, and I'd got a spoon in my hand an' I threw it at him and it went through the kitchen window! Oh I had to lose my pocket money for a long time to help pay for that window!

Then when I got a bit older, I used t'have to get down on my hands and knees with a brush and dustpan and brush the dining room carpet, oh it was *all* done by hand in those days. Of course, you didn't have carpet-sweepers or anything like that, you used to keep the tea leaves for a day or two, get them fairly dry and then sprinkle them over the carpet and sweep it every so often to collect the dust up. And we *did* get dust in those days, 'cos I mean not like the macadamed roads then. On every cart that went up and down the road was dust all round everything, used to get it in the windows. And my mother was very grace on having open windows, so we'd get the whole lot in!

Another job was, we had coloured tiles from the front door, there were two steps down and then there was a width of coloured tiles down to the gate. *That* all had to be scrubbed every Saturday morning and steps had to be whitened. We had to take our turns at it. But kids nowadays never seem to help with anything in the house – ask them to wash up and they make a fuss! They don't know what work was!

There were no washing machines in those days and no laundries, and most houses had a copper in the scullery. On Mondays a woman would come to do the washing, how we children hated those days! Ours was Mrs Spet Jeffery, she was a little short woman with a very red face. All the water had to be carried in in pales and tipped into our old-fashioned brick copper. And you had to bale it out, no taps. We used to have 'balers', small round bowls with a wooden handle. Then light a fire under the copper to get your water boiling. After you'd boiled the things from the copper, you had to take them out in the big tubs and really rub them to get them clean. If you were lucky you'd got a wringer, and you had to turn the handle all the time and then keep on emptying the pale where the water had come out of them. When she was finished, she had to hearthstone the copper and all over the floor, got down on her hands and knees with a special piece of stone stuff and rubbed it over with a cloth afterwards and then the floor came all white.

We had a shed outside where all the garden tools were kept and where all the odd jobs used to be done. All the shoes had to be cleaned out there. Then

## Chapter 14 – On the Home Front

we had to clean knives in those days on an emery board with knife-powder, and on Saturday mornings our boys would rub them up and down on this board till they got all the stains off, there were no stainless knives then! And then later on there came knife-machines, semi-circular wooden things with holes in the top which you put the knives in with the powder, turned a handle and inside were brushes which cleaned them. And even then they had to be washed and dried afterwards!

## More Village Stories

We used t'have German bands come round the village, and they would say it was always a sign of rain after they'd been. And a one-man-band, he used to come round every now and then, walk round the village playing. Then we'd get Johnny Onions coming round, Frenchmen, with long strings of onions on their bicycles.

We went by train to Freshwater on May Day once – we were only about seven – all the way to Farringford and danced the maypole. That was quite an occasion for us!

We used to go out in the woods and gather ivy for Christmas decorations. We'd be busy getting ready for Christmas from the summer, almost.

All us schoolchildren had mugs given us for Queen Victoria's Diamond Jubilee in 1897. We had a short service in church, then we all marched round the village with our flags before we had the sports. Then in 1901 my mother went to Osborne House to see Queen Victoria lying in state, I remember that much. We all had to dress in black in the village, of course. Then she was taken over on the royal yacht and buried at Frogmore.

I remember my mother knitted balaclava helmets during the Boer War, then most people were knitting in the First War, scarves and so on.

We used t'have baptisms in the children's service in those days, and the font was at the back of the church and you all knelt up on seats. Well now they have them during the morning or evening service, don't they?

Those days there used to be big camps of Boys' Brigades here every year up at Whitecliff, from different parts of the country [*a tradition maintained to the present day*]. Our chief one was Reigate, and we had boyfriends among them. They used to come down year after year, and we got to know them when we were quite small and kept up a correspondence. But we didn't *marry* any of them!

Well at one time I was holiday governess to Sir John Thornycroft's grandchildren, that was *Mr* John Thornycroft's children. I used to go up to Steyne Battery every morning, that was when I was about seventeen [*1907*]. They needed to make up a bit with their schooling, and their father insisted on them having some lessons during the holidays, and of course their own

Thornycroft family at Steyne House, with latest grass-cutting machinery and pony wearing leather 'boots'. *Courtesy of Peter Chick Collection.*

governess was having *her* holiday at that time. So while she was away, I'd go and teach them reading, writing, arithmetic. Mr Collister was the gardener and he lived in the lodge.

Now Albert Pocock who lived in Foreland Road was the verger, he was another of those *sharp* people. He'd got quite a good voice and he used to sing sometimes at our village concerts, and we'd watch for his hand: all the time he was singing his hand would be moving up and down in short, sharp jolts and we used to giggle about it! And he had a couple of boys, one was named Eddie and he was always in mischief. Anyway, there was some trouble or other with the choir, and the old man said, "Couldna bin you, Eddie! Couldna bin you!" *His* boy couldn't do anything wrong.

Corny Orchard lived at Harbour Mount, he was a very *fussy* sort of man, couldn't do anything quietly, always very important, you know, really, in his own way. He and his wife came with Mr Freeman, who had something to do with the building of the embankment, the business side of it. We used to call him Humpy Freeman, he wasn't married but lodged with somebody or other.

Doctor Payne lived opposite us when we were at the Cedars in Foreland Road, he was a dear old chap. Mrs Payne was a little busybody, she often used

# Chapter 14 – On the Home Front

to borrow my mother's sewing-machine. Doctor Gordon came afterwards, he and his brother were in partnership. One had been a ship's doctor and he came and joined his brother in the practice here. Well for one thing doctors then always had their surgery in their own home, and they were friends of the family, you might say. And then we used t'have one come from Brading, Dr Chick-Lucas, he'd travel in a high dogcart.

I remember a big elm tree at the side of the road just in front of the piece of spare ground next to Excell's [*in Foreland Road*], outside Tompkins' house, and my brother Dick fell out of this tree and broke his arm. Now old Tompkins was a retired seaman, and there was some story about him being on a yacht that brought a princess who'd fled from France [*probably Princess Eugenie*]. They had like a biggish room out the back and they used to live out there instead of in the house, they thought the house was too *posh* for them!

Farmer Morris at Stanwell Farm couldn't bear anybody going into his fields and things – he wasn't even very keen on them stopping at the pond to see the ducks!

I remember old Tom S – well we were having a birthday party, and he was one who came. And he happened to get a cracked cup when we were having tea, and he turned round to my Aunt Tops an' said, "See – you – still – got – some – **cracked** – **cups** – then – Miss – Duckett!" Everybody laughed, of course! Tom used to push a tank of paraffin round the village and sell it: in those days there was no gas here, it was all coal or oil. And a young nephew of mine, John, he couldn't have been more than four, well he got out and turned the tap on an' let the paraffin run down the road! He was a young demon, was John.

## A Rough Crossing

I just remember the old man Robert Newman the pilot, Newton Newman's father, he lived where the Marine Hotel's been extended: there were cottages there before and he lived in one of those. I recall going there once when I was very small, but as far as I remember he'd be by the fire always, he was a real *old* man.

There used to be a good deal of gunfire practice, and we'd have notices round to open the windows when there was going to be practice from Nodes Point. They were terrible guns, and the vibrations were liable to smash the windows.

Occomores used to go across to Portsmouth as carriers, and they always got our butter for us, they'd go over every week and get all these orders for different people.

And o' course in those days there was *Fanny Grab*, the dredger. It had a 'grab' thing at the end and it used to keep the channel into the harbour clear.

Then there was a wall running round the harbour from the Spithead Hotel, and it was six or seven feet high, and we used to dare each other to jump down from it, because we were scared to do it.

Well, I was about twenty and we were coming home to Bembridge for a holiday an' it was a *terrible* night, very stormy, and we had a rough crossing as far as Seaview pier, and I begged them to get off at Seaview and have a cab out, but "Oh no! we'll be alright. There's a low tide, we've got to land under Tyne" – and that meant jumping down into a rowing-boat. I quite expected when we got to Under Tyne they wouldn't let us land and they'd send us back to Seaview, but they didn't, they risked it and let us land. And I'll never forget, they stood holding me on the boat, one on either side of me and each holding onto a mast because it was blowing so hard, and how we ever got into that boat without jumping into the water I don't know! I was never so terrified in my life! You had to watch until the boat came close, you see, and the next *second* the waves'd take it away and there was a gap. Mr Townsend, the man from St Helens, caught me as I jumped into the boat.

Queen Victoria II Lifeboat, with a rare photo of PC Toomer in the foreground.

## Chapter 14 – On the Home Front

The minute the lifeboat rocket went most of the menfolk of the village 'ud be tearing down there, and when we were kids we used to go tearing down too, to see the lifeboat go out. In those days it was up in the lifeboat house on the cliff, and it had to be hauled down with ropes. The ones who got down there first were the lucky ones who got an armlet and were allowed to help pull it and got paid for doing it. The cox'n would throw the armlets out. You could go and help pull if you wanted to anyway, but if you got an armlet you could claim money for it, I think they used to get about eighteen pence. Our boys would go down anytime, often in the middle of the night. The rescues were more or less commonplace in those days, the boats seemed to get more on the rocks and so on – well for one thing the boats couldn't *move* like they can now, and they didn't have so many pilots.

# Curiosities

## Home from the Front (Boer War)
*(IW County Press archive for 14th July 1900 – amended)*

The loyalty of the people of Bembridge again asserted itself on Wednesday evening, when they turned out at a very short notice to welcome home a neighbour who had rendered good service to his Queen and country at the front – Col. R. B. Mainwaring, assistant adjutant-general 1st Division South African Field Force. He arrived at Southampton in the *Kildonan Castle* on Tuesday, having charge of the consignment of the sick and wounded from the Cape… These facts were enough to stir the enthusiasm of the people of Bembridge and to lead them to do honour to one who is every inch a soldier and who on many a field has risked his life for Queen and country. The train was due at Bembridge at a few minutes past six, by which time a goodly number had assembled at the Station. Fog signals had been placed on the railway metals, which 'discharged' a salute as the train entered the Station. On alighting three hearty cheers were given for Col. Mainwaring and also three for Mrs Mainwaring, who accompanied him. Ropes were attached to the dog-cart in waiting and willing hands dragged the Colonel and his lady through the village via Ducie-avenue, passing under streams of flags which were flaunting in honour of the gallant soldier, to his home at Bembridge Lodge, the entrance to which was gaily decorated with bunting. On arriving at the entrance door the gallant Colonel said: "Gentlemen, I am very much obliged to you for this reception. I have had a good many receptions from the Boers, but not such a pleasant reception as this. I thank you all very much." Three more cheers were given and also cheers for the other officers at the front.

## Blanket Torn by Shell of Destroyer
*(Newspaper cutting about 1908; entry in the old WI Scrapbook)*

Live shells from destroyers engaged in target practice off the Isle of Wight startled the little seaside resort of Bembridge out of its usual calm on Tuesday. Sir John Thornycroft, a local resident, is instituting enquiries into the matter.

It seems now to be settled beyond reasonable doubt that the shooting in the British Navy is greatly improving. A few evenings ago, for instance, a man was taking a stroll down a lane towards the sea at Bembridge, when a shot from the British torpedo destroyers off the Nab ploughed up the

## Chapter 14 – On the Home Front

earth and stones a few yards ahead of him. In another part of the village a lady who went into the backyard to collect a double-folded woollen shawl, hanging on the clothes-line for airing, discovered that a shot had made a hole through it.

We are asked respectfully to inform the Admiralty that the inhabitants of Bembridge do not for a moment desire to stand between the guns of His Majesty's destroyers and any target which they may select for practice, but at shooting at such articles of attire as they may select on the clothes-line, will naval commanders oblige by giving a few hours' notice in order to enable living creatures to get out of the way? Also, shall the owner send in her bill now for damage to the shawl, or shall she wait until one of the gunners has scored a magpie on her husband's pyjamas, or made a bull's-eye on the southern aspect of his trousers, and lump the items together?

## Letter to the Editor – Carriage Charges
*(IW County Press archive for 10th November 1894)*

Sir,— Before we think of growing early potatoes or anything else in the Isle of Wight we must join in getting cheap conveyance, as the present rate of carriage is not only stopping commerce, but also preventing residents settling in the Island. Last week I sent a hamper of vegetables to London worth about 4s. and was charged over 5s. for carriage. Enclosed I send you the charges, made up to 4s. 5d., for a rat-trap.

Your obedient servant,<br>A. H. MACDONALD MORETON<br>Hill-grove, Bembridge, Nov. 8th, 1894.

## Bembridge School
*(IW County Press archive for 12th April 1919)*

A Public School on progressive lines for boys between 9 and 18, with large playing fields, overlooking the sea. Special features of the school are the position given to arts and crafts as instruments of education, modern international history and languages, civics, science, the organisation of leisure time, etc. The school will open on May 16th. A prospectus giving full details may be obtained on application to the Secretary, Bembridge School, Whitecliff Bay, Bembridge, Isle of Wight.

# Chapter 15

# A Seaman's Story
## – Mr Frank Brooks

*Frank Brooks was born in 1890 at Henley-on-Thames, and moved to Bembridge in 1894. He was 85 years old when recorded at his home in Swains Road during two visits in March and April 1976.*

## Up To Mischief

I came to Bembridge from Henley-on-Thames when I was about four, in 1894. My father Joe Brooks came here as the cap'n of a yacht for a man named Mackenzie, used to live at Vectis Lodge [*in Kings Road*]. 'Course, Mr Mackenzie was friendly with all the big nobs, and my father knew all the servants an' that. We first lived in one of the two cottages by the pumping station down by the embankment, then after about a year we shifted up to Elm Cottage [*also Kings Road*], which is where I was brought up.

Mr Mackenzie was an engineer really – plenty of money, you know – and he had that place round the embankment, that long building where you go round the turn, he had that full of model machinery. And my earliest recollections are going down there and stealing copper pipe and sawing it up in short lengths, then selling it to the rag-and-bone man that used to come from Ryde.

The first teacher I remember was Selina Matthews. Olly Robinson was another mistress, she was quite a character. She always used to ride a bicycle, she lived at Lane End and we used to put tin tacks in a piece of string and put it across the road. She was great on punishment, keeping us in and that sort o' thing.

As for Daddy Acre, we *all* passed him, he just stopped in one class, I don't think ever he had a Standard Two or something like that. And there was another one, Pudden Jeffery, and he lived down Bug Alley. His mother used to sit over the fire like that, with her elbows resting on her knees and her hands on her face (she used to drink a bit, I think), and where she sat she had two horns growing out of her brows, it used to push her skin up an' it grew.

Well we used to go round at night-times – down Bug Alley there was some excavations down there and we'd pick up the little bits o' clay and

## Chapter 15 – A Seaman's Story

roll 'em up and then go round and throw it at people's windows. When the spring came, we were always birds-nesting. Then we used to pick the rocks up with a crowbar and catch the lobsters.

They used to have Ashey Races then – proper races, they came over from the mainland. And old PC Toomer always used to go to Ashey Races, well I know we boys 'ud always meet him off the train an' play about with him, knock his helmet off and pull him about. And Jim Gawn lived opposite Sothcott's shop down Point, well he got married for the third time, very late in life. And we boys all went down there and called, "Why can't every man have three wives?" – that was a very popular song at that time. And his son went out and called Toomer, they came back and caught us lads. Toomer didn' half lay into us, took his belt off and cuffed us. I know we fell over the hedge – 'twas only a low hedge and low gate but we fell over that. But Shotter when he came was a great contrast from Toomer, there was no skylarking about with Shotter.

Then on another occasion – there was a reading-room down Love Lane on the left-hand side, and Tom Jordan was on the committee. And I know we boys got a bit obstreperous one night, I suppose, and they sent for Tom Jordan. He came down and laid about us: cuffed us an' took his belt off to us and so on. It was a boys' club really, nobody ever did any reading there.

An Early Bus in Ducie Avenue, 1908.

When we had measles at school, I worked for Denison's down Balure [*in Ducie Avenue*]. Old George Fry was the gardener and I used to go down and pull the mowing-machine, it had a rope on the front – one-and-six a day they used to pay me. That's the first work ever I did. Then on the left as you down Love Lane all the chickens would lay in the hedges there, and I'd go round and collect the eggs.

My next job was at the Bembridge Hotel – Watneys the brewers lived there. Well I went down there, cleaned the knives and boots an' so on. I had a little dog called Nipper and we used to take him in there, and they had some dogs – we used to bath them all together in the bath. That's the only two jobs I ever had ashore. I remember at the back of Watneys' place, they had a big shed there. A man came here called Aran Moore, he was about seven feet tall, and we all paid tuppence to go in and see him – he was the tallest man ever I'd seen, ever I'd heard of!

We used to bring the bullocks down from Bembridge Farm to the slaughterhouse, and we'd go down and help scrape the pigs after they'd been killed. They'd just cut their throat, then they'd put them in hot water, pull 'em out and we'd scrape all the hair off ready for hanging up in the shop. Louis Jones was the slaughterer and he'd stand with the poleaxe and hit the bullock. We'd pull the bullock down onto the block, an' I've seen him hit the bullock four or five times before he'd knocked it out!

## A Life at Sea

My brother Tom Brooks was eight years older than me [*born 1882*]. He was captain of a yacht called the *Sagitta*. He was a sailing-ship man, he was in a ship called the *Laureston* and they took a hundred and ninety-eight days from Australia to here. I was only a schoolboy then of course.

When I left school, the first job I had was in a small yacht called the *Claymore*, belonging to Fitzgerald. We went from here to Scotland; Ned Rooke was the captain, and the engineer was Frank Powell, and with old Mr Dyer from St Helens. We went to Sandbank to fit out, then all round the canals and up the Caledonian Canal, and I know I used to go out trout fishing with a man named Haig – one of the Haig whisky people; I used to row him out in the boat on the different lakes.

Then my next job was as a boy down the Sailing Club. I helped Harry Love get the Club boats ready and that sort o' thing. The Ismays were great people down there then, they lived at The Cottage.

Harry Love was a character down there, I remember some sayings of his. I know when I used to go up the mast to clear the rigging of one o' the boats, my hat used to blow off; he'd say, "Well you never knew your bloody hat blow *on*, did you?" He lived in one of the two cottages opposite the Sailing

## Chapter 15 – A Seaman's Story

Club, then afterwards he shifted up into Queens Road. But Harry and his brother George and Toby Bannister, they were inseparable in going to the pubs and playing violins an' that.

Then there was a man working there named Stripéd Stevens, he was telling us a yarn that he was gardening and he was sowing parsnips an' he threw some in the well, and the bloody parsnips that he threw in the well grew so much that he had to split them out of the well with bittel and wedges!

Then I was in a small yacht down there called the *Elsie*, belonged to a Mr Harrison, he was a magistrate that lived in Ryde. It was kept in Bembridge Harbour, and Fred James was cap'n of it, there was only about three of us there.

When I left the Sailing Club I went in a yacht called the *Vagrant*, and we went over to Holland and around the canals. Then I left the *Vagrant* and went into a ship called the *Ginette*, and old Newton Caws from Ryde was the captain and we went up to Scotland that time. And then I started thinking about getting my second mate's ticket, which I did. Well then I went over to Havant and taught a family sailing in Chichester Harbour, that was through the Sailing Club. I stayed over there about a fortnight and then the [1914] War broke out. I got the third mate's job in the *Caledonian*, that was a troopship; I did 'bout a couple o' years there.

Then I got my mate's ticket and I joined the RNR [*Royal Naval Reserve*]. I got in a destroyer there, but I was sent to Belfast to join the 10th Cruiser Squadron. I was picked out for boarding officer because I'd been used to small boats. Well then I came back to Portsmouth and got in a destroyer called *The Boxer*, which we lost in collision off 'ere, just off Shanklin.

After the War I got my master's ticket, and I went first officer of a yacht called the *Sagitta*, which was Cap'n Southcott from St Helens. Then after that I went to Nigeria, I went out as mate of a collier, we used to run from Lagos to Port Harcourt with coal. I got on the pilotage out there an' I used to pilot the ships from Lagos; I was out there for about 14 or 15 years, and that's where I finished up.

And before that I was in two merchant ships, I've been to Australia several times, and America. I've never been to China and Japan, 'bout the only places I *haven't* been to. I was in a yacht chartered by some Americans, we did ninety ports in three months in the Mediterranean!

Then when I finally came home after the [*Second World*] War, I started Lane End Nursery Garden.

## Village Characters (and More Mischief)

Albert Mead was a little man, I've been chased by him lots of times! I had a gun, and I went down Folly Hill and along the bottom, and I've shot several pheasants there. I know I shot one pheasant one morning early, I fired the gun and all the pellets that didn't hit the pheasant went down an' dropped on Elias Jeffery, he was just starting gardening at Old Garth, next to the Lodge. I know he shouted out, and I picked this pheasant an' soon disappeared!

Just after the First War there was an aerodrome just where that car park is by the Spithead Hotel, they used to launch the seaplanes over into the harbour. And before the War there was always an old dredger called the *Fanny Grab*, which worked every day and all day. Then when they built this aerodrome 'course they wouldn't let anything move about in the harbour, they just stopped it all, and that's when the harbour started to fill up.

Of course, that was the hub of the universe down there, down Point as we used to call it. Trooper Weeks was at the tollgate for years: he used to chew tobacco but you never saw him spit. I've been into the Marine Hotel many times for an ounce o' shag an' a clay pipe, threepence; in those days it was just a sawdust bar, sawdust on the floor an' that.

Vern Toogood used to be captain of the *Bembridge* that ran from here to Portsmouth; a man named Townsend used to collect the tickets, he belonged to St Helens. The *Lord Kitchener* went to Gibraltar after she was finished here, I saw her there three years afterwards. Then the *Dandie Dinmont* used to come in here and lay up top o' the harbour where the Brading Haven Yacht Club is now. She wasn't in service here, they just used to lay her up during the winter, she was a passenger boat. Then Dick Churchill always went by the name of 'Captain', but he never had any certificates or anything.

Toll Gate, Bembridge.

## Chapter 15 – A Seaman's Story

Bob Jordan had a stable down Weaver's yard at the Point, Weaver's the undertakers. We boys used to play about with *him*! There was no lights here then of course, and he used t'have a lantern: he'd always go out and pull the lantern down, and we used to go and put his lantern out of his hand an' pull him about. 'Twas just boys' pranks.

King Edward VII's coronation in 1902 was on my birthday, August 9th – that's when that oak was planted at the top of Point Hill. A Mrs Osborn lived near there, she used to send me for a bottle o' stout, tuppence ha'penny. And *always* when I came back she'd say, "D'you warnt the ha'penny?" 'Course I always said yes!

Albert Pocock was the churchwarden: he used to whisper in the church, and his whisper was louder than anyone's speech, you could hear him wherever he was!

Barber Potts charged tuppence for a haircut, three ha'pence for a shave. We used to send boys into Ashford Mursell's for a penn'orth of something or other and he'd blow up a bag and give it: "'Ere's a penn'orth o' wind for yer!" People named Butler used to make sweets to sell, and we generally went down there on Sunday afternoons for a penn'orth of toffees. And Old Devon an' his wife used to come round with a vegetable cart, blackcurrants were always tuppence a pound.

The old Preston's fish-shop was a down-and-out old shop: all you saw in the window was bloaters and kippers and salt-fish an' all that sort o' thing. And they also sold sweets there!

Major Windham lived down Lane End. He had religious mania, he used to stand about calling little meetings if he could get anybody to listen to him. And I know we found an old stocking, filled it up with sand, and we threw it and wrapped it round his neck.

Freddie Searle that had the boot shop, he used to live down Swains Villas. When I was a boy there was no houses in this road at all [*Swains Road*], only the Swains Villas. It was all cornfields each side belonging to Way's of Foreland Farm: you'd climb over two or three stiles. Then Chamberlain bought all the land round here, he lived in Windy Ridge, and Jack Gouge was his gardener. Then a man named Cap'n Don had the Elms built: he used to drive about in a little bath chair with a donkey to draw it along.

Jim Mackett was a kind of an indoor servant, he'd go anywhere and help, and he used to do gardening as well. They lived in Foreland Road. And we boys would make up parcels, tie them to a piece of string and pull the string just as the lady of the house was gonna open it. We'd send in Duckfred Woodford with the parcels. And I remember Mrs Mackett was very house proud – and she took this parcel and put it on the table, and we pulled the string an' it was all dried horse dung! All over the place! Mackett put the wind up us boys, because he worked for a magistrate named Harrison (used to live here in the summertime), and he said he was going to see Mr Harrison about this.

Bill Pope lived in that Thatched Cottage up Steyne Cross, it's derelict now; he worked for *old* Sir John Thornycroft. Old Neddy Pope that lived up Peacock Hill, he used to say, "Can – yer – tell – us – the – toim – within – an – 'our – or – two?" 'E didn' care *what* time it was! Kids used to go up there for an ha'porth o' skimmed milk and a penn'orth o' pears.

Old Tim H–– didn't know the name of the house he lived in! It was called Norfolk Cottage, down Lane End. Somebody asked him where Norfolk Cottage was but he didn't know. So they said, "D'you know a Mr H–– that lives there?" "Yeesss!" he said, "I'm the very man! Didn' know the name of the house because all the artificial flowers were growin' up over it an' hid the name" – artificial, mind you! But he just couldn't read, of course. He did nothing, mostly, but he was a renowned character for always putting things arse over head, sort o' thing.

## Chapter 15 – A Seaman's Story

# *Reports*

## A Sunken Barge

*(IW County Press archive for 17th December 1898)*

A small vessel, belonging to Bembridge, foundered off Ryde on Monday evening through striking the wreck of a sunken barge, which has been allowed to remain there for about a year, proving dangerous to navigation. Who is responsible for this? Is it not time that the Trinity House authorities were moved to move in the matter? Or must one of the Elder Brethren be sacrificed first?

## Terrific Gale – Disastrous Results on Land and Sea – Effects of the Storm in the Island

*(IW County Press archive for 12th September 1903)*

…The gloomiest piece of news comes from Bembridge, where it is feared that two visitors who were out in a small sailing boat on Thursday have been lost. Many small craft have been sunk or driven ashore. Excursion steamers have been driven to shelter and their passengers have had an anxious time, but thanks to the skill and prudence of the captains no serious casualty has to be chronicled…

Mrs Bull, the lady cab-driver, on driving over the Bank, had her carriage blown completely over. The shafts were broken, but she escaped with a few bruises.

## Heroic Brothers: Bembridge Fishermen Risk Their Lives to Rescue a Wrecked Crew

*(Newspaper cutting January 1912; entry in the old WI Scrapbook)*

It is to the heroism of the fishermen of Bembridge that the skipper and crew of the schooner *Romola*, wrecked on Bembridge Ledge in a fearful sea last evening, owe their lives. The lifeboat, after struggling to reach the wreck for an hour, returned to find that two young men named Attrill, in a small fishing boat, had rescued the skipper and two men.

I heard the full story of the heroism of the Brothers Attrill from their aged father, Edmund Attrill, formerly for twenty-seven years coxswain of the

Walter and Fred (Teddy) Attrill with their wrecked boat, following the 'Romola' rescue in 1912.

lifeboat. "Walter is thirty-two and Fred is thirty-one," he said, "and they are not in the present lifeboat crew. We heard of the lifeboat being launched and went to the foreland near the wreck, where we could hear the men calling for help.

"I did not want my sons to go out, for the sea was fearful, but at last I cried to them, 'For God's sake, go! and do the best you can, lads!'

"And they did the best bit of work ever done on this coast. They were able to get quite close to the wreck at their second attempt, as they started only 500 yards away, and they secured the three men left on board by holding on to a rope thrown from the ship while the men slid down it."

"We did not think the lifeboat could get to them," Walter told me. "As we rowed back we broke an oar, but luckily had a spare one."

They were brought safe ashore and two taken into Coxswain J. Holbrook's house, and the other to the Crab and Lobster, and looked after by Mr Wilson.

# Chapter 15 – A Seaman's Story

## Wreck Visitor's Exciting Experience
*(Newspaper cutting circa January 1912; entry in the old WI Scrapbook)*

On Wednesday morning Mr Percy Watton, in company with Mr John Holbrook, coxswain of the lifeboat, Mr H. Holbrook, and Mr J. Attrill rowed out to inspect the remains of the wreck *Romola* and met with a curious accident. When some distance from the wreck a huge wave caught them and pitched the boat right on top of the wreck, and stove in two or three of the planks of the rowing boat. Mr Percy Watton was pitched right out of the boat, but fortunately was able to swim to the wreck, and held on until rescued. The boat was pulled to shore with all possible speed while two were busy baling out the water, one with a tin and the other with a hat, and all reached shore safely, none the worse for their experience.

## Island Fishermen in Peril
*(IW County Press archive for 6th December 1913)*

Two Shanklin fishermen named Bert Kemp and Ernest Beynon had a perilous experience in the Channel during the recent rough weather. They left Shanklin in their open sailing boat on Thursday morning, and when off the east of the Island were caught in a squall, the rudder was broken, and the boat became unmanageable. A torpedo-boat towed them into Bembridge, where, after effecting repairs, they started to row home and fish on the way. They got round to Sandown Bay in the evening, but in the heavy seas their little craft was again badly knocked about, and when their position had become quite perilous another torpedo-boat fortunately came up and took them aboard, where they remained until daybreak yesterday, when they again took to their boat and arrived safely at Shanklin yesterday afternoon.

# Chapter 16

# A Pride in His Work – The Local Carpenter
## – Mr Walter Sillence (Part 2)

### I's Some Jolly Glad

One time down Love's shop in Northclose Road you could look from the shop door and you could see all round because there warn't no houses there then. One day there's a reg'lar thunderstorm and somebody says, "Look, Ellis's chimney's been struck down!" see, bin cut *off*. Well that there lightning struck and cut the chimney, come down through the glasshouse, pots with bulbs in all on floor an' that. Well I had to go d'recly after breakfast with the boss – I was still only a lad – go down and get up there, 'twas pretty windy too, and cover down with ruberoid and all sorts to keep the wet out of the house. And the fireplace in the bedroom was shot out into the room, yeah! Then after that they had a mast put up outside, and I had to help with one of the sons [*of Loves the builders*] to put it up. And what a good job that was, we was down there to put that lot up and raining all the time! So anyhow we kept at it, wet right through to the skin! He says: "Now look 'ere, nipper, go on home, an' don't you get showin' up down shop not 'fore three o'clock." Cor!

When you started building a house, first you had to get yer water for to make yer mortar and all o' that. Well do yer know how you had to do that? You had to dig a well, then make a jack pump stand and a well-curb. A well-curb is a great big circle. And you gotta use all whitewood, not red deal. Now d'you know why? If you used red deal, you tasted turps, but white you don't. Now why d'you wanna curb in there? Well I'll tell yer. As they're digging, there you are, you got it all rigged and made, now they puts the bricks on and they keeps lowering as they go, so she gradually lowers down, loads up with the bricks as she goes. They're safe! Nothing can cave in on 'em, and you can't bring a bigger circle into a smaller circle, so you got your men in safety.

And that would 'a taken a bit of time to do, about three weeks I expect, if not more. Then you gotta cove it in at the finish. Well I've seen a bricklayer building that all around, and then just when he's gonna finish, put his first foot up and get up out! Now there, I was surprised, there y'are, they know

## Chapter 16 – A Pride in His Work – The Local Carpenter

how to do't, yer see. So you had your jack pump stand and you pumped your water through a lead pipe. And if you didn't know how to make a jack pump stand, you always had it rickety, there was a proper way to do't. Well anyhow, all them houses in Foreland Road got a well. Well at Madeira Villa in Foreland Road – I dunno what they call it now – well we had a well for drinking and a rainwater tank there. And Mr Smith the schoolmaster had one o' them built, too.

O' course, Love and Watton used to work together at one time: Mr Watton would do the brickwork and the plastering. Now Watton Mews was a club he had built there and he wanted Mr Love to do the carpentering but he was too busy, so then he had Weavers to do the carpentering. Anyhow, Weaver's man went away on holiday so then I had to go up there. I done the counter for the place and I done also a big seat in a big window, I had quite some jobs there to do, 'cos they wanted to get it open, yer see.

You know The Elms, that was one house Loves built. I know I was down there, blessed great high roof we was up on and 'twas blowin' hard and you was right up on high trestles on a nine-inch plank, and you had to look out for the wind not to blow you over too much. I's some jolly glad when I had me first rafter, "I'm alright now," I had something to steady your gusts of wind then, you had to look out not to get blown orf. I used to like it, though, I thought what a priddy view all round!

'St Denis', High Street, under construction.

Loves built a lot of the houses in Bembridge. I helped build St Denis, that was built for the Reverend James.

And Portland House, Loves built that, then Old Garth, that was built for a Miss Collins. Another one I helped build was what they call Warner's holiday camp now, that was for a man named Paul Waterlow, he was from a big printer's in London, notepaper, five-pound notes, that sort of work. Anyhow, Pease had it next – they was iron people – then Warners took it over. O' course, that's been enlarged since then. And then we built a place there on the cliff for Derry & Toms in London, that's years ago, tell yer.

Oh yes, you had some good work in them days, you had to build your skirting up here somewhere, so high, well now it's only a little bit, about three or four inches and that's all you get. We used t'have to do a lot more work than they do now in a house, 'cos there you are, they can't afford to have it and they don't get the wood to go round. That's another thing. We used t'have some proper good wood, and Mr Love would get a lot come up from Poole, a bargeload of roof timbers, floors an' all that, and he'd keep that for a twelvemonth for his joiners – oh, nobody'd touch that, not for a twelvemonth. So he always had seasoned timber ready, yer see. Now, well beggar, you can't get seasoned wood, it's either cured an' dried or something like that but 'tisn't the same.

There's another one, White Cottage, along the cliff there by Lane End, we built that for an architect, Mr Ball (then afterwards he went and had Whitecliff Hotel). Well now then, he was having that painted up – and he used to dress as if he was a butler feller, sort o' white shirt and black in it. So a painter feller from away, I dunno if it was from Sandown or what, so he thought this 'ere was the butler, and he says t'him coming down the stairs, "We got a good job 'ere, we're gonna hang on to't". He had the sack that night! Aw haw haw!

## Round the Village

Jordan's Farm used to be on end of the shops [*in the High Street*]. Just out over the gate there was a pond and there's the ducks on there. Then top o' Foreland Road, well that used ter be the cow stables there. One brother had the butcher's shop, that was Tom Jordan. The man that had the farm was John Jordan, the oldest son, that was. Then they had a coal business, used to run it from down over Point Hill, just opposite what was the blacksmith's. Well the blacksmith Perkins used to shoe horses, then his son come into it afterwards and he built that garage place in the High Street for motor coaches [*occupied by Hodge & Childs garage at time of recording in 1975*]. But I tell yer, when motors come in *first*, well they had to be mechanics to do their own work, yer see, there warn't no *garages*. Mr Couldrey, he used to sell

## Chapter 16 – A Pride in His Work – The Local Carpenter

Stanwell Farm milk cart, with Stan Nightingale, c.1905.

petrol, cans of petrol an' oil too, for 'em. Then just opposite the blacksmith, that's where Weaver's had their carpenter's shop.

Another thing, the farmer used to come round with the milk. Well there y'are, there's the blinkin' feller dripping it off his hat into the milk bucket, dipping it out as pints, yer see. Well now look how much better 'tis with the bottles! That was Morris, up at Stanwell Farm up near the duck pond, he was really a wheelwright by trade. Anyhow, he used to come round with horse 'n cart, just a pony and milk float, and he'd come round with a bucket, morning and afternoon, every time they milked. Tuppence a pint. Then Prestons, they got on, well they took Wallsend Farm, and then *they* had a milk round.

Now top o' Foreland Road, that was a old school there, but was never used in my time, and Osborne used t'have that for a paint shop and run a bit o' plumbing and one thing an' the other. But it wasn't what so much plumbing in them days as there is today, 'cos Foreland Road, well they had no sewer and no water, see. And there's the old bakehouse by Foreland Road, where old Bastiani used to bake the bread, yer see, with the old brick ovens and that.

When we moved from the Lodge to Foreland Road – 'cos there warn't no lodge at East Cliff for the head gardener when my father took over that job – well then there was no houses, there was just the Limes and the Hollies as they called them two, then there was nothing but allotments. Then you come to two belonging to Jordan's, and up near Slaughter House Row the three Salisbury cottages, that also belonged to Jordan's. And also afterwards that bungalow what Lacey the farmer had. Well then this coastguard feller Weeks and Walt Caws' father – he was a pilot – had a pair of houses put up next to where my father lived in Foreland Road. My father's was called Madeira, Weeks's was called Lucknow, and Cawnpore was Caws's – that's all different now, all renamed. But Weeks was never in the coastguard services from what *I* remember, he was all retired before.

And years later when my oldest daughter was born, that was the first time we had lights in Bembridge, in the streets. That was in Foreland Road – we used to live in Number Two the Cedars.

Where Frampton's estate is [*Meadow Drive*], that was all Lacey's Farm. That goes as far as East Cliff fields, and they used to hire a cart an' all sorts, they did.

I remember when there was no Swains Road, none o' that was there! From Love's shop you could look and see anything goin' round, on the sea. But all this stuff's bin built since, yer know. Tommy Staples must 'a been one of the first t'have a house built in Swains Road, and Osbirn [*Osborn*] had a house built there. And on that other side, that was a man named Mr Barlow, he had that built, and that's how it came to start, I think. Then Love's done Tonacombe down there.

Down by the Point there was the three pubs down there: the Marine Hotel, the Pilot Boat on the corner, then the Prince of Wales just up the hill a bit, see, what later became a shop [*Ship 'n Shore, itself long since gone*].

There'd be the Point Coastguards and the Foreland Coastguards. Now, down the harbour the coastguards used to go on th'end o' the wall, but you can't see it now, all silted over with that there sand, right up level – well there

Bembridge Coastguards c.1906.

# Chapter 16 – A Pride in His Work – The Local Carpenter

used to be a sea wall there. I've seen it years ago with a barge right alongside of it, see, floating. You had fourteen steps on the end to go down: now it's all up level.

Now Captain De Bully [*Du Boulay*], he had that house there what's Greylands School [*i.e. in 1975*], right down the bottom o' the Ducie. When he left there, a Mr Cookson come there: that's the first motor car I see, 'twas a steam car too. I dunno how they used to get the beggar along, I'm sure. I 'spec that was back in the 1900s sometime.

And Colonel Moreton, he had Hill Grove and he also had Denison's built, and Pitt House, and also Swains House he had built.

The only houses that was built in Lane End then all belonged to the Smith family. There was Quilly Smith the oldest son, he had his – Milverton House, right on the front there. Then there was Henley Smith, he had his house up the top o' the garden. There was that there Mr Blake, he married a Smith; well then there was the Prestons and the Robinsons, a Smith girl married into each of those. And all of 'em had a plot of land of theirs, in that Smith family. Right down to the youngest, that was Blanche Smith, and she married a man that come 'ere to be the ganger when they built the sea wall at Lane End.

Well then there's that Miss Orchard, she married a man named Humphray, he come 'ere – him and a man named Wilcox – as a nurse for Sir John

Colonel Moreton and family.

# An Oral History of Bembridge – Isle of Wight

Lane End Road, c.1880s.

Thornycroft, that's up Steyne. Well Wilcox later took on the Crab and Lobster. Anyhow, Sir John Thornycroft, he was a man that built torpedo boats an' all that. He had Steyne Wood Battery built for a test tank he got up there, where they could run their model on there, he could tell what speed the things go.

## A Pride in His Work

I knew how to get round jobs many a time. We went to fit a key, and back in less than half an hour, we done that *any* amount o' times. Yet yer see some people don't know how to do that. We had one man go and fit a key and then after a bit they come back and say, "Well yer can't undo't, it won't do the other side!" You gotta put a key in *both* sides of the lock to fit him. But any rate, the country yer see, you got *everything* to do in the country, there 'tis.

Well I tell yer straight, I've never bin beat at anything that I went at, I've got over it somehow, there you are. And I've had some tricky jobs. I'll tell yer one job I had, that was to fit a blinkin' key through a oak box. So, this

## Chapter 16 – A Pride in His Work – The Local Carpenter

man kept sending up to Loves. Charlie Love told me, "You tell that man, we don't like ter send anyone where someone else is doing the work". Well I know who it was, 'cos he used to work for Loves at one time, then went on his own. Well I suppose he couldn't *do* the job. Anyhow, I had to go there and see about it. I kept filing away at this 'ere skeleton key I was making, crikey alive, if this 'ere beggar lock don't soon go, this is gonna break orf! Anyhow, at the finish, up she went, I got it. "Ooh," he said, "you *are* a clever man! I've wanted that box open for months!" With me all the time he was, you know why? When he come to get the blinkin' thing open, it was all full of silver cups and things, he had all sort o' silver in there! I said, "Well I can't leave it, this key—" "It don't matter about the key—" "You can't have this, I'll fit a key proper in me vice at the shop, I can't leave it—" "Oh yes, you—" "I shall take the lock home and fit the key proper." I took it and fitted up, well there you are. D'you know, some time after somebody else wanted a lock seeing to or something, so this man's wife said, "Oh you want to go to Loves, they got a very clever man there!" So yer see, one job gets you another!

Now, Robert Tuffley used t'have the windmill and John Jeffery was the miller, and I've seen the windmill going round but it haven't been done for *years* now. When the wind was right, he'd be making flour, grinding it up. And then it all got dilapidated. Well I had to go up there once, with others, and put a great big bit of pitch-pine on, where it had all gone. Anyhow, I got it up there. You had the end of the chain right up top; now you had hold of this big bit o' wood down there. Well Bert Parry was right up the top on the ladder, and I was below, ready to start hauling this bit of stuff up. So the chain's coming down, instead of goin' up he was coming down, yer see. Now when it was getting up there as like to sweep him off the ladder, "Now Bert," I said, "I wants a rope on there". He: "We don't want a rope——" I said, "I'm havin' a rope on there. If that there chain breaks, where're you gonna be? Swept off that ladder and killed!" Speak a bit of heavy stuff like that. "Oh I never see that, mate, I never see that, mate." Anyhow, I had it. And what you thought was a little wheel for to turn her round – and that had to come down and be renewed – it was like a blessed great waggon-wheel when you got up there, I'm beggared if it wasn't! I'll tell you what, it's summat ter lower the thing and then get it back up there too! Cor!

And there's one of the Loves, the bosses, and my son there, he's only a nipper, and Love says, "You do what yer father tells yer". See, if there's a job on, I should warnt to be there mesel', I wouldn't want to put nobody else there if I couldn't be there mesel'. Anyhow, we got it up there alright. Cor! One time it come on to blow up across the harbour when we was on there. He was one side and I was the other. I held on t'him, I says, "Alright, Bert,

Love & Sons workforce renovating the Priory, St Helens, c.1925.

you're alright, I'll hold yer!" And regular blowin' wet, we couldna moved, not before it was slacked off.

Yes, we've done work for an architect come from Brighton, on Foreland House. That was before *I* started, Foreland House was built. Then they had a tower, and old Mr Love asked these architects, "Well how d'you reckon to put it there?" Oh they didn't know how to put it there! They could draw it, but they had no idea how to go and fix it there. Orright, *he'd* do it. Well he used to think it out. "Aw, wakes up about four o'clock," he says, "an' thinks out the job," and I used to do the same. When I got the work, I wanted to know what I was gonna do. I used to wake up at four o'clock even if I didn't think I had it on me mind, and I'd have that made up in all different ways, and I knew what I was gonna do when I went to work. But you'd never believe you could think like that, would yer? Quiet in bed you could do't, better than when you was in the shop with others!

Same as I say with these box frames, sash cords, I was down round there at King's Oak [*in Church Road*], and there's a gentleman there, he says, "The worst windows there is!" I says, "The best, sir!" "Ho," he says, "how's that

## Chapter 16 – A Pride in His Work – The Local Carpenter

then?" I says, "What's a matter with 'em?" "Well," he says, "Look how they gets knocked about when you gotta put a sash line in". I says, "It *needn't* be, sir, if yer knows how to do 't". I bet he had a good look when we's finished, too!

Well at one time Mr Savile used to have King's Oak, he warn't at all a bad chap. I mean to say, you had to know how to talk to him, y'see, but he was alright, never interfered when I was working there. Well one time there we was building a great big place for several tons of coke, there was gonna be a shortage. Well anyhow he opened a window from upstairs: "I thought that place'd be done in a certain time" – I s'pose Love's had given him a certain time. Well I was 'long with the young Mr Love, not the boss, he never said a word. "*Yes* sir," I says, "so it would've been, but we're salignumin' the edges an' all the boards! That takes a bit longer but you got a better job!" He never said no more, shut the window and never heard no more. See, you gotta know how to talk to people, that's a blinkin' fact. I knows how to get round 'em alright!

## Wreck of the *Romola*

Now, old Joey Attrill was Cox'n of the Lifeboat for years. He used t'have the Crab 'n Lobster Inn and he was a fisherman, but when that feller was eighty years old his teeth was as beautiful as yer like – and talk about a constitution! He got the highest award, old Joey did, from the Institute, like you get the Victoria Cross, and his two sons got it, Johnny – well that's Walt Attrill, his proper name – and Fred Attrill, they used ter call him Teddy.

Well, they went out to a boat that come on the Ledge called the *Romola*. And his daughter was born on that day, his first-born, and she was born on the day when they went out in their open boats to get them fellers off that wreck. The lifeboat couldn't get in over the outer ledge, and they went out in a regular south-easterly wind, blowin' in there an' dark as yer like. Now ol' Joey, he was out o' the lifeboat then, I know what Joey said, he said, "I didn't know how ter contain m'self ashore. I thought I oughta went with 'em, I didn't know whether the boys should do't or not".

That Joey Attrill, 'twas in the rowing and sailing days he was a cox'n, and I'll tell yer, there was a vessel in the Channel showing signs of distress, distress signal. They launched the lifeboat, and they couldn't go, they was going up Channel and Joey says, "Well I'll have 'er, I'll go on up to Dover". And they got off Brighton and there's a tug that had her in tow, see. Well then he had all head wind back from Brighton in this 'ere open sailing boat. Old Joey got back with 'er, though. Talk about a sea dog! Cor! And that was different, there wasn't none o' this 'ere pier then, yer see, 'twas in the lifeboat house on the top, see, then they had to run her down over on a wheel and then out over Ledge. People used to go up round their waist and that ter get her away in.

## All Keep in Order!

Well when my father first come here they was just finishing the embankment, shutting the water out from going up ter Brading, that was over ninety year ago [*c.1880*]. At the same time, now I think 'twould have been better if they'd never had the embankment, and had a big harbour there.

Mr Occomore when he was in the Post Office, well he had the boats that used to run from the harbour over to Portsmouth, calling at Seaview, you could go over for eighteen pence return, see, old *Bembridge* and *Island Queen*. *Lord Kitchener* come in afterwards in place o' the *Island Queen*, she was sold and went to Spain. Well they used to come into the harbour, but when the tide was out, they'd land them Under Tyne yer see, then they'd have ter *row* 'em ashore there, but o' course people didn't come if they'd have to get out in a little boat, lots of 'em going back and waiting till they could get in th'harbour and come in next time. Yeah, frightened to get out in a little boat 'cos you get those big rowing boats, two men to sort o' row it in, yer know. Then when you got in there he said, "**All keep in order!** You get up close ter keep 'er trim, not the whole lot be…!" – and tip her over, yer see.

Well I went and steered the old *Lord Kitchener* once. Somebody wanted a ticket – the skipper, nobody on the deck, so I said, "What! I'll take the wheel if yer like, skipper". Well I took the wheel, cor! When he come back: "How d'yer get on?" I said, "I've never known a thing sheer about like this in m'

'Bembridge' and 'Island Queen' at their winter quarters.

## Chapter 16 – A Pride in His Work – The Local Carpenter

'Lord Kitchener' Steamer.

life!" And we was towing a feller, yer see. Occomore's boat, they had a little sailing boat Occomores did, years ago. They'd bring over timber and that from Bayley & White's for Mr Love; then Mr Occomore's son Herbert got to be postmaster afterwards, but he was a boatbuilder by trade.

They used t'have a pontoon down the harbour then. Well the boats wouldn't go Sundays, there they was afloat, because they dredged it out and there they was tied up alongside the pontoon, see, then they'd start off again Monday.

Yes, I knew what rowing was when we built Woodnutt's big boat store over there [*on St Helens Duver*], Loves and Wattons built *that*, yer see. And we had a big ironmaster come down for where the boss used to buy his stuff up, and he was a great big feller. Anyhow, 'twas blowing a lot of wind; they say, "Oh, you get in the dinghy, row 'im back ter Bembridge". Cor! What a job I had! The blessed feller stick in the stern, the bow all stuck up and the wind blowing me all over the place. I had a reg'lar job to get her to Bembridge, with the wind, I ain't jokin', 'tis hard work!

Now Saturdays I used to go with Walt Caws, he was a pilot's son. Well he was a boat bird, he built a little boat for hisself and these working chaps, would have like a three-cornered course, yer see, so you'd have a bit o' tacking and running and yer wouldn't haul her up. Anyhow, he used to put a bit to't and race for it. Well we used to go on a Saturday afternoon and get wet through, only a little boat. I've had him drive her and he's said, "Look out, keep 'er baled out!" – 'cos his father being a pilot used to say, "Oh, a bit o' strong wind today, son," and we'd have about two or three pigs o' ballast out there in the little boat! she was like loaded, yer see. That Charlie Love, he had the same sort o' boat and he'd have about three in his boat to sit her upright. Well, just me and this Caws, together, then we have all this pig [*iron*] ballast, and we'd have ter shift that and one thing and the other, cor blimey alive! We was always loaded, you couldn't get in, but he'd drive her as hard as ever he could, yer know, and this water 'ud be just lapping over – 'cos if I didn't bale her, she went down with the weight of the ballast, we'd have been left without our boat.

Years ago there was several pilots in Bembridge lived here, to take the boats in, to take the liners in. There's Josiah Caws, he lived in Sherbourne Street, and his son Charlie; the youngest one was George Caws, he worked for Mr Love, anyway he was a nice comical chap, always had a bit o' fun.

## A Glimpse of the *Titanic*

Another thing, years ago there was the Review of the Fleet, out off Ryde. Well you had any amount o' battleships, battlecruisers, destroyers, oh and submarines come in. And you'd have the passenger boats running trips round the fleet, yer see, and you'd go down through three or four lines o' ships. Some of the warships would come from other navies, what they call on the Mother Bank mooring there, that's what they call that. Then at night-time they'd be illuminated, all lit up. Well that's things we used t'have years ago but yer don't get 'em today.

Then years ago you had several excursion boats, paddle steamers, just to take you round, well, we could watch 'em going round from Love's workshop in Northclose Road. All that excursion work's finished now, coaches 'a got it now. Southampton Pier used to run a boat straight up to Brighton or down to Bournemouth – I been both places – and another one p'raps to Cherbourg. An' I tell yer, they fellers knew their job. Come on a fog there once, and one was going to Cherbourg, another one gone to Bournemouth, they come up and let go o' their anchors within about a stone's throw of Shanklin Pier but they couldn't see it – let go of their anchor but they done their course! They're doing their bit, yer know! They gotta know their navigation – outside work, and especially with passengers.

I can tell yer one thing I think a lot of people wouldn't know. I saw the *Titanic* leave here. She went from Southampton and she stopped off here by the Warner Lightship there, and she come out and dropped her pilot. And I was working in the Foreland House at the time, and I said to the lady, "Here's the largest liner comin' out". And she got her binoculars then handed 'em over to me. There she blowing orf steam on all four funnels on the steam-pipe. Little did I know she'd never reach New York. So ain't many

## Chapter 16 – A Pride in His Work – The Local Carpenter

could say that, is there? Well there you *are* – *challenging the Almighty*! We had an unsinkable ship – but did we?

Anyhow, the *Britannia* and the *German Emperor* would meet at Cowes Week an' all that, and we used to see all them big yachts come out here and go out round the Nab. Nab Lightship then, there warn't no Nab Tower then, that was made after the War, they was making them towers to block the Straits of Dover with. Now you know on the end of Southampton Water the lightship there was called Calshot. So they used to say, "Why was Cal shot?" Well d'yer know what they'd say? "Because the Nab didn't warn 'er." That was the Nab, and the Warner Lightship – didn't warn her, that's how they bring it in, see.

## Any Part o' the Island, Sir!

Well, Brading Harbour Railway 'twas then, yer see. Now I'll tell yer one thing – they made them *pay*, years ago. Why? well now, a man that worked on the Brading Railway, there's H.K. Day, he was the manager. Now then, they wants some fencing. So what did he do? He bought up a lot of old wire that they had for telephones or summing, got somebody to clean it orf, and he put all that wire for his fencing. But now it's all under the government, you gotta have all *new* every time. Then they made things go, and when he got his copper wire there, it was there ter *stop*, wasn't it? You take all the blinkin' things that have bin nationalised, well beggars, none of 'em pay, they're all in the red, yer see. Well they had to make 'em pay, one time!

Oh yeah, Bembridgers and S'n Helens used to use the railway, then there's a junction at Brading, you change there for to go to Ryde or to go to Sandown.

Well we had a lady cabby here, that was Mrs Bull. And everybody likes her, she had like a little trap, yer see. Her husband was John Bull, and he had a landau he used to drive. They used to meet the trains an' all, yer see. And they had Barfield built up there [*in Steyne Road*], that's where they had their stables; but before that they was up the High Street, next to the Grange, they had a place there when they started off. Well anyhow, these visitors come – oh, they'd have ter go in the *lady* cabby's, oh they thought summat of *her*. She was a very good lady cabby too.

And Sothcotts, they used to let out carriages and that, they had one or two chaps to drive for 'em. I know there's one, Harry Chappell – we used ter call him Ad Chappell – he would drive for 'em. Well there's a Sir Owen Slacke, he come here as a summer visitor and he was in Willow Cottage up there. So anyhow, he come out, they wanted a drive, yer see, so Harry Chappell come up, blinking ol' horse tired, yer know, summertime. So: "Where d'yer propose ter take us, driver?" "Any part o' the island you like ter say, sir!" Aw-haw-haw! The blinkin' horse couldna done it, it was too tired, ah-ha! "Any part o' the island you like ter say, sir!" Oh there bin some cards about, I tell yer!

## Humbuggin' About with Curtains

Now how'd you like a job like I had there, well twice, one at Saviles' and one at Tottenhams': blessed great windows, you had to go and take that out and put a new one in. Well you gotta know yer job to know how to do't, yer see. Oh I went and got it *done*. I know once I went there then, Tottenhams', and they sent down to us to come and put this 'ere new sewer in. Well I got all prepared, I'd been and got the lengths and all that. So got this 'ere round there and had another man with me, and her ladyship comes in: "What yer comin' ter do?" I said, "We're comin' ter put the new sewer in". "Oh you can't do that!" she said, "I'm goin' out!" "Well I thought you sent for us." "Well it don't matter 'bout that," she said, "we can't have it done!" Then ol' admiral come: "What's up? What's up?" "Well," I said, "her ladyship says that it can't be done. We're just packin' our tools ter be orf, sir". He says, "Well how long will it take?" I told him. "Oh," he says to her, "You go on, you go on and get yer hair done. That'll be alright". Anyhow, so when she come back after her hair-doing, she come there, says, "If yer like to go round the back door, there's a cup of tea for yer" – altogether different, yer see! Ha ha ha!

Then somebody had it after Mr Savile, a lady, oh she was a nice lady to talk to when I went to work there, but I don't think she could get on with the Sailing Club people, 'twas a bit sort of uppish or summat down there. I don't think she could hit it with them very well. Now a bad one I worked for was Mr M–– at Glenowen, just down the end of Foreland Road there. He was a brewer. Well, if you had a magic wand like that, wouldn't be quick enough for him. Always on, a reg'lar *brump*!

Now a Reverend Francis had Westhill built [*also in Church Road*] – we didn't build that one, somebody else come away and built that house. And Savile's house was built be a Ryde firm.

I'll tell yer one job I had, years ago. I was round there on Harbour Mount, the one nearest to Admiral Tottenham's, and there's old lady lives there, and I was on doing, well I was sick an' tired o' that flipping job. And while I was there, she was there. "Oh Sillence," she says, "Er, that them curtains down and put them other curtains up today". Anyhow, and then another day: "Oh er, I think I'll have them altered, have them back". Keep on humbuggin' about like that. Then, yer see, she had a drop-leaf table. "Oh," she says, "oh, er, I'll do away with that there, Sillence, that top'll come in for the top o' the

## Chapter 16 – A Pride in His Work – The Local Carpenter

cupboard in the dining-room. You make a cupboard for the dining-room, then it'll come in for the top of it". So anyhow, I took *that* down. Well then she says another day, "Oh, Sillence, I shall have t'have a drop-leaf table. I had a gentleman ter dinner the other night, and there's nowhere to put his hat an' gloves – I must have a drop-table". Had to make another one then! There's the maid showing orf to me. Well I said, "Tell 'er I don't want the job, tell 'er I don't want the job!"

Anyhow, Alf Love said to me one day, he says, "Are you doin' anything round there?" "No," I says, "I've not got nothing to do!" "Well," he says, "pack up yer tools and come away then, I wan'cher come an' start hanging doors at Conquest's house". We was building a house for Freddie Conquest, in Lane End – the actor. I was summing glad when he said, "Come down to the building". I thought, "Just right! I wanna get out o' there!" So I went down there, then anyhow, he come down there an' he say, "You'd better pack yer tools up again". I said, "What's up then?" He says, "Ol' lady wants yer round there again". I says, "I got nothing ter do round there!" "Ah," he says, "you'll have ter go *round*". I had ter go round, and she got up every morning and let me in at six o'clock! She was at front door and let me in, yeah. "Oh, oh, good *morning*, and where were you yesterday?" "Yes I had ter go on another job, madam." "Yes," she said, "and I went down an' give 'em a round o' the guns!" Aw haw haw! So I had ter go *back* there again! Begg'ed if I… I was fed up with the blessed ol' job, warn't nothing of interest to me, didn't want no blinkin' curtains ter be humbugged about with, I didn't want *that*! But anyhow, I s'pose she just took to me, she just wanted me to be there!

I tell yer one thing, she was bad in bed, and she told me, "Now," she says, "er, the doctor's comin' today, now keep quiet – if he hears you about you'll have ter go, an' I don't warn't yer ter go!" See? So I had to keep quiet while the doctor was there. Well then, while she was still in bed, I'm begg'ed if she didn't have two of our painter chaps to do the ceiling while she's in bed! Yeah, do this blinkin' ceiling! Haw-aw! I tell you! Anyhow, I was real sick an' tired o' the job, you had ter go shopping, or go out or anythink, yer see.

I had a priddy job down Tyne Hall once. Cor, was I down there for a long time! I had baths an' that to case in, and all the wardrobes ter bring out wider; then when I looked in the wardrobe, there's dresses right down to the… *thick* as ever they could be! I had ter make the kitchen table, I had all sorts o' jobs down there, yeah! She was the best lady I ever worked for! She was Admiral de Robeck's sister. She came with her list of a morning, tell me how much she wanted done, I get on and do't. And never wanting any alteration or nothin', like some of 'em. Then when I come to the finish, I said, "Well, is there any other job you wants done?" "Oh no, but wait a minute," she said. She went and give me three quid tip, yeah, that's money them days, yer know!

Another one up to Chetwynd in High Street there, that was Mrs Mertie Thomas, she was a Hanley and Mr Merton Thomas married her, then they lived up Chetwynd when he come out o' Tyne Hall. Well there y'are, she was always losing her keys, she was. I had to keep going up there ter fit keys. Every time I went up there I had half-a-crown. Well one day, they wanted a key to the wine-cellar and I had to go up there. "Oh," she said, "oh Sillence, I think I shall be gorn out before you've finished, I haven't got half-a-crown today" – give me two shillings. Well I got the key fitted: "Well, madam," I says, "I've fitted the key, it's all in." "Oh wait a minute," she said, "I must give you something." I said, "You did when I come in." "Did I?" she says, "well I must keep on giving". She found half crown, I had four-an'-six that day! Ha-ha-ha! I got some tips out o' some of 'em, I tell yer!

## I Like a Good Root

There was a chimney sweep, 'e was a regular doughty character, name Blow, he used to do the chimneys then he'd go up the Village Inn and spend it! that's how 'e got on with it. But he'd do a bit o' turnip-hoeing sometimes for the farmers an' all that. And he'd know how to measure up too for that! he could tell, although he never had much education, yer see.

Now the cobbler's name was Freddie Searle, and he used t'have his shop still where the shoe shop is in the High Street. It come into a greengrocer's there at one time, that was Warne's. But anyhow, old Freddie used to *make* yer boots, they'd come out alright! He used to measure us as nippers, and we'd have these 'ere boots made for us with him, yeah! Anyhow, old Mr Love, he liked a bit o' funning, and Mr Jordan he liked a bit o' fun too, the butcher. O' course, they were sort o' cronies, I s'pose, 'cos old Bembridgers again yer see. Well, Mr Love one day he come from the shop over Sothcott's and he had a bit o' glass in his hand, flung a bit o' stone at the door [*of Searle's shop*], flung another bit o' glass down, nipped into the butcher's. Out comes ol' Freddie Searle, yer know, and he see a nipper down the road there just beyond Lindsey Cottage, he went after him… oh and this nipper didn't know anything about it, he couldn't say – and then come down, as innocent as yer like, Mr Love and Mr Jordan: "Well what's up then, Mr Searle?" "Somebody bin an' flung a stone an' broke my window!" he says. "Well then, where, where?" They couldn't find it! Ha! Yeah, that's the game they had! He liked a bit o' fun like that, Mr Love did.

Then George Caws, he was the youngest son of Josiah Caws and worked for Mr Love, anyway he was a nice comical chap, and *he* always had a bit of fun. People say about, money is the root of all evil; he says, "*I like t'have a good root,* I'd see it never die for the want of water!" He could always put summink in like that, yer know.

## Chapter 16 – A Pride in His Work – The Local Carpenter

Bert Baker 'shoving' his fishing boat in, 1950s.

Then old Fred Weaver was a real good comic, too. He had the Marine Hotel, then in th' afternoon when they're slack he'd p'raps come out and do a bit o' painting for the firm. But he was really the publican down there. He used to say, "I've got the ooper-suitin'… in me parallelogram" or somethin', all comic, long time ago now. But he used to sing very good comics, people were laughing, yer know!

Well there's Bert Baker, he was a cox'n but got his living always off fishing; then he come on and he took the Lifeboat on. He had such big toes on his feet, he used ter stand there and just pick up a stone like that and fling it down onto the beach as accurate as you'd throw it with your hand! Funny to watch, that was. And Bert had a little black dog. And he had a carrier bike, and on this carrier bike he always had a withy basket fer taking these shellfish home, but he'd never take his dog with him fishing. And this little black dog, if you went anywhere near that bike, he'd *'ave* yer! And he'd sit all the time the man was gorn out in his boat, couple of hours or more that dog 'ud sit patiently by that bike, and it wouldn't do for you to touch it either.

# Chapter 17

# The Bembridge Lady Cab Driver
## – Mrs Maggie McInnes & Mrs Isidora Whitehead

*Mrs Maggie McInnes was born in 1892 in Bembridge and was 90 years old when recorded together with her sister Mrs Isidora Whitehead – also born in Bembridge in 1902, and aged 80 – at their home in Steyne Road during a single visit in August 1983. They were the daughters of Mrs John Bull, well-known to older villagers as "the Bembridge lady cabbie". The recording is prefaced by two newspaper reports. The first is of uncertain date but most certainly the first two decades of the 20th century, and taken from the old Bembridge WI scrapbook; the second appeared in the IW County Press in 1933.*

Mrs Bull the Lady Cabbie.

### Chapter 17 – The Bembridge Lady Cab Driver

## Only Coachwoman:
### Mrs John Bull's 26 Years with Horse and Cab

The only woman coachman of the present day, as disclosed by the census of occupations, lives at Bembridge in the Isle of Wight, and bears the truly British name of Mrs John Bull. She may be seen any day on the rank outside Bembridge Station attired in blue coat and skirt and hard bowler hat plying for hire with a smart landau. For twenty-six years she has held a licence, and it is her proud boast that she grooms her own horse and can harness him and be in attendance at any residence in the parish within ten minutes of receiving an order.

For funerals and weddings she assumes the additional dignity of a top hat. She started business with a pony and gig. From her earnings she purchased her horse and landau. Now with the business of cab proprietor she combines that of pig breeder and may frequently be seen taking stock to Newport market. She attends market personally and strikes her own bargains with the dealers.

Mrs John Bull has but one eye, the other having been kicked out by a restive cob which she was bringing over Ashey Down fourteen years ago. Before her marriage she was in service with Sir Donald Currie. She lived in France for five years and also in Texas, and knows something of prairie life.

## The Bembridge Lady Cab Driver
### (IW County Press for 8th July 1933)

A correspondent in *The Times* of yesterday wrote: With sorrow I read of the passing of Mrs Jessie Bull, the 'lady cab-driver' of Bembridge. Well do I remember as a child sitting proudly on the box of her Victoria carriage while she told me how she lost her eye. "There," she cried, triumphantly waving her whip, "on a thorn on that very bush." The horse meanwhile careering full tilt down Howgate-lane, she turned and over her shoulder shouted cheerfully to my petrified mother: "This is the very horse that threw me out!" The mention of Bembridge, even now, always conjures up a picture of this fine old woman, sitting erect as a soldier outside the station on her carriage, long since, alas! ousted by cars and omnibuses. It was with a pang that I missed her at her post on returning to Bembridge after an absence of some months a few years ago. I called upon her and found her surrounded by kittens. She had sold her last horse. "Too slow," she said, sadly, "though one time there was no-one could go as fast." Her customary cheerfulness returned as she took me over her house, so spotless that she lived in a

Mrs Bull the Lady Cabbie.

hut at the end of the garden for fear of soiling it. With her some of the charm of old English rural life seems to have died; and lanes and hedges seemed to make way for noise and tarred streets, raucous horns, and petrol fumes.

> **Isidora Whitehead (ISW):** My mother was born at Kern Farm, Brading, in 1862. Her father was a horseman sort of thing, and so she was well in with the horses. She travelled quite a bit to France and America, then she came back and took this job in Bembridge with the Reverend Nelson Palmer. My father had already started a small hackney carriage business at the Grange [*in the High Street*]; well when they married in about 1882 or 3 she went into business with him. She was the only lady cab driver of the Isle of Wight – of the whole country, I believe. I was born at the Grange on the 23rd November 1902, and then my parents moved the business to Barfield [*in Steyne Road*] when I was 18 months old.

## Chapter 17 – The Bembridge Lady Cab Driver

**Maggie McInnes (MM):** She had three horses – Florrie, Betty and Nelson – and she was going to Newport one Easter day and Mr Warne said, "Oh Mrs Bull I can drive the 'orses just as good as you". So she handed over the reins and the horse shied at some paper in the hedge, reared up an' kicked my mother's eye out. I was with her, I was very young, that was before 1900. She was taken in a trap to the hospital in Newport.

**ISW:** My father used to take the footballers to Cowes in his big wagonette. Mother had a wagonette and a landau and a pony-trap – between them they had three landaus. Father had also helped to make the road round the embankment, and odd days I think he used to work at the windmill too, grinding corn.

**MM:** I was born in Bembridge [*almost certainly at the Grange*] on 6th December 1892. I went to work when I was 12 years old for old Sir John and Lady Thornycroft as a scullery-maid, then I took on the cooking – great big kitchen, great table! I used t'have to make bread three times a week with a machine. I had to save the beef drippin' for mother, y'see. There was a dinner-party on one night, and I put the wrong coffee on, we'd run out o' the coffee-beans an' I gave 'em Camp coffee. I got into trouble, o' course! And I learnt a bit o' French: "Oui, oui, ma'moiselle," and a bit o' German: "Ja, ja!" "Pommes-de-terres" – potatoes, oh my goodness! Then when Lady Thornycroft died, she preferred to have the hay wagon to put the coffin in to go down to the church.

**ISW:** I used to work as cook for Sir Montagu and Lady Eddy at Steyne Battery, and I lived in the little cottage at the entrance, which as it was built as a battery the kitchen was like a prison cell, and they had a door an' a tiny peep-through – well I lived there for seven years.

My husband was a north countryman, and he came down and worked on the *Empress Queen* when it ran ashore on the ledge [*in 1916*]: he was an acetylene burner, and his uncles had bought the ship for salvage.

These houses [*in Steyne Road*] were being built in 1912 when the *Titanic* went out; they had all the scaffolding up and I climbed up and saw it go round.

SS 'Empress Queen' paddle steamer later to become wrecked on Bembridge Ledge in 1916.

My mother used to say to Tom Jordan the butcher: "Oh Mr Jordan, you always make an odd ha'penny." He said, "I can make it a penny if yer like!"

**MM:** I used t'have to go down to the slaughterhouse when the slaughterin' was on and bring back the innards to cook them for chidlins [*chitterlings*]. I heard the pigs crying, awful really.

**ISW:** Tom when he used to come round with the paraffin, he'd sell toilet rolls, and gas mantles, boot polish, everything. And he used to call on Mrs Wheeler in Dennett Road regularly every week, and he'd say, "D'you *warnt* anythin' today?" and every time he went there she refused him. Anyway he went this day and it was pouring with rain and she says, "Yes Tom, I'll have a tin of boot polish".
And he laughed at her and looked her in the face an'

## Chapter 17 – The Bembridge Lady Cab Driver

said, "Mrs Wheeler, I *thought* I'd get yer custom one day!"

**MM:** I had a little trolley made when I was a kid, an' tip my sister owt on it! Took her t'school in it, I said to mother that I always turned it up if it rains. Well she thought she'd go round and see and o' course that day I hadn't turned it up, it was all wet inside.

When Queen Victoria died, we paid a pound to stand in the grounds of Osborne House to see her coffin go over the water.

**ISW:** And the children had a saying if their mother called them in: "She bin callin' we, us don't belong t'she!" Ol' Neddy Pope used t'say, "If I sniffs tomorrer I shan't go ter work".

Quilly Smith used t'have a boat that went across from Lane End to Portsmouth, and they were going over one day and the ol' lady didn't think the boat was goin' fast enough, so she says, "Put another knob o' coal on, Quill!" Ha-ha-ha! And they took passengers over from Bembridge for half-a-crown.

Pewey Mursell and Mr Occomore went out in a boat one day and the weather come on very bad. And Pewey – he couldn't speak very well – 'e said, "Oppomore, Oppomore, you blubber fool, row fer the blubber shore!" Ha-ha-ha!

# Chapter 18

# You Never Seen Anythin' Like It!
## – Mr Arthur Orchard

Arthur 'Curly' Orchard and his Model T Ford Van.

# Chapter 18 – You Never Seen Anythin' Like It!

*Mr Arthur 'Curly' Orchard was born at Thorpe, Surrey, in 1890. His family moved to Bonchurch in 1892 and then to Bembridge in 1900, where he had lived the remainder of his life until a move prior to my visit. He was 93 years old when I recorded him at his new home in Carisbrooke during two visits in March and July 1983.*

## Early Days with the Royal Mail

I was born in February 1890 at Thorpe, Surrey, and we came to Bonchurch when I was two – my father came as head gardener. Then we came to Bembridge in 1900, market garden down the harbour, he took over from his brother Cornelius Orchard.

I was telegraph boy in Bembridge for years. Years ago the Royal Mail used to come to Bembridge with a horse and van, and the man's name was Jim Foss, he would get to Bembridge every morning at six o'clock, that's when postmen had to be there. Then 'e used to be there again at seven o'clock at night to take the mail to S'n Helens, Seaview and Ryde. And we used to work from eight o'clock in the morning till eight o'clock at night for five shillings a week, two suits o' clothes a year, an overcoat once in three years, and two pair o' boots a year.

And as telegraph boy I used to pretty well *live* in Bastiani's bakehouse, 'cos telegraph boys never had anywhere to go, so when it was cold and wet we used to go in there! Poor ol' Basti! And I remember at the football matches up the top o' Dennett Road, us telegraph boys used to get round Bastiani, an' if you was anywhere near 'e'd up with his foot an' *kick* yer!

Well then they was drillin' the well at Bembridge waterworks, at the same time they was also building Culver Cliff Battery up on the down. 'Course, Billy Muggins being the… "Telegram – the waterworks!" Had ter *walk* down the harbour with this telegram; if it was a reply-paid, you had to wait for the reply and bring it back. P'raps when you got back to the post office – "Culver Cliff!" an' you's had to march up orf to Culver Cliff with a telegram. Well then it got so like this we couldn't cope with it – 'twas waterworks, Culver Cliff, nothin' else *much more*, and they made the arrangement in the finish for Brading Post Office to telephone the messages up to Culver Cliff, so we was relieved of that eventually, we only had the waterworks!

There was one messenger there, won't mention any names, and at eight o'clock at night p'raps a telegram would come for – 'Love Pilot' – well that was Forelands. And what they used to do, the telegram generally used to say, "Look out 'bout three". Well pilot Love an' old Judd Bartlett that had this pilot boat used to go orf and wait for the P&O liner to come down, and bring the mail off this liner into Bembridge. Well this particler time

Bastiani and Osborne's baker's cart.

this feller – ah, he wasn't gonna go, 'e never took the telegram; 'course, the P&O boat was waiting out there for the pilot and he never turned up 'cos this nipper had the telegram. And there was a proper mess-up about that – an' "No!" he'd put it under the mat, 'e'd done all sorts o' things, he wouldn't own up – but he tore it up, that's what 'e done. Well then after that, ol' Mrs Love, she said, "You boys, you bring the telegram an' I'll give yer a shillin' for every one you brings over after eight o'clock" – ha, ho! We used to wait then, I tell yer! We used to get the bob! No more trouble after that.

Well after I got too old for telegraph boy I used to do the postman's holiday work: we used t'have to do a collection every evening, there was no bicycles, we had to walk from the old post office to Hillway, empty a box there at six o'clock, from Hillway go to Steyne Cross, empty a box there, from there to Lane End, through to Swains, down to the Point, and be back up there an' ketch the mail at seven o'clock! How many postmen would do that today? I was hoping to get a postman's job but those days the government brought in a scheme where an army reserve man that done three years in th' army could come and take a postman's job, an' us poor telegraph boys got done owt wi' that!

## Chapter 18 – You Never Seen Anythin' Like It!

Gardeners at Tyne Hall – Arthur Gouge? (left) and Frank Orchard (right). Frank Orchard was the brother of Arthur Orchard and grandfather of Ken Orchard.

Then I had a horse an' trap over Forelands y'see, pick up anything, and this particler night it was a mowing machine, take him into Ryde for repairs. Well, left the horse and van up on the green and went down and got the machine – 'course, me, fool-like, started drawing it back with a tick-tick-tick-tick... Horse run away! Ha! I was runnin' up the road, and some voice in the hedge showted owt, "***Whose horse is that?***" Ha-ha-ha! never answered, I kep' on runnin'! And I had to run right to the top of Howgate before I caught the horse! Those were the days!

And when I couldn't get a postman's job, that's when I took up gardening. I started at the vicarage for the Reverend Tapsfield, and worked at several houses in the village. I was gardener at Tyne Hall for twenty years, for Major Peel. All that land opposite used be a lovely great wheatfield farmed by Preston, and look at it today, all built on.

## You Never Seen Anythin' Like It!

There was three boys in standard seven at school – me, Brooks and Woodford – and o' course Mr Smith, 'e always had his eye on us. "Brooks, is that you talkin'?" "No, sir." "Well then it was you, Orchard." "No, sir." "Well then it was you, Woodford!" "No, sir." "You three boys come out here." We went out there, we had four cuts each, and we got back to the desk rubbin' our hands an' laughing at each other. "You three boys, come out here again!" We went out again and had another two cuts. Ha-ha-ha!

And in those days when the village was in darkness 'course us boys used to get to all kinds o' tricks, we used to put stinging nettles on the pub door, they'd holla as they went in, ha-ha! And we'd look out for PC Toomer of a night, no lights in the village, and if you spotted him you'd say, "A B C – A Bobby Comin'!"

When the No Man's Land Fort was being built at S'n Helens, what's called Nodes Battery, Daddy Acre used to work there, there was two of 'em. And there used to be a great big stone at the end o' the fence. This other feller says, "When I go by, I'll put a stone on the top o' this one an' you'll know I'm gorn." Daddy says, "Yes, an' if I gets there first, I'll knock 'n orf!"

And when the Bembridge Carnival was on, ol' Daddy Acre used to lead the procession, yes 'e did, used t'ave a khaki uniform and a peak cap. And on one occasion Tim H— showted owt, "Larnch the lifeboat, man lorst in withybed!" 'Course, he must have been drunk. And ol' Shep used t'like his beer, too. He was persuaded to join the Good Templars, signed the pledge, supposed not to drink any more, but 'e hadna' bin long before he busted owt again, yeah!

Freddie James always used to play 'the Duck' at the Bembridge Regatta, the duck hunt. They'd have to try and catch 'im – he'd dive down and swim

Bembridge Harbour Regatta Crowds on the Ferry Pier, early 1900s.

## Chapter 18 – You Never Seen Anythin' Like It!

under the boats and come up somewhere else! Oh he was a star turn at the duck hunt, ol' Freddie.

Old Nat Ingram used to live just up by the almshouses and they called her that 'cos she kept on about the *gnats*. And she used t'help Albert Pocock the verger in the church. Well we lived next door to her at the time, I used to keep rabbits at the top o' the garden, and she'd come out, an she'd be "Nn-nn-nn, nn-nn-nn" up the garden path wi' bits 'o bread, and feed those rabbits! And I told her time and time again not to feed 'em. Y'know, she must have overfed goodness knows how many and killed 'em!

And we used to go down to Hapgood's the tailor to get the football results, the County Press would phone the football results through to Hapgood and he'd put them up in his window – and you'd be surprised the crowd of us that went down there for the results. No wireless then for football results!

Barber Potts was tuppence a time for a haircut, and he'd shave yer for a penny.

Old Jim Bond used t'have the bathing-huts Under Tyne. Well he got married, an' I remember the lads – I believe 'twas on the Fifth of November or summat – I know they had a lot of fireworks and set 'em orf in his garden. And the policeman come round, ol' Toomer, and 'e got in among these boys and let go like that and hit Charlie Love right in the nose, made it bleed. Oh and there was a devil of a row about it, a proper upset! And Jim would sell lemonade down there by the beach, well boys went down and found it an' pinched it, drunk all his lemonade and took the bottles away. When they asked him about it, he said he wouldna minded so much if they'd 'a brought the bottles back!

The passenger service to Portsmouth was an old paddle-steamer called the *Bembridge*, and down at the Sailing Club there used to be a pontoon, and at high water they'd depart from there and come in there, but if it was low water they had to go and land Under Tyne, and there's a gully there where they'd keep a big boat to row ashore with passengers and luggage. And the cabbies used to come along the sand with the horse an' trap and pick up the passengers, yeah that's true! That was summertime y'see, then at the end o' the season they'd run a trip to Southampton, a shillin' return – time you got there it was time to come back!

Dickie D–– used to come round with a horse an' trap selling vegetables, 'e was a rough old character. Bembridge was playing football away on this Saturday, an' o' course always like it was they started fighting, and Dickie got foightin' with Teddy H––, who used to play centre-forward for Bembridge. And Teddy said to 'im, "Orright," 'e said, "I'll 'ave you when yer comes ter Bembridge!" Well when next Dickie was selling his vegetables in Foreland Road, Teddy set to 'n and pounced 'im, yes he did. He was summonsed and he was given a month imprisonment. Someone offered to pay the fine for him instead, but Teddy said no, and he done the month in prison.

Tom Warne was a roadman, and in those days they used t'have the gravel put on the road, bloomin' great pebbles, and then the steam-roller to roll it in, then they'd water it with a water-cart drawn by horses, 'course d'recly there'd be all the mud. They had this gravel stacked alongside the road, then when they wanted it they'd just put it down. Just for horses, you couldn't ride a bike over it. What a way of goin' on!

I'll tell yer another little instance. When they wanted to put the lighting rate on – 'cos the village was in one mass o' darkness – well they had a meeting at the infants' school. Ha! These ol' boys was against the rates being put on, so they went to this meeting wi' jam jars with a candle in! Anyway, the lighting got through – twelve lights with incandescent burners, and a clock that used to come on at night and go orf, but get a rough night there was always trouble with 'em.

Major Windham used to get in the street with these religious tracts. An' I always remember him, one Sunday, he was up where the war memorial is, and he was offering tracts to people. And there was some person there refusin'. Major Windham said, "Him that refuseth me refuseth him that sent me!"

When the Isle of Wight Rifles was first formed, there was thirty territorials in Bembridge at that time, thirty. And what we had to do, we had to get thirty drills in for the first year, and then you did not many a year after that. We used to go up on S'n Helens Green to drill, march round the bank to S'n Helens, drill and then march back again – wha' for? I can't see anybody doin' it today! Yeah. I remember once there was a snowstorm. Old Bill Couldrey was made sergeant: "Come on lads, come on lads," 'e said, "let 'em know we're not made o' sugar!" You never seen anythin' like it in yer life – in a bloomin' *snowstorm*!

### Chapter 18 – You Never Seen Anythin' Like It!

# *Features*

## Bembridge Parish Council – Fire Safety
*(IW County Press archive for 18th January 1902 – amended)*

Mr Couldrey called attention to the want of some provision in case of fire, and thought that a manual fire engine, worked by a volunteer brigade, could be formed in the village and a very good manual could be bought for £75 or £100. Mr Weaver thought they ought to get a water-supply first. Mr Orchard did not think that the village could bear the expense of providing and keeping up a manual engine, but fire buckets might be provided or something of that kind that could be used and passed from the nearest pond or pump. After further discussion it was proposed that a letter be written to the Superintendent of the Sandown Fire Brigade asking if their fire engine and appliances would be available for Bembridge and if their brigade had power to come if they were sent for in case of emergency.

## Three Hay Ricks Destroyed by Fire
*(IW County Press archive for 18th September 1915)*

On Saturday a fire broke out in the corner of a meadow near Longlands Farm, where there were three hay ricks, the property of Mr Thomas Urry Taylor of Bembridge Farm. The alarm was given at about 11 o'clock to Mr Alfred Watson, captain of the Volunteer Fire Brigade, by a Boy Scout, who was passing on a bicycle. Mr Watson immediately called his men together, and with their hose-cart they proceeded to the fire. Before doing so Mr Watson telephoned to the Sandown Fire Brigade. On arrival they found the ricks, which had got well alight, being fanned by a strong east wind. As they were on a high part of the land, the fire could be seen for miles around. The nearest water was a small pond on the lower ground near where the old village of Wolverton once stood, just above St Urian's Copse, but this was soon exhausted by the Sandown Brigade… The hedges were burnt down. On account of the shortage of water it was found impossible to save any of the ricks… The fire was smouldering for three days, and the ricks were entirely destroyed. The fire is supposed to have been caused by some boys playing with matches near the ricks.

## Otters in East Wight
### (IW County Press for 19th December 1931)

Otters have made their appearance on the land of Brading Harbour, writes Mr Cornelius Orchard of The Retreat, Bembridge. Mr Albert Mead, gamekeeper to Lady Thornycroft, found one dead last week, having evidently been killed by a dog. There is abundant proof that they have located there and bred during the year, as Mr Mead has seen evidence of their depredations. It is surmised that they have found their way there via the Medina or the West Yar, as they had been seen last year at Alverstone. They are very destructive, not only on account of the fish they destroy, but will undermine trees growing on the water's edge, tearing the rootlets and causing them to list and eventually to fall.

# Chapter 19

# More Village Characters and Tales
## – Mr Ernest Butler (Part 2)

### Forelands and Howgate

Crab 'n Lobster pub was 'ere then – not like it is now, though, ha-ha! You go in the side door there, there's the little seat along the wall there where 'bout three can sit on, or four, and the counter was a little bit like that, a beer barrel or two over behind, ha! Ol' Joey Attrill kept it one time, Frank Mursell had it – he come from Mursell family down harbour somewhere – then Coopers had it one time, Wilcox had it, they were the older ones.

Then some other feller had it. Some people were staying over there one time, one of 'em was the harbour master from Bombay or Calcutta or somewhere. They were pokin' fun and grumbling about the food over there, so my wife jokingly said to 'em one day, "Ah, you'll have chicken and

Crab & Lobster, Forelands c.1904.

Forelands, c.1900.

pheasant an' everythin' else up there tonight." "Ah-ha-ha! Yes, you bet we will!" But anyhow, when they went up there they put the dinner down in front of 'em, there's ol' beef, pork an' all the lot mixed up an' stewed up. And they say, "What's this?" He told 'em. They pick up their plates, throwed 'em right through the window! "Now go an' sort that lot out!"

Lady Fawcett used t'have Ledge House, she used to keep a lot o' budgerigars there, and let 'em all out. Hundreds of 'em flying about in the garden, in the trees. That wall 'long there, they had a plate-glass window put there, so's you could look through there into the aviary. And they had a trap in the top o' the aviary which they used to let the birds out. All day long they's flying, and night-time the birds 'ud fly back in and they'd shut it down. She lorst one or two, not many. She was a *real* lady, no doubt 'bout that. She used to give Christmas parties for all the children in the village, always summing for everybody. And ol' Ernie Wheeler used to dress up as Father Christmas. That's more *modern* times, really.

Judd Bartlett lived over Rose Cottage, and Ev Love lived in that little black cottage over the back of it [*Aida Cottage*]. But it was mostly just cornfields round Foreland that time, all come under Sir Egerton Hamond-Graeme.

There used to be a brickyard down Howgate what belonged to Love and Watton – Harold Hobbs worked there, and his father before him. All the houses round 'ere at that time was *built* with the bricks what they made

# Chapter 19 – More Village Characters and Tales

up there. Southcliffe was built 'bout the 1900s on the opposite side o' the brickyard. Some people b' the name of Adcocks had it built, I knew them well. It was a brother and two sisters, and the brother was a doctor, but he didn't practise *here*.

There was an old cottage where the chicken farm is now – man b' the name o' Morant lived there, he worked in the brickyard. Well then the next one below was the old cottage Harry Hobbs was brought up in, and the others was put up a little bit afterwards. No other ones wasn't there at all. And from when I was a boy up till 'bout 50s, some people had Howgate Farm b' the name of German. The son was in the aviation business.

## A Blessed Great Lump o' Bacon

An' another thing – as a boy I had a marrow, you seen 'em hollowed out, with eyes and nose an' mouth with a candle in. I was putting one down on the gate there one night, and I heard somebody comin' up the road scufflin' and falling about, so I run indoors, I was frightened see, I only a nipper. Dad was home at the time, he said, "What's matter?" I says, "Oh, there's a man drunk I think comin' up the road." He says, "Orright, I'll go down. Come 'long with me, we'll go down an' see." So I went down 'long with him. That was chap b' the name o' Sam M––, he used to live at Sandown – eventually he came 'ere to live, but anyhow at the time he lived at Sandown. He come up the road and 'e fell in the pond – well he walked in I s'pose, he was reelin' about. Dad fished 'im out o' there, and Sam was wet right through, lathered up with mud and one thing 'n another. Morris the farmer, he come out and he says, "Come on," he says, "I'll put yer in the stable on some straw fer the night." Oh ho! Next morning Dad went down t'have a look around, and Sam was there lookin' for his hat, and the mud out o' the pond where he bin flounderin' about, his hair was stood up on end, oh dear! Ah-ha! There was ever so many things like that, I s'pose. 'Course, nipper like, that just amused me!

Young used to go down an' have a tidy drop o' drink too. And Bernie Woodnutt kept the pub there at the time, and Young paid him summing, and Bernie give him the change. He says, "That's right mate, just right to a ha'penny!" That was a catchphrase for a long time! Beer was tuppence a pint then.

Ol' Shep lived in Hope Cottages, he was a character, orright. He liked a drop o' drink, cor! Used to come down to Crab. "Beer won't kill yer!" Well, we was comin' home one night when we lived up Howgate, an' along Walls footpath there was a big ditch, used to run the water away an' that. And the two boys was ahead of us and they stopped and walked back towards us, said, "Ol' Shep's layin' in the ditch there." There he was, floundering about in the ditch, 'e couldn't get out. So we got him out o' the ditch, and got 'n on his feet, and left 'n. We wasn't gonna handle any more o' that, 'cos he was soaking wet through! We looked back in the ditch, and there's a blessed great lump o' bacon floating about there. I dunno where he'd got it from, but he'd left it in the ditch, anyhow. Anyhow, we dished this bit o' bacon out for 'm and give it to 'm. Next morning, this is the funny part of it – tap at the door. It was Ol' Shep: he'd cut a lump o' this bacon orf. He says, "That's – fer – gettin' – me – owt – o' – that – ditch – lars' – night!" 'e says, "I've – brought – you – a – bit – o' – bacon!" I says, "Thank you Mr H––, but we got plenty o' bacon!" Oh dear, oh dear, he was a character! He was a general anything, mostly on the buildings.

Ol' Ned Pope had Peacock Farm them days. He had some *beautiful* cows, the ol' feller used to wash 'em and brush 'em – had about six I s'pose, summimg like that. After milking he used to bring 'em out o' there p'raps ten o'clock in the morning, toddle 'em down the road, let 'em have a drink in the pond. He had a dog and always an old sackbag tucked under his arm. Then toddle 'em down the road. When they got to a bit o' grass anywhere, ol' Ned used to put his bag down on the side o' th' hedge, and they was feedin' all the time, all the way round. Took nearly all day to go down the road, 'long Woodclose Lane, come out against where airport factory is now, round that road an' back to the pond again. The cows was feeding all the time, all along the road. That was reg'lar. Anybody comin' along – there used to be a Dr Lucas come from Brading, he had a coachman chap used to drive him in a little landau-thing – but any carts or carriages or anything there was about, ol' Ned 'ud get up and jogging his cows along, see. Soon as they was out o' sight, he'd sit down an have a pipe o' baccy, and let the cows feed all the way round till after dinner, then he'd put 'em in his field 'longside the stable, then the afternoon milk, I s'pose.

He never done much other farming. He used to keep some pigs, admitted. He had a field or two 'e used to make hay. We nippers used to collect all the hay for 'n, yeah, Alf Smith, Charlie Smith, me, Bill Merryweather. He used to get Ben Jeffery to mow it down with a scythe. It's dry one side and 'course green the other, all let down in rows where they mowed it down – well when it was ready we used to go up and turn it over for 'n, see. Then when it was right for carting, he used to borrow Farmer Morris's little wagon an' a horse, and he used to say, "I'm gonna hay-kiert t'night, miert!" [*hay-cart tonight, mate!*]. I says, "Right-o! That'll get the boys up!" Ha-ha! Three or four of us, we used to go out, take the horse out in the field and load up, then bring it up and put it in the barn. Ol' Ned 'ud bring out about a gallon o' skimmed milk for us! Oh dear! He was a character, 'e was! Then they had some pear-trees there, and when the pears was about he'd always give us some.

## Chapter 19 – More Village Characters and Tales

Ned had some bad corns, 'e used to cut his boots, take a nip right out of his boot. He had one good boot and one cut with holes in front. And I said t'him – well I's only a nipper – I said, "Cor!" summing about his... "Agh!" he says, "I can only afford one boot at a time!" He done orright, Ned did, he had some money when 'e packed up, mate! Somebody asked him where he banked his money. "Bank?" he says, "up under Down!" I 'spect he was seventy when *I* knew him, as a kid.

Mrs Pope she was a very nice person. She used to go to Bembridge with butter and eggs once a week, yeah, two little shallow shopping-baskets, one on each arm, one with butter and the other eggs. Mother used to get our butter and eggs an' that off of her. She had her reg'lar customers, reg'lar round, you know. And away she used to trot. I often run errands an' that for her, y'know, she'd always give yer summing for it. Yeah, she was very nice lady she was, no doubt 'bout that. She was so much the ladylike an' everything, y'know. She used to show orf about 'Edward' – "Edward this, Edward that"!

Then Clarkes, well they were relation to Popes, and they come up from Wales, ol' Mr Clarke was gamekeeper down at Wales, and they took it over when ol' Ned finished up there.

Mr Toomer the policeman used to walk round all the farms and he used t'have a good drop o' wallop everywhere! Bembridge Farm, and Stanwell, an' up ol' Ned Pope's. And Toomer was a big policeman, once round him was twice round the Isle o' Wight! Then PC Shotter came 'ere then, which turned out afterwards he was Sergeant.

Tom S–– used to come round wi' the oil. Ol' Frampton fitted him with a flippin' great hand-truck thing with a big tanker on, and Tom used to come round and sell paraffin. And he pushed that thing to Hillway, mate! How he used to lug that blessed great cart about, I do not know! People used to give him farthings an' everything, and he'd count 'em out! There was a feller b' the name o' Mr Poupart, and Tom used to go there with oil, y'see. And Tom says, "Yes, Mr Pou- Pou- Pou-..." He says, "Not so much o' the 'Poo- Poo-'!" "Orright, Mr Pou- Pou-..." Tom went there every week, the same thing used to happen. But figures, mate, figures, he could reckon it up just as quick as that. Yes 'e could, mate, a list o' figures like that, he'd have it before you added up two of 'em. That's a gift that he *did* have, I'll give him his due there, and Alfie Smith the schoolmaster 'ud tell yer the same.

I remember ol' Tim H––, he had two left feet! He was looking at the paper one day and someone says, "You got that paper upside down, Tim!" He says, "Well any damn fool can read 'n other way, can't they?" 'E couldn't read or write, mate! He was more of a general labourin' about, anythink, yer know. He didn't do *much* fishing, but he used to go out in the rocks, put his toe in, caught lobster or two like that! Oh dear! With a stick in his foot! Not as a proper boatin' fisherman.

## Defences

There was Barrack Battery, that's at the top o' Sandown where the Battery Gardens are now. Then there was Granite Fort, where the Zoo is now – that used to be muzzle-loading guns there, they used to fire a shot like that. They used to wheel 'em back, ramrods there see, rammed in the powder, and a great big shot. Well we nippers used to go over there after they'd bin firing, pick up the great lumps o' powder that didn't explode. And we had some toy cannons, me an' my brother, and we used to load up these cannons with this powder – *prrrh! prrrh!* Yaverland Battery was a little way's up; there was Redcliff Battery between Yaverland and Whitecliff Bay, that went over cliff; then the old Bembridge Fort up there.

And then later years when I was fourteen or fifteen [*in 1904/5*] they built Culver up 'ere, that was the ninety-two guns there. They landed the first one opposite the Yaverland pub there, between Granite Fort and Yaverland Battery: a large barge brought it over from the mainland. One chap was badly injured when they landed that one, so I think p'raps that's why second one was landed up on S'n Helens Quay, and a big army traction engine pulled that and got that up Culver. They was trindling it up to go up over Culver, and I was goin' to work from Peacock Hill to Sandown one morning, 'bout quarter six, and that gun was *right* across the road. I was riding me bicycle down there and bein' half asleep p'raps, an' I just ducked in under 't like that! Cor! they shouted at me! ha-ha-ha! called me everything – but I kept goin', mate!

Only other forts there'd be are White Fort – that's S'n Helens Fort – and Nodes Point up there, that was ninety-two guns there.

And the first plane I ever saw was, Gordon England and Grahame-White & Co, they flew from the mainland up on top o' Saint Boniface, gave a little exhibition up there, then they went on to Bournemouth. I was up Whitecliff Bay when I saw 'em go over.

Me brother was in the Princess Beatrice's Rifles, he was one that went down as a guard of honour when they took Queen Victoria away [*in 1901*]. Then I joined Princess Beatrice's Isle o' Wight Rifles when I was 'bout seventeen [*in 1907*]. I s'pose half Bembridge belonged to 'em then. We used t'have to drill up in the school playground and in the new hall up at Grange there. I did three camps out o' the four, one at Salisbury Plain, one at Yaverland, and one out Yarmouth there somewhere. 30,000 troops up at Salisbury on manoeuvres. Ho-huh – thunderstorm! Heavy brigade was next camp to us, blessed great carthorses stampeded down through the

# Chapter 19 – More Village Characters and Tales

Hauling the 9.7 inch guns to Culver Battery, c.1928.

lines, hundreds of 'em. Tents blowed down, cor! Then we went three days roundin' up all these horses!

## The Lifeboat

Well the *City of Worcester* was the first lifeboat that was ever 'ere. And my father went out with it one night. They had the horses from Foreland Farm, dragged the boat to Sandown. Halfway along they had to pull out a couple o' trees that's laid down across the road, shunt the horses out and shunt 'em on the trees and pulled the trees one side to get through. And they launched the Lifeboat over at Sandown that night [*in 1877*] to rescue the *John Douse*, a French boat. And in the morning they got one or two o' the lives orf, and the Coastguard launched their big boat and took the rest orf. And the Cox'n Charlie Searle was washed overboard but he never went *right* over, his leg was stickin' up in the air, and they saw his leg an' pulled him in.

I remember a regatta down at Lane End when it come on, oh, blowin' and raining, and there was a little sailing boat missing. And they larnched

'City of Worcester' Lifeboat c.1880s.

the Lifeboat, but I don't think they got them, I think they were drowned. I was only a nipper at the time.

Then there was the *Empress Queen*, that wreck out 'ere at Foreland. You can see part of her boiler in dead low water. She was running shuttle service for troops, wounded, and those coming on leave, from Southampton to Le Havre during the '14 War, but actually she was an Isle of Man to Liverpool passenger boat. And she run on the rocks out 'ere 1916 in the thick fog, tore her bottom right out, they couldn't do nothin' with 'er. But the Lifeboat got 'em orf orright, all of 'em.

There was a French sailing boat got on the rocks out 'ere [*Foreland*] on the outer ledge, and I think the Lifeboat saved *them* orright. You could hear 'em shouting an' that, couldn't understand what they said, though!

## Lessons in Seamanship

There was a lieutenant commander down Tyne Hall before Merton Thomas. Well there's a lot o' boys in the village all went to sea. Well when they come home, this commander took these boys down there and learnt 'em seamanship and navigation. Every time they come home, he goes, "Come down an' see me, and I'll give yer somethin' to take aboard the ship fer yer

## Chapter 19 – More Village Characters and Tales

Master. Now you write that..." He used to write out summink an' he'd say, "Now you ask yer Master t'help yer wi' that". And that's how they all got on. There was two Wallises – Bill Wallis and Edmund Wallis Trinity pilots, there's Walter Osbirn [*Osborn*] Trinity pilot, Ev Love Trinity pilot, there was Cap'n Frogbrook, Josiah Caws Trinity pilot. They was all boys running about together. Cap'n Frogbrook lived up S'n Helens but he was a Bembridge lad.

And at that time Ev Love, Trinity House pilot, and Judd Bartlett had a boat called the *Undine*, and they had the contract with two or three different shipping companies to take the pilots off the big ships. Walter Burden the fisherman, what was my wife's father, was one o' the crew that went in 'er. A London pilot would bring the ship out o' London, round so far. Well the ship would come straight on 'ere, and the boat 'ud go and take that pilot off – he'd go back home, and the ship'd go on. They'd go out in that big sailing-boat, go up as close to the ship as possible an' larnch the small boat and go 'n pick up the pilot. He was only the London river pilot, boarded out p'raps to Dover or somewhere, see. Well instead of stopping there, which was very uncertain place of getting landed all along the rough south coast there, this being a sheltered water they got the contract every time to pick 'em up.

There was a fine harbour there then, y'know. Well later years, after the harbour was reclaimed, I can remember when the two colliers used to come in 'ere with a thousand ton o' coal, the *Allerwash* and the *Ellington*. They

SS 'Allerwash'.

used to cross, go up North and get the coal, come down with a thousand tons. David Newman was the harbour pilot, lived in Woodbine Cottage. He used to pilot 'em in the harbour, take 'em up the Quay. When one was here unloading, the other one was up there loadin' up. Unloaded at St Helens Quay into coal trucks when the railway was on – little railway engine there called the 'Bembridge' used to take this coal to Sandown, Shanklin, Ventnor, dump off so many trucks, take a lot up Brading and leave it there for other railways to take it to Ryde, Newport, or anywhere. And that little engine, when the '14 War broke out, they took her over to France – proper little ol' square-tank shuntin' engine they called her.

There's two brothers b' the name of Henley Smith an' Quilly Smith, they fished from Lane End. They went in the Lifeboat, and so did Henley's son George Smith when Joey Attrill was Cox'n of 'er. Well Henley and Quilly also used to run a little passenger boat called the *Blanche* across to Portsmouth. There was a joke one time. Henley was sort o' skipper of 'er and he spoke down the speaking-tube, "Stop 'er Quilly!" And Quilly says, "Stop 'er? Wha' for?" Huh! Crunch – into Seaview Pier! Oh dear! "Tha's what for!"

## All in a Day's Fishing

George Bannister was a fisherman there, he used to look after Mr Waterlough's sailing yacht in the summer, *Atalanta* [*Ashford Caws called it 'Alama'*], then all the winter he went fishing, under Tyne. His father was fisherman, too. They used to go netting in the winter, bass, mullet or anything, see. I used to see him go round the village with a shallow basket with a few bass an' that in. Charlie Mursell fished from Swains, and so did another one what I can just remember, his name was Harbour, Crabby Harbour they used to call 'n.

Well then there was ol' Edmund Attrill himself – Joey Attrill as everybody called 'n, he was Cox'n o' the Lifeboat for years. Then his three boys George, Walter and Fred (Teddy). They was all Lane End. When ol' Joey Attrill gave up the Lifeboat Cox'n, John Holbrook took it on. Well then there was his son Dick Holbrook, he was a fisherman, and Teddy Holbrook that had the café here at Foreland, he was another son. They used to go way out in the Channel, mackerel fishing an' one thing 'n another. Holbrooks always used to moor up in the Run – that's a little river bed that comes in just on Foreland 'ere, and you can always get the boats in there when tide is out. One time they used to live in one o' the ol' cottages on edge of Foreland cliff, just about where Ledge House is now.

Now Tim Gawn took over the Lifeboat from John Holbrook, Tim was ex-Navy man. Then when he finished, Bert Baker took on Cox'n o' the Lifeboat for several years. Well he was there till he was over age and they

# Chapter 19 – More Village Characters and Tales

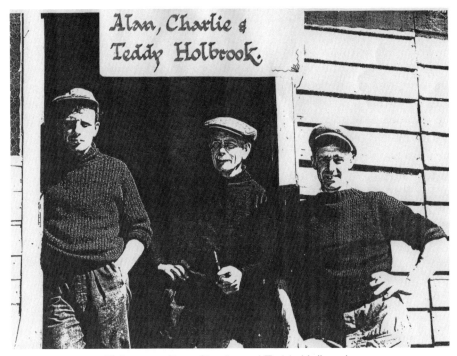

Fishermen Alan, Charlie and Teddy Holbrook.

asked him to stay a twelvemonth longer till they got another cox'n, see. Well then Peter Smith took over.

Then there was Bakers. Jim Baker, he had Alf Baker, Sid, Bert, Ev, and Frank Baker – well all that lot was fishermen, and the family was brought up in Isabel Cottage. They worked from Forelands, and they used to keep their boats in the Pool there. That's where Bakers always moored up there, Holbrooks over in the Run. Then theres the Gritton, which is outside the Pool, it's like a big lagoon place, *low* water, just a small mouth o' water comin' in. The Bakers had one girl, she married a chap b' the name o' Bert Lacey, an' he was in the army, and he got wounded in the Boer War.

Sam Mursell used to work from the Harbour. He was a smart bloke in a boat, Sam was. He lived in one o' the cottages by the Marine there.

Now summertime they baited the pots overnight, then when 's daylight just after ha' past three they's up early and out an' haul the pots, according to the tide. No good going out there unless you had slack water. They got bickerns* on the rope with corks on. Well when the tide's running strong, they what they call 'run under'; then when the tide's slackened up, the corks come to the surface, then you can pull your pots up, bring 'em in a boat, what

---

*a bickern = an anvil with two projecting taper ends.

they call "boat 'em". That's the inshore ones. Come back about breakfast time, seven or eight o'clock.

Then the next slack water they'd be out to the Nab Lightship an' haul in round the Princess Buoy for lobster pots, see. And that's why they had to be there on time to get 'em or else they run under. When the tide's running strong, you wouldn't see any corks or anything, but soon as the tide slacks up they comes up to the top. Then they'd be back somewhere 'bout midday. That's lobster and prawn fishing. Then in between that, they used to bait a trot – or shoot a long trot – a cord with a length o' hooks on, hundred or two hooks, anchor that and haul that, get a bit o' fish *that* way.

For the rest o' the day they'd ha' got their heads down, had a nap! Then up again, shoot their pots overnight. Go down teatime, bait up the pots, go out and shoot 'em over.

Well in the winter months they used to make up their lobster an' prawn pots. You gotta wait till all the leaves are off the withies, then cut 'em up, bundle 'em up and make 'em. And go and do a bit o' net fishing for mullet and bass and different things like that.

Well then they'd have to cook their fish, shrimps or lobsters or whatever it was. Now lobsters and prawns you gotta put in boiling water, but the slower you can cook a crab, the better 'e turns out. If you put him in boiling water, they scream and throw their claws, then you got a crab in pieces, haven't yer? So you must cook him in cold water, but when it boils well then you can let it boil, see. And you can always tell a good crab when he's cooked. Where they're joined together like top and bottom, the back part should be just hove up like that. And he hadn't oughta rattle at all – if he rattles then he's eatable, but slack.

Now if you go down and pick winkles, well the first thing to do is bring 'em up, put 'em in water with some salt, and change the water two or three times a day for a coupla days. That makes 'em spit out the sand then. That's the proper way to do it. Then cook 'em, spread 'em out on the draining board, sprinkle some salt on them, and rub 'em all over like that. And with a lobster, when he's warm – get a bit o' butter paper what you unwraps the butter in, comes up shiny, beautiful.

The fishermen had their reg'lar rounds, 'course all big families in the village then. Well they all got a living out of 't, mate, and shrimps an' prawns was about eighteen pence a hundred then. Teddy Attrill used to go round the village with a couple o' shallow baskets, shrimps or prawns in one and p'raps a lobster or two in the other. And if he didn't sell 'em, he'd jump on the train and go up to Brading and sell 'em there. Lobsters were four or five bob, I s'pose.

Holbrooks done lobster and prawn teas up 'ere at Forelands for years. They'd sell some and keep some for what they wanted. When they wanted

## Chapter 19 – More Village Characters and Tales

any lobsters they'd go down to the penner and take 'em out and cook 'em. Fishermen used to pen the lobsters in a wire cage in the sea, keep them alive yer see, and tie some string round the claws else they'd fight one another, wouldn't be nothin' left of 'em! 'Cos p'raps they wouldn't want all those lobsters that day, so they come and put 'em in there from the pots.

They'd have had boatbuilders to make their fishing boats. I made any amount at Sandown, meself. I built one for Caws, Charlie Mursell, Fred Attrill, Walt Attrill, George Attrill, ol' John Holbrook, Alan Holbrook, one o' the Bakers. Cor lummy, yeah! And they used to row their boats frontways, mate, they stood up and rowed wi' crossed oars, forewards. That was just always the way it was done, I s'pose.

Well then my wife's father Walter Burden was a Lane End fisherman, and he used to go in the Lifeboat. They lived at Elmlie, Steyne Road, and Rose 'ud come out o' school and have to go down shore winkle-picking for her father – frozen stiff she'd be, but she had to do't. That's what made her feet so bad. Then another night go round with a couple o' shallow baskets selling whatever her father had, pick a few crabs or a lobster or two. She daren't go back till she sold some of 'em! They had so many orders from the big houses – somebody'd say they'd like some winkles, or like a lobster or a crab, well she'd have to take 'em there, see. And what wasn't ordered, she used to go and rang the doors, she had a little mug, so much for a pint o' winkles. And I've seen her cook a copper-full o' crabs, with her mother.

## Another Tour from Harbour Gardens up to the Village

My wife's uncle, William Burden, they called him Bill, he had the market garden down by the harbour – Harbour Gardens they called it. It belonged to Thornycroft o' course, but it was let out on lease, y'see. Roses was his speciality, he had some beautiful roses there. He used to put muslin round grapes to save 'em, and put a little band round the roses to keep them just that size. Then he'd deliver round the village, and go to Sandown with apples and asparagus an' all things like that. My wife was housekeeper there for years till we got married, 'cos his wife died and he had two boys. She used to go to the shows and do decorations an' all that. She used t'have to pick all the fruit, and get up in the morning and bundle up the asparagus and one thing 'n another, and look after the animals. They used to win lots o' prizes all over the Island, even shows up in London. Before a show they used to sleep out in garden in a little tent and patrol at night-time! People 'ud have anything mate, if they wanted it. But he was a gardener, no doubt about that!

Tom Fry looked after the pumping station down Harbour Gardens. Then Jack Pittis, which was a Foreland Coastguard, he got the job after Tom.

Mr Burden with pony 'Stella' and trap, at Home Farm.

You could go down to Hapgood's the tailor's and get measured up for a suit o' clothes. You get anything there in the way of men's clothes, yachting stuff for the Sailing Club people an' all that, see.

Now Frank Attrill down there they used to call 'Copper King' – any metal or anything like that, if it was the least little thing he'd pick it up and save it! Had everything in that shop mate, *everything* you could think of – boating, yachting, nails, screws, tools – 'cos he was a sailmaker, really. Mention it, he got it – he says, "I've got it somewhere or the other!" An' he'll find it – anchors, chains, ropes, shrimp nets.

After Damp come up from the Point, he had a little workshop next to Sothcott's stables in Point Hill, and he used to live opposite.

Alf Weeks was the Guard on the train which used to run from Bembridge to Brading.

## Chapter 19 – More Village Characters and Tales

Sandown Band used to play down Ducie Avenue at the regattas when I was a nipper. And that field up the top o' Ducie Avenue, Hill Grove field, they used t'hold the sports there. Running races and sack races for kids, coconut shies and allsorts there. And the Italians used to come round to the regattas. They used to make up these wafers, s'posed to be ice-cream, but it's only a lot o' cold custard, frozen – well that's what we thought it was, didn't think much of it, anyhow.

Jerry Goodall was a big bird egg collector, he had one o' the finest collections in the world.

Alf Chick's father worked for Riddick's for a time, then he started that bakehouse in Sherbourne Street in 1913 – he used to come round with the bread. It was a little cake shop before that, 'cos my wife's cousin had it, name o' Jacobs. They sold up and went to Vancouver. Albert Jacobs used to work for Tom Osbirn [Osborn] that had that shop before. He used to drive the little pony with a covered-in cart with all the bread in, he used to do the village and up Hillway as well. Well then he took over from Tom Osbirn – he was married, and lived there. He was there about a twelvemonth, and he reckoned 'e could do better if he packed it up, and he went abroad. Then Alf Chick come there.

You could go in Bastiani's bakehouse and buy a cake or bun, a loaf o' bread or anything there. He lived up Abingdon Cottage, Steyne Road.

Potts's barber's shop was a proper den that was! Tuppence t'have yer hair cut, then. Well I'd go in there and sit down, there's everybody in there waiting, an' ol' Potts was yap-yap-yap-yap-yap all the time, and snip-snip-snip-snip-snip. You had to wait yer turn, p'raps half an hour.

I remember the Woodford's shop where the War Memorial is now. That was a different Woodford, they came from Sandown way. Nothing like a butcher's shop really, no. It was a nice shop, but there were never much in there! Ha-ha-ha!

When that big snowstorm was, in 1881, I heard my father say that you couldn't see Lodge Wall, the snow was so deep that you was up there and you didn't know where the wall was, all the way down.

Lacey had Jordan's Farm before Jordan had it, he used to live down Foreland Road. When Lacey had it, that was before the Council buildings was built there – there used to be a big farm gate there, and they used t'have the sports and the roundabouts in that field. Lacey's didn't have a slaughterhouse, they had it just as a little farm place there, they used to go round with milk an' that.

When we was at school we used to go in that shop that belonged to ol' Charlie Preston's mother and father. They used t'have a few boxes o' sweets an' that in there, as well as fish, and we used to go in there for sweets before Winters ever come 'ere.

## Chapter 20

# I'm Not Blessed Well Jokin'!
## – Mr Ashford Caws (Part 3)

### Where're You, Dick?

We didn't take no notice of rowing from 'ere to Portsmouth, no 'course you didn't! We went over three or four times a week p'raps. You had t'have nice little breeze for sail, but if you had no wind, you had to *row*. When you caught yer anchor, you'd go straight over, driftin'. I bin over Portsmouth with four thousand mackerel. You know where the ferry used to go across ter ol' Portsmouth, well that place there was laft purpose fer fishing boats. I've seen quite forty boats off there come down from Littlehampton and go out in the Channel and shoot the net; 'course, they couldn't do't now, there's too much traffic. Well if they had just a hundred mackerel they'd sell 'em for about a pound.

I used be 'long with Dick Mursell. Well we was over there picking these mackerel out, and very often used t'have a policeman stand there 'long by us for hours, talking yer, well I s'pose passing his time away. And a chap come down from up 'long the camp there, he says, "Another boat up there full up". So we guessed it was Ern Baker, 'e used to change about his partners. By an' by Ern Baker come down there. Dick says, "Oh," he says, "I thought 'twas you!" Ern says, "Finished?" Dickie said, "*We* bloody well bin asleep!" When we come ter reckon up, they only had eighteen hundred, we had four thousand! Lot o' difference, yer see. And mackerels not like herring, no, mackerel if they gets stiff you gotta sort o' lift the weight off their gills.

I used to laugh, I used to like to be over Portsmouth when they's selling fish. There's a man come down there, Pledge, I always called him *Mr* Pledge but they used to call 'n Dave Pledge, plenty of money. And there used to be all the men come down there to auction the mackerel, yer see. Well it didn't seem go up very high one day, several times it happened. He says, "I'll have every fish on the market at that price." 'Course, there you are, he had 'em! Well yer see, them other men that wanted fish, they knowed they could get it cheaper orf of him than if they'd run it up there. But he had hawkers used to take it round ter people, well the others didn't warnt too much 'cos they only had fish-shops, I s'pose. Well when me an' Dick went over there once,

## Chapter 20 – I'm Not Blessed Well Jokin'!

eight shillings a hundred we was getting for herring, they wasn't getting none down from up the north, 'twas a bit rough. Thought we had a bloody fortune!

We was down Portsmouth one night pickin' out mackerel, and a fisherman there 'long with us. Someone says, "A woman just fell down up the street there." "Ah," he says, "that's a bloody game, that is, don't take any notice o' that!" He knowed who it was. He says, "Somebody'll pick 'er up in a minute an' take 'er to a pub." 'Course, they *did* as well, he knowed!

We never used to go over unless we had a thousand mackerel. Went over there with about a thousand one night, put our mackerel ashore, and we's gonna book a bed for the night in a eating-house just off Broad Street – I ain't bin over there for sixty-five years! Well you could book a bed fer a shillin' *then*, yer see. An' only a man and his wife. "Cor!" he say, "good play on up the Hippodrome this week! David Devant up there, magician from London," he says, "me an' the wife in it last night, 's a good turn-

Fishermen – most likely Dick Mursell and Ashford Caws – setting off for the day's fishing.

owt!" So he says, "Why don't yer go up there, a very good turn-owt!" Dick says, "Can't go up like this, sea-boots on!" "Oh," 'e says, "borrow mine, borrow my shoes." 'Twas only leather sea-boots in them days: we used ter get 'em made up at Gosport. 'Course, I had *no* sea-boots on, so we went up there, we got in. Very good though, he done some good tricks. And then he had some gal, 'course all in it, up on the stage. An' a lot o' sailors all round, yer know, and this woman was in amongst this lot; an' after he done a good bit o' talking, took the cage away and she was gorn, she wasn't there!

So we comes back over to Bembridge, and next day: "Aw," Dick says, "we won't go out tonight," he says, "we'll give it a spell" – 'cos 'twas next day before we got back, yer see. So I said, "Orright." Dick come round after dinner, he says, "Er, yer game ter go owt again tonight? Perce W–– wants ter go over an' see that show tonight." (Perce warn't a fisherman.) "Aw," I says, "I don't feel–" "Well," he says, "it won't cost yer a ha'penny!" So I says, "Orright then, I'll come." So we went out, pushed the nets over. And they had a bottle o' Johnnie Walker whisky with them, yer see – I didn't know much about Perce W at that time. So pulled this net over and they drunk this bottle o' whisky, keep on sayin' ter me: "You're a bloody pretty feller, havin' no drink!" I said, "I don't want that, I know salt an' water won't carry too much o' that stuff!" So anyhow, we sailin' over, an' I s'pose I picked owt 'bout a hundred, little bunch. Perce says, "Haul the bloody things in!" – he's strong language chap – and then what I had, 'e says, "Chuck these b– lot overboard!" So he chucked them overboard, what I'd already picked owt!

Anyhow, we got over Portsmouth and Perce 'ud say, "Steer fer the red, steer fer the green," then he says, "I warnts ter b– well steer," three parts shot away. Dick says, "You knows what do, don'cha?" I says, "I know" – put a rope over the end o' the tiller, I knows how ter back her, I was up ter them games!

Anyhow, when we gets over Portsmouth – we must ha' bin a bit late goin' over – we booked up a bed first in this place, they had a good drop o' drink there. Then we went up the Hippodrome: full up, no standing room! Ol' Perce W says, "Now we shall 'ave ter b– well go *somewhere*!" So we went round to the Coliseum, and get sit right up the blessed front we was, and the first bloke come on sort o' taking a parson orf, see. 'Course, Perce shouted bit of his language an' that. Ah ha! down come an attendant, he says, "If you don't behave yourself, I shall 'ave ter turn y'owt!" Perce says, "Needn't do, we're bloody well orf!" So I thought, "Now I don't quite know where to get the tram down to the floating bridge from here. Now if I can get 'em down to the town hall, I knows then." So I had ter walk 'em down there, three parts shot away the pair of 'em.

# Chapter 20 – I'm Not Blessed Well Jokin'!

So we gets on the tram, 'course gets inside, Perce lights up a cigar downstairs, see. The chap says, "Can't smoke down 'ere, three of yer'll have ter go upstairs." O' course Perce, strong language again, wouldn't go upstairs then. Anyhow, gets down there, went in the pub that used to stop open all night for fishermen, *they'd* know who come in fishermen, yer see. Well I knows what that was, it was blessed cold. He'd say, "We'll 'ave a coffee royal" – half rum an' half coffee. We stayed down there till turnout time, then this other pub I s'pose. Well I didn't used ter drink. Some gal used to come round the pubs singing, yer know – I dunno where *she* used ter come from, I'm sure – 'She is My Mary', a song just come out at that time, yer see, and somebody go round and collect with a hat for 'er, I s'pose. Stayed there, then we went back up this eating-house where we booked our beds. Anyhow, had a bit o' supper – first time ever I tasted pickled walnut, it warn't *my* cuppa tea.

Then went to bed, we had a bedroom each, an' I could hear Perce W shoutin' all night. "Where're you, Dick?" Dick: "I'm in 'ere!" Perce: "I'm in the bleedin' prison! Bloody bars up the windows – can't get owt!"

An' I could hear all this goin' on. I think he got in bed, sea-boots an' all on, Perce W did! 'Course they had a good bottleful o' drink, them two had. So in the morning when we gets up, woman said, "Well what d'you want fer breakfast?" "Oh, fried steak an' plenty o' gravy, a blessed good thing for us!" 'Course, they blessed couldn't eat it, they had ter go outside an' heave all that lot up then. He says, "Think we'll go down that pub again!" So went down the pub again, and Perce looked at the chap who was stood in there: 'e says, "Yer face's pretty familiar!" "Yes," he says, "I had a job turn you owt last night!"

## More Fishermen and More Characters

Walt Mursell and his son Charlie, they used to do the same as we did, used to go potting summertime and then netting wintertime, only up t'about Christmas, then they'd make their pots outdoors, yer see. Used to live in Sherbourne Street. Charlie'd go round the village selling fish, and Walt 'ud send the prawns to London in the spring when nowhere else to sell 'em, nobody 'ere to buy 'em.

Now Ernie Baker, he used to do a bit o' yachtin' too. They used ter call 'n 'Fly-at-yer': if it didn't suit 'n, he'd fly at yer! He lived down Flint Cottage *[in Station Road]*. In the winter once or twice he went out to the Mediterranean, racing. He said he used t'have two oilskins on, one back and one front, keep the spray orf! Dear oh dear! Ern Baker used to go over Portsmouth 'long with Daddy Acre, wi' the mackerel or summing. Well there was a gal over there singin', I told yer, 'She is My Mary', when that song first come out. Irish she was, and she used to come round the pubs singing. An' Daddy says,

"Where d'yer come from?" She says, "Northmeads". Daddy: "I've a good mind ter come 'ome with yer!" He only said for a bit o' fun, anything! She used go round collecting, a few coppers I s'pose, I dunno how she done.

Bill Love used to live in what they call St Veronica now, where the nuns was [*in Lane End*]. He was getting on yer see when *I* remember him, he used to do lobster pots an' shrimp pots, that's all.

Ol' Joey Attrill couldn't get no king crabs once for baiting his pots, so he went down to Ryde to ketch him some – he went on the spree and stayed down there all night! Dunno whether he got any crabs! His son George used to go fishing but then sometimes he'd work for Tom Occomore carrying across from Portsmouth. It was hard work. George nearly had accident: the chain broke when they was liftin' up some crates or summat.

Ol' Teddy Attrill was a bit of a devil, yer know, 'e was *orright*, but anything went with him. He used t'have outboard engine fitted on his boat and if it wouldn't go he used to set fire to't – an' it nearly blessed well got blowed up! Then eventually there orf Whitecliff he fell overboard, lightin' it. Now

Teddy Attrill, fisherman.

## Chapter 20 – I'm Not Blessed Well Jokin'!

my brother Herb, we had an inboard motor, afterwards, on the boat. He was a couple o' mile orf an' he couldn't get the motor to go. One o' those hoppers come in, so Herb put his hand up to 'n. He had a sail in the boat, only a low sail, so he thought, "If I can get a tow into the No Man's Fort, I could sail down then t'Under Tyne." Anyhow bifore they got up there he got the motor to go, and then he went out and towed Teddy Attrill in, orf where he was bifore, yes he did! You'd ha' thought he'd 'a come on home, wouldn't yer?

Reuben Mursell used to live down Mentone Cottage, down the Point. His father Frank used to keep the Marine Hotel. Reub couldn't make pots, he had to *buy* his pots. He used to go winkle-picking and the money he got from winkle-picking paid for his pots. He went fishin' from Under Tyne; then during the First War he didn't want ter join up so he went orf on a lightship for 'bout a month, then he got a job down Cowes. Then after War, well he had his two boats up Fisherman's Square, and a tree fell down and smashed both of 'em, and so he couldn't go fishing no more. He only had one insured, and he got fifty pound for 't. He just did a bit o' shrimpin' then. The tree smashed one o' Dick's up too, so Dick only had one boat then.

Spratty K—— [*from Sandown*], he'd have any boat he could get! He oughta bin a millionaire, the money 'e wasted, ha! true 's I live. But the police was always after him, always reckoned he's drunk, *but he blessed well warn't drunk*, he went straight after down Sandown, larnched a canoe an' rowed out round the pier somewhere and the police was frightened to go after 'n, he's in a canoe! He warn't drunk, was 'e? He used to go over Portsmouth and buy anything he could buy cheap. Then when strawberries out, he used to go and get a load o' strawberries. He came down by Lane End as well: "Anything you warnts tomorrow? D'you wanna anchor? what 'bout anchor?" "No, don't think so." "I can *get* yer one!" "That's orright, that's orright." Next morning yer'll have a anchor in yer boat, I dunno where he got it, but it'd be in the boat! ha-ha! "How much?" "'Bout 'arf a crown!" Oh dear, oh dear!

Now Crabby Harbour was another fisherman and he lived next door 'ere [*in St Helens View*]. I think his wife must 'a bin Sarah (Sally) Smith's sister. He lived downstairs and slept in the kitchen. He was a very strong man – yes 'e was, I knowed 'n – and he used t'have the rheumatism: you could see him put his stick down in the road and hold onto his knee, the pain. Well he went fishing afterwards, I don't think he went fishing first. He an' his nephew used t'have a barge and load up wi' sand and take it up 'long the coast. Now he'd chuck in sixty ton o' sand – *chuck* it in just with a shovel – not trolley it wi' barrels but throw it in over, sixty ton in a tide! He were *very* strong, he was. Well he and his nephew afterwards walked from 'ere down Foreland to go fishin', and they got a place down there called Crabby's Run, near the pool, and he used to keep his boat down there. Then after he finished fishing when he retired, they had two boats pulled up there: the *City of Worcester* was one, the first lifeboat, yer see.

Sam Mursell used to do a *little* bit o' fishin' but he wasn't a proper fisherman. He used to sort o' do anything, any barge wanted be loading, he'd be up load a barge. And he had a few lobster pots, he used to go round Whitecliff with 'em, he was a Sandown Mursell really.

Now Tim H–– used to reckon he put his foot in the water and the lobster 'ud get hold of his toe an' he'd pull him out, but agh! blessed lobster wouldn't bite on yer toe like that! He didn't know where 'e lived, tell yer the truth! Some people were wanting to know where he lived – they said, "Where's Norfolk Cottage?" He said, "I dunno, who lives there?" "A Mr George Reed." Tim said, "I'm the very man!" But you couldn't beat him playing cards or anything like that, by gum! They used to come in the Village Inn there – they say, "'Ere's ol' Tim comin'." Charlie Keeping 'ud just pick up a hand before he comes in – that was done purpose, yer know, so he shouldn't play. Tim 'ud say, "That's that blessed Charlie Keeping, I knows who that is!"

There was a little crowd Under Tyne: Kingy Woodford – his name was George really – and his brother Ern, Jimmy Holbrook – his real name was Arthur, and the other George Woodford, they used to come down there nearly every night for a row. And they'd train down there for the regattas

Sam and Charlie Mursell.

# Chapter 20 – I'm Not Blessed Well Jokin'!

– always wanted to borrow the boat after you put yer pots out, then by 'n by they got a racing skip from Bonchurch. And they rowed round Frank Holbrook and Fred Love, they rowed round *them*.

Well Kingy an' Ern were Wreaf Woodford's brothers. Kingy used to work for Tom Jordan the butcher, that was bifore Wreaf had his shop 'ere. He married a girl from down Balure and went out to Canada. Ern Woodford just started gardener for Mrs Philips what was down Hill Grove. Then when she left there, he went gardener 'long for Denison's, he was under-gardener for George Fry.

George Woodford came from Bonchurch, he was a gardener down the Vicarage, but he got killed in the First War.

## Some Pretty Lucky Escapes

I caught a lobster once, ten pound after he's cooked! Now I's very lucky getting *him*, 'e was on the top of a shrimp pot, that big lobster, I reckon he'd ha' weighed 'bout eleven pound an' half, before he was cooked. We caught 'n just this side o' the lifeboat house, well you could nearly paddle there when's low tide, there warn't no more than nine foot o' water when we caught 'n. I had t'have two hands ter get around him. Ol' Curtis was comin' at that time – he said, "Well I could give yer thirty bob for it, but it'd pay you to let me raffle 'im orf, I knows Charlie Kitchen" [*landlord of the Marine Hotel*]. "So m' son," he says, "can I have 'im?" Well we got four pounds five shillings for him, and there, I s'pose Curtis and Charlie Kitchen got two or three pounds each, they didn't do it for nothin', yer know!

Now if yer going fishin', you mustn't take no notice o' the weather – if you *gotta* go, you *gotta* go, if 'tain't too bad. You gotta risk a little bit, you know, sometimes. You mun't think that every day's gonna be fine, because it *ain't*. You had ter sort o' study the weather round, sort o' work it out for yerself, you can't get people to work that out for you, you understand that. But I don't think we gets the weather now we used t'have, yer know! I seen Ernie Baker and Dick Mursell going down shore wi' their jersey, well not *on* but just put round an' under, just their sleeves tied round the neck, yer know, chucks over their shoulders.

I think I've had some pretty lucky escapes in my time, one way an' another, **I'm not blessed well jokin'**! When Bert Baker an' Alan Holbrook an' Spratty Kemp and we was after herrings down Little Forelands, it was blowin' a proper stripper, it was. And me and George Bannister, we rowed down there and shot our nets, and it come on ter blow, and Bert Baker an' Alan Holbrook an' Spratty Kemp, they lorst their nets! They were drove away, well not really drove away – they would ha' bin if those steamers hadn't been there, 'cos they went and hold on behind one of 'em, tied on, and they larnched the lifeboat and brought them in afterwards. And me and George was down well orf the Coles [*Cole Rock*], and George says, "We'll have ter try an' get the nets". I said, "Well you try back an' I'll haul in," and I think we had about three thousand there. We was outside the fort, an' he was rowing, and I was pushin' and shovin', yer see, and he says, "Orright, we're holdin' our own, we'll get up by the side o' the Coles, we shall be orright". And so we did, we managed to get in, rowing we was, mate. And o' course years ago, 'tisn't like 'tis now, yer know, if the wind was blowin' it warn't nothing ter see about twenty big steamers all being brawled up 'ere, yer see. And p'raps they'd go then in the evening, p'raps next day they's *back* again! Now they got television, they can get the weather whilst they can. Bert Baker and Alan Holbrook, they had a motor-boat, the *Patter*, she was a nice little boat, belonged to Lord Herschell, I think he give it to Bert Baker.

I had a small boat, the *Dorothy*. Then I had one built for fourteen pound. Fred Burden walked over Sandown and picked the timber out and brought it up on the lorry, and they couldn't get up Steyne Hill, so they had t'unload and go back and get another lot. And Fred Burden 'e built one for me, one for Dick Mursell, one for Ernie Baker, and then he built one for Jack Holbrook. Me and m' wife was orf in the boat the time Bleriot flew over: that's the first time she came out wi' me in the boat I think. We didn't know what it was,

At the Fishermen's Hut, Swains Beach c.1910.

## Chapter 20 – I'm Not Blessed Well Jokin'!

yer see – just up in the air a bit! He flew from over Gosport down to Ventnor.

Well they only put names on boats during the First War, when you had t'have names an' numbers on, see. And then you had t'have a permit to go fishing, yer see. And they come down one day and rounded all the boats up. And Henley Smith, 'e didn't have his permit and he left his boat down Lane End and went on up home. I said t'Herb, "Oh," I said, "I got mine in a little tin in me pocket" – an' I couldn't find the blessed thing! So they started towing us up towards the examination boat, yer see. I say, "Lemme 'ave a look," and then I found 'n, an' I says, "'Ere's the bloomin' thing!" So we had permission to go. But Quilly Smith: "I'll see my solicitor 'bowt this!" He didn't know 'bout permits then.

We used a truck down shore, used to take it 'long on the sand for winkles – that's when the soldiers was on guard down there, see. We went along shore one day wi' this blessed trolley, a soldier really looked over our passport when we went along, then when we come back the same soldier's on, damned if he didn't stop us again! Herb says, "You stopped us just now." He says, "I know, but I warnts to make *sure*!" And George Bannister was out fishing one day and he saw a bomb land right on top o' one o' the trawlers: 'twas anchored orf there and was blowed up d'recly.

I always used to haul a net when I was on with Dick Mursell or George Bannister. In the *May Queen* we had ten nets, yer know, and didn't take any notice of it. We had them mackerel nets, and they'd be heavier than nylon nets, too! I was out 'long with George Bannister once, hauling some nets up against the Coles, and a *blessed* swell come there, and we only had a big anchor and the rope in. And I said to George, "Look owt!" – George Bannister big, big man he was – a blessed swell come in and took the anchor overboard, the anchor rope wrapped round his feet. That tipped 'n arse over head into the bow o' the boat! "Cor! Gracious me!" I said, "we gonna let the net go now?" He said, "That's orright". No nother swell didn't come, only seemed to be that one, I dunno!

George and me used to go down as fer as Bonchurch, and one time we got down Ventnor, short off there to the south'ard, 'twere blowin' pretty *hard* too, we's nearly upside down! Yer see, when you got ten nets in, yer don't have no ballast, you depends on getting fish for yer ballast. Going down through Sandown Bay we's nearly upside down! But we was very friendly with the Shanklin fishermen, the Loosemores.

'Course, when you goes out with anybody like that, you gen'lly only gets a third of the share. They have's a share for theirself, and a share for the boat an' their nets, yer see, and you have's the other share. You don't get *half*. But now when I was on with George Bannister, well he never had a big boat like others did. Eight bob a hundred, eight eights are sixty-four shillings, that's what we got for the catch. Wi' George I used to go half, so I got thirty shillings, that was for a whole bloody night! Now they want 'bout ten pound for that now!

George Bannister was comin' over cross the shore there one day and there's one o' them bull terriers there, and he growled at George when he got out the boat. So George thought, "Aw, I'll take a oar along wi' me over cross the beach." So he took oar, and the dog sort o' followed 'n and – "Aw," he thought, "'e seems quiet now". But then eventually he picks George, he had hold of him up 'ere, on his jersey. An' he shouted, and Tom Cole the gardener come out an' had to choke him orf. *I* never liked blessed dogs – one bit me up near home, well I only had knickerbockers on 'cos I was taking my sister down the Regatta. The blood was running down m' legs, and I had five teeth marks every year, each side!

Well Fisherman's Square was left free to the fishermen, but then the Council wanted to claim that, so you had to pay half a crown a year for that there ground, yer see.

Dick Mursell was about one o' the strongest fishermen there was. And he knowed how to charm warts away! Paddy [*Mr Caws' daughter-in-law*] had one on her hand. He did it! I said t'her, "How did 'e do't?" "Aw," she said, "he just gimme a penny an' said, 'E'll go!'" ha-ha! And yet yer know, he strained hisself pullin' up a flat dinghy. Dick used to live up Roseneath [*in Mitten Road*]. His first wife was a cook down Denison's at Balure, for years. Dick had three or four sisters. There was one married Harry Parkes, the son of Parkes what had the Village Inn at one time. A gardener says to Dick, "What time d'yer pull yer bean-sticks up?" O' course, *his* was fallin' down, they didn't want no pullin' up!

## The Lifeboat

[*Regarding the wreck of the Romola, 1912.*] I was going in the ol' *Queen Victoria* lifeboat at that time – I only went with 'er four or five years till 1915 – and it got called out, yer see. An' well, blowed a gale o' wind from the south-west. Somebody'd seen a buoy, couldn't fetch down there, we should never 'a got down there. After that we tacked, we got a flare up Lane End recalling us back, 'cos Teddy Attrill and Johnny had picked them up. Now Couldrey got sort o' the praise for that, but Couldrey didn't *do* that, now that was Johnny Attrill and Teddy. Well the boat smashed up down Sharpus – lot o' rocks just off Foreland – I never seen not a word of 'er. We heard that she was loaded wi' coal, so George Bannister and me went down there – there's blessed great bits o' coal there, you'd 'a filled up a boat 'bout half-hour! Lovely coal, too. Jack Holbrook, he come down, 'e shoutin' out, "Don't you touch that, that's my coal!" Well we didn't take no notice of *'im*! Then by 'n by the Coastguard come there and they told us to stop, so we stopped. But I don't

## Chapter 20 – I'm Not Blessed Well Jokin'!

think we *need* have, because if we'd 'a take that up, we could've claimed that as salvage – I *think* we could, that would be jetsam yer see. Well Jack Holbrook reckoned he bought it in the end, but don't think he ever *did* – well if he did, 'e never got none of it!

When I was in the Lifeboat you had a job to get down to it, because of the Coastguards. There were about seven to eight men there all free to go in the Lifeboat. They used t'have two crews once upon a time.

The only time I went down to really rescue anybody was the *Mint*, she was a little Plymouth trawler, only had two men an' a boy, a billy-boy's crew – a man, a boy and an ol' bugger! It warn't very rough, and me an' Bill Adams was stood down the Church corner when the Lifeboat gun went, an' I run down, I'd time to get to the Lifeboat then. And 'course they larnched the Lifeboat – well only gone 'bout hour I s'pose, take these two men an' a boy out. Perce Watton bought that boat afterwards for twenty-five pounds, I dunno what happened t'er, I think she must've had holes in her.

Now Lammy Etheridge was a bit of a card, y'know. He was out in the Lifeboat once. We gen'lly used t'have a naval man for inspector. And 'course, you know what a chap is if he *likes* a cigarette, he likes a cigarette, don't 'e? don't matter where he is. So 'course, he lit up a cigarette Lammy did, and this inspector: "Owt that cigarette! Owt that cigarette!" You know what a Navy bloke is. So Lammy: "Uh-uh you, uh you talkin' to me?" "Yeah! Owt that cigarette!" Lammy says, "You can land me soon as ever yer like. We be only volunteers, we're not in the Navy!" 'Course, Cox'n Jack Holbrook, he had to quieten the inspector down a bit then, yer see!

## It makes yer feel bad!

'Course, we had to sort o' *foind out* a lot o' ground, if you can make out, you had to get that out from where you put yer pots. As long as you can get a cross-section like that, you can get your exact position in the sea. You want to get one mark one way, yer see, and one the other to work that out. Now we missed Seaview Pier a good bit when that went, well that was a really good mark for us. And so's that ol' church mark over S'n Helens. If you was come up from Shanklin night-time, always keep Shanklin lights open, and when you got up far enough, when the old church come open at the Point there, you was up clear o' that ledge. We went down to Shanklin and Ventnor for herrings, not for mackerel. They'd come up *'ere* for mackerel: I've seen seventeen boats off 'ere, from Sandown to Shanklin.

When I first went fishing, 'course we used to make our own pots, but you could buy them sixteen shillings a dozen, already made, from a man named Cook over at Brook. Or, if you got your own withies, one o' the Attrills 'ud make 'em up for a shilling for yer. We used t'have withybed down

Carpenters, we borrowed that off Miss Moreton down the Ducie: she just as well give it to us really 'cos we only paid a pound a year for it. I used to go up there and cut 'em, blimey, it'd take us two days to cut 'em. Because they're very high, we used t'have to stand up on a harrow against the stumps and cut orf a handful and get down again – took yer a *devil* of a time to do it! You had to be careful, 'cos it was always half full o' water. And [*brother*] Herb warn't very keen makin' pots, he always left me to do *that* blessed job!

Well one time me an' Dick Mursell, we's be in Shanklin after herring, and several boats down there. And we's comin' up from there and it come on ter blow a proper stripper. We was in the *May Queen*, open boat. O' course, I could see it afterwards, if you were a bit nervous you warnts to steer so you can't see the waves goin' behind yer – if you're lookin' at it you think the waves gonna overpower you. Oh, I bin out in a boat before with a load o' pots, and a blessed great swell comin', and yer think to yourself, "By God!" 'Course, the smaller the boat, the quicker the motion. The bigger the boat, the slower the motion. Anyhow, it was blowin' a stripper, and we only had a trysail set, and d'you know, it took us longer to get into the harbour than it did comin' up all that way! The tide was coming out the harbour and we only had that small sail, we couldn't get to windward very far. And Alfie Mursell told me, he said, "We's frightened ter put ours up, we *rowed* up from Shanklin!" He says, "I wonder how *you* got on?" I says, "Ooh, I dunno, we got up there orright!" I could see what I had to steer, I could see these blessed great swell, I've seen 'em before!

The last time I went down to Shanklin was just before the First War. And one o' the German princes was there, and Ernie Baker was sailing with him in the boat! 'Cos Ernie Baker used to go down and work for Loosemores, yer see, an' he reckoned the Germans *alright* – he said, "They pay you orright, you get plenty o' money owt o' them!"

But I bin down there fishing well up to midnight. We was very friendly with the Loosemores, they'd do anything for yer. So one night we was down there, oh midnight an' p'raps later. Somebody said, "Er, haven't seen Crappo an' Poppy tonight" – they's a couple o' ones about there, they used to go up the workhouse wintertime. "No," someone says, "han't seen 'em". He stuck his stick under – they shouted! they was under one o' the sheds, asleep! "Ah," he said, "I thought they'd be 'ere!" *He* knowed where they was.

George Smith and Bert Baker was fishin' together at one time, fer herrings down Shanklin, Ventnor. And George Attrill and his brother Walt, they was goin' out fishing together. And the water was pretty theck [*cloudy*] for daytime. And George Bannister says to me, "Oh," 'e says, "let's have a try down ol' Foreland". And we tried just up where Sharpus [*Rocks*], where the *Empress Queen* was there [*lying stranded*], and we loaded up. We warn't down there more than half hour! And I remember since it was yesterday,

## Chapter 20 – I'm Not Blessed Well Jokin'!

Bert Baker, George and Walter Attrill, and George Smith.

we comin' up by the lifeboat house, and Tim Gawn – 'e was Cox'n o' the Lifeboat – he was down cleaning the lifeboat station. "Oh," he says, "you got a good lot, but wait until them chaps comes up from Ventnor, they'll be loaded right up". George Bannister says, "Well they can't 'ave more than *we* got, we's loaded!" The water's loppin' over the side, you couldn't have no more! What d'you think they gonna have? When they come home, they never had none! No, they never had any! And Hewison from down Ryde, he bought some off Attrills the day before, four bob a hundred they charged 'n – because you didn't get much money for fish them days, yer know. And when he come after some more the next day, well o' course they never had none! So he come along there where we was an' he says to George Bannister, "Can I have some?" George says, "I don' mind *sellin'* yer some but I ain't gonna *give* 'em to yer!" He says, "If you wants 'em orf us you'll have ter pay six bob". He paid 't!

Cor blimey, I've seen the price of fish go like that, **makes me feel bad**, honest it do! I've seen bloaters over Portsmouth a shillin' a box, fifty-four in a box, but you had to buy twelve boxes, yer see, that was on the market. Now what could the men who caught 'em, what could they have got, eh? It makes yer feel bad!

Bert Baker first looked after a boat for a Colonel Logan what lived down Lane End, at Banavie. And one day I was out fishin' and I seen the boat a little way orf an' I thought t'myself, "Well she's no business orf there." So I went orf by and shouted an' I didn't get no answer, so I pulled up on the chain and found her wi' no shackles going. So I towed 'er in Lane End, then

George Smith and Bert Baker 'shoving' the pot boats.

## Chapter 20 – I'm Not Blessed Well Jokin'!

I went orf and got me pots what I had to get, and when I come in Colonel Logan said, "You picked up my boat?" I said, "Yes". "Well," he said, "I can't afford to give yer the full price, so I'll give yer five pound". So five pound was five pound them days!

Then afterwards Bert Baker worked for Lord Herschell, lived down where Warner's is now. And when Lord Herschell went away, he give him his motorboat. Then after Lord Herschell moved away, Bert went fishing, yer see, but he couldn't make pots very well, he used to buy 'em, I s'pose.

I was lucky one day. Bert Baker come up from Foreland, an' I was down Lane End, and I let a oar overboard, yer see. And the oar was going down wi' the tide an' I couldn't get down fast enough to get 'n. And he happened to come up round and he picked th'oar up for me. An' after that I always carried three oars, I carried a spare one in case one slipped overboard. You never knows, things happens, I dunno.

Then Bert's younger brother Frank, he says, "Anybody got a fag?" "No." "Well I'll have one o' me own then!"

Me and George Bannister was going up to Hill Head just by Lee-on-Solent, we was goin' down through Priory Bay with a little breeze east'ly, and the blessed mast broke orf! He said, "Better go back in harbour." And I said, "Oh, p'raps I could sharpen that owt"; so I cut off the broken bit and shortened it and put it in the back in the step – then we went on up there.

# Notes

## Town and County Notes
*(IW County Press archive for 3rd September 1898)*

Lord Fitzwilliam has been staying at his place at Bembridge [East Cliff]. The inhabitants of that rising resort will be interested to learn that a London contemporary has made a discovery which is by no means new to them – that the country surrounding Bembridge is simply delightful.

# *Feature Article*

## When the Sun always Shone
### by Angela Whitcombe

*(Adapted from an article in the magazine Wight Life October/November 1972)*

As a small child, the most exciting event of the whole year was the annual removal of our household for two summer months to our home in the Island.

The little paddle steamer, called the *Bembridge*, ran directly to the small pier of our village; neither boat nor pier still exist, but if I shut my eyes I can see them still. The forty-five minute crossing over, the *Bembridge* would manoeuvre alongside the pier with much clanging of bells and reversing of paddles. On disembarking, our whole party would clamber down a long flight of slippery, seaweedy steps, where three rowing-boats were waiting to take us to our own steps; one boat for the family, one for the servants, and one for the hand luggage. The heavy luggage was taken down the pier by a horse-and-cart and went round to the house by road. The boatmen were old friends and we all solemnly shook hands before starting on the last lap of our journey, half-a-mile by rowing boat.

How I loved those little village shops, and how good their owners were to us. The postmaster was a lovable but eccentric old man, and I do not think he would have made much money out of his shop unless he had had an eagle-eyed assistant. He was always giving away his goods to the children who came to the shop; but the old postmaster's assistant was a rather severe spinster, and she would nip out of the door after me and forcibly remove the treasure trove. The little baker's shop was another favourite haunt; nowhere else were there such shiny currant buns or such beautiful doughnuts. The

## Chapter 20 – I'm Not Blessed Well Jokin'!

speciality was a large flat tea-cake called a Coronation bun. I have often wondered which coronation it celebrated, as my father told me that he used to eat Coronation buns when he was a little boy, and he first went to the village in 1859. Was it Queen Victoria's coronation or an earlier one? Alas, that little shop has passed away and also the charming old lady who kept it.

A great delight to us as children was the barrel-organ pulled by an old grey donkey and complete with Italian organ-grinder, and a monkey wearing a little red coat who used to pick up pennies in his tiny black fingers. This barrel-organ toured the whole Island and would come to our village about once in three weeks. The old Italian had known us for years, and sometimes allowed us to turn the handle and grind out the old music-hall tunes. One day he handed it over to me and a small friend and disappeared in the direction of the pub. We were delighted. As we collected the pennies, the monkey was kept busy taking off his little round cap to say thank you. We took it in turns to grind the organ. Eventually our arms began to ache, but there was still no sign of the Italian. Though tired and hungry, we could not leave the organ unattended, and felt honour-bound to go on grinding out till the old man came back. At last he came swaggering down the street, very merry indeed, with his wide black hat on the side of his head, and singing 'Santa Lucia' at the top of his voice.

Our whole life in the Island was centred round the sea and boats. Sometimes we would sail out to the Warner Light Ship, taking fruit, vegetables and newspapers for the crew. In those days the men would have to stay aboard for many weeks at a time and fresh supplies only came out at intervals; as there was no wireless, news was also scarce. We would sail round the lightship as close as we could and the men would hold out a net on the end of a long pole, rather like an outsize shrimping net whilst we threw in the things we had brought. This was not as easy as it sounds, and

Warner Lightship.

sometimes we would have to 'come about' several times before getting into the right position.

It is well over a hundred years ago that my father first went to the Island; he used to tell me how very different sea-bathing was in those days; anyone who wished to bathe had to book the one horse-drawn bathing machine the day before. It would then arrive at the door, pick up the bathers, drive them down the village street, down the slipway and into the sea; there it reversed so that the door was facing out to sea, and the bathers, who on no account must be seen, crept down some steps hidden by a sort of canopy, and modestly slipped into the water. The bathe over, they crawled back into the machine, and dripping wet, were driven home.